THE REVELATION OF TRUTH

THE REVELATION OF TRUTH

A Mosaic of God's Plan for Man

JOHN HAGEE

THOMAS NELSON PUBLISHERS®
Nashville

Published in Nashville, Tennessee, by Thomas Nelson, Inc.

Library of Congress Cataloging-in-Publication Data

Hagee, John C.
    The revelation of truth : a mosaic of God's plan for man / John Hagee.
    p. cm.
    Includes bibliographical references (p.).
    ISBN 0-7852-6967-3 (hc)
    1. Revelation. I. Title.
BT127.2 .H24 2000
231.7'4—dc21   00-037980
                                     CIP

Printed in the United States of America

1 2 3 4 5 6 7 8 9 10 BVG 09 08 07 06 05 04 03 02 01 00

He who gives a book gives more than cloth, paper, and ink.
He gives more than leather, parchment, and words.
He reveals a foreword of his thoughts,
a dedication of his friendship,
a page of his presence,
a chapter of himself,
and an index of his love.

—Author Unknown

This book is lovingly dedicated to the memory of Wanda Webb, who served as my secretary for twenty-four years.

CONTENTS

INTRODUCTION

An ancient Chinese wise man was the first to say, "One picture is worth more than ten thousand words." The Russian novelist Ivan Sergeyevich Turgenev amplified the idea. "A picture," he wrote, "shows me at a glance what it takes dozens of pages of a book to expound."

If your family is like mine, you've been snapping pictures for years. When our five children were born, Diana and I took their pictures as soon as possible. Over the years, we've taken pictures of gap-toothed children, children in the kitchen, children at play, children at work. Our family album includes pictures of not only our children, but also of our friends, our pets, and our home. We carry a camera on vacations, on special trips, and to visit family members. When our oldest daughter graduated from high school, we behaved like every other parent and nearly blinded her with flashbulbs. When our first child married, we had a photographer at the wedding to record every significant moment.

We take pictures because we know time is fleeting and memory is fragile. We organize photos into priceless albums because we want those who follow us to know the stories that explain who we are as individuals and as a family.

Most of us wouldn't think of letting a major life event slip by without taking a picture to freeze the moment in time and preserve the memory for the future.

Every picture tells a story; the stories are surprisingly similar. Without even looking at your family photo album, I can guess that you have pictures of toothless babies, candlelit birthday cakes, teenagers with their first cars, gray-haired grandparents, and young adults in graduation caps and gowns. Pop artist Andy Warhol once said, "Isn't life a series of images that change as they repeat themselves?"[1]

God takes pictures too. He doesn't use a camera or a camcorder or even a paintbrush, though I suppose you could say the universe itself is His canvas. His pictures are recorded, not on Kodak paper or videotape, but in the Bible and the annals of human history. God's pictures, which theologians call *types*, are like the novelist's tool of foreshadowing or the movie teaser that entices you with a glimpse of an exciting coming attraction. God's pictures are situations that represent an eternal truth or prophecy about an event to come.

A few years ago, Robert Silvers, then a student at the MIT Media Lab, designed a computer program that created stunning large pictures out of smaller images. His artistry was so unique and his work so outstanding that after graduation he founded his own company, Runaway Technology. You may have seen some of his recent work—a *Newsweek* cover featured a photo of Princess Diana composed of smaller pictures of flowers, and a Master Card ad featured a picture of George Washington created from the images of five thousand credit cards. The cover of this book is one of Silvers's photo mosaics.

Like Silvers's work, God's pictures are a mosaic. Studied individually, these revelations of truth and the stories they tell are beautiful and moving, but studied collectively, they are almost overwhelming in scope and intent. God is a prolific artist; His pictures are scattered throughout Scripture. But from the beginning, He has been painting variations of the same picture and emphasizing the same story: there exists a Redeemer for fallen man.

Acts 15:18 (NKJV) tells us, "Known to God from eternity are all His works." In the beginning, God knew what would be required of His pictures. He knew that Satan and sin would color the creation black and that only blood red could restore mankind. Still, He dipped His finger in the blue of an ocean and painted a sky, then nudged His thumb into the clay and formed a man. Knowing everything that would be required of man and himself, God continued to create . . . out of love.

God has never ceased to demonstrate His faithfulness. Like an eager suitor, He is still pursuing the hearts of men and women today.

In Genesis, the first installment in the Book of books, God has included thirty clear pictures that portray His plan for the human race from creation to eternity to come. As we study these revelations of truth found in the first book of the Bible, we will be using the chart on pages xviii–xxi, which shows how the pictures revealed in Genesis fit into the span of earthly time.

There were no cameras in Jesus' day, and though artists and sculptors abounded in Roman culture, we have no definite record of His earthly image. But as we look at God's revelations of truth in Genesis, *you will see Jesus.*

You will come to know Him far better than you could from a photograph or video. You will come to understand that He is the Alpha and Omega, the First and the Last. He is from everlasting to everlasting. He is almighty, all-knowing, and the Eternal God. On creation morning, He was the Light of the World. During Noah's flood, He was the Judge of the Earth. At Passover, He was the promised Lamb of God.

Presently He sits at the right hand of the Father, making intercession for you and me. He is coming soon in the clouds, with power and great glory, to take His church to heaven. Seven years later He will come to the Mount of Olives to rescue His people, Israel, from the bloodiest battle the world has ever seen. He will then reign for one thousand years, sitting on the throne of His ancestor, King David, and of His kingdom there shall be no end!

Hallelujah! I am thrilled to have this opportunity to open God's family album with you and share these wonderful revelations of truth.

The Thirty Revelations of Truth in Genesis

1. God is a Trinity.

2. Every individual must be tested.

3. Satan is a real being, not a myth.

4. The work of salvation requires the shedding of blood.

5. Good works cannot hide your sin.

6. Believers will not go through the Judgment.

7. God will honor those who honor authority, even when that authority is wrong.

8. Babel and Nimrod are pictures of the Antichrist and his kingdom.

9. Babel represents Mystery Babylon, which God will judge during the Tribulation.

10. We are to be separated from the world.

11. We are justified by faith.

12. The promised Son will be delivered from death.

13. The Church is the bride of Christ.

14. Prayer has real power.

15. God, the Great Shepherd, is still seeking the lost.

16. The marriage of Isaac and Rebekah is a picture of God's betrothal to Israel.

17. In Jesus, God was incarnated in human flesh.

18. Two trees tell the story of man's fall and God's redemption.

19. God will discipline erring believers.

20. The life of Enoch vividly portrays the Rapture.

21. The Antichrist is Satan's seed.

22. The story of Joseph pictures Christ's second coming.

23. Grace has been available to man through every age.

24. God will bless those who bless Israel.

25. God blesses Gentiles through the Jewish people.

26. In Genesis, the Sabbath, a time of rest, foreshadows the Millennium.

27. Israel will enjoy a glorious, triumphant future.

28. Jesus Christ rules by royal right of inheritance.

29. Eden is a living portrait of heaven.

30. Abraham yearned for the New Jerusalem.

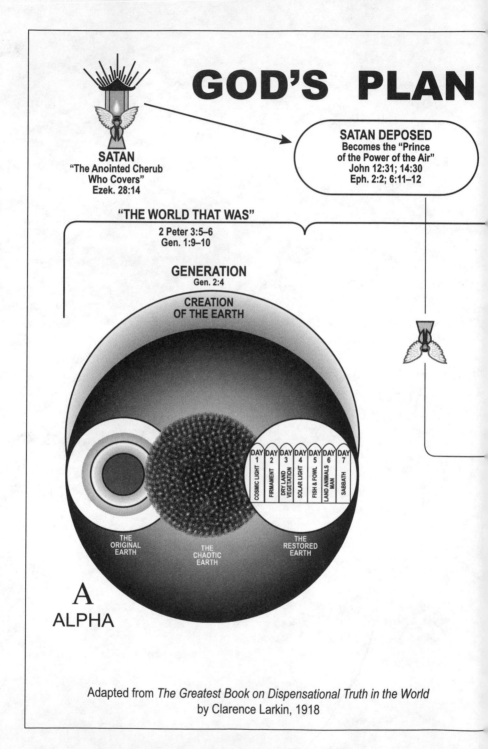

GOD'S PLAN

SATAN
"The Anointed Cherub
Who Covers"
Ezek. 28:14

SATAN DEPOSED
Becomes the "Prince
of the Power of the Air"
John 12:31; 14:30
Eph. 2:2; 6:11–12

"THE WORLD THAT WAS"
2 Peter 3:5–6
Gen. 1:9–10

GENERATION
Gen. 2:4

**CREATION
OF THE EARTH**

DAY 1	DAY 2	DAY 3	DAY 4	DAY 5	DAY 6	DAY 7
COSMIC LIGHT	FIRMAMENT	DRY LAND VEGETATION	SOLAR LIGHT	FISH & FOWL	LAND ANIMALS MAN	SABBATH

THE
ORIGINAL
EARTH

THE
CHAOTIC
EARTH

THE
RESTORED
EARTH

A
ALPHA

Adapted from *The Greatest Book on Dispensational Truth in the World*
by Clarence Larkin, 1918

FOR THE AGES

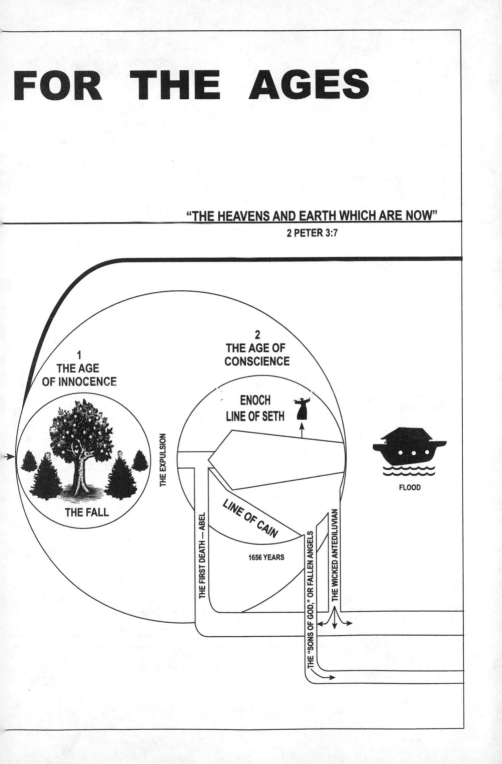

"THE HEAVENS AND EARTH WHICH ARE NOW"

2 PETER 3:7

1
THE AGE
OF INNOCENCE

2
THE AGE OF
CONSCIENCE

ENOCH
LINE OF SETH

THE EXPULSION

THE FALL

LINE OF CAIN

1656 YEARS

THE FIRST DEATH — ABEL

THE "SONS OF GOD," OR FALLEN ANGELS

THE WICKED ANTEDILUVIAN

FLOOD

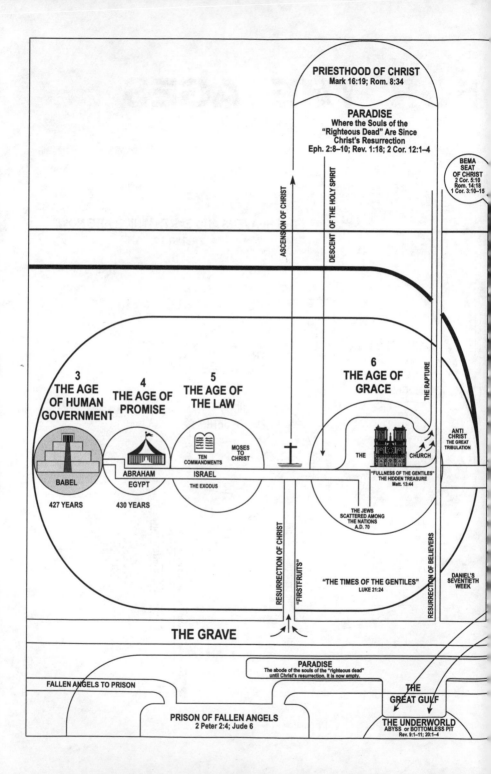

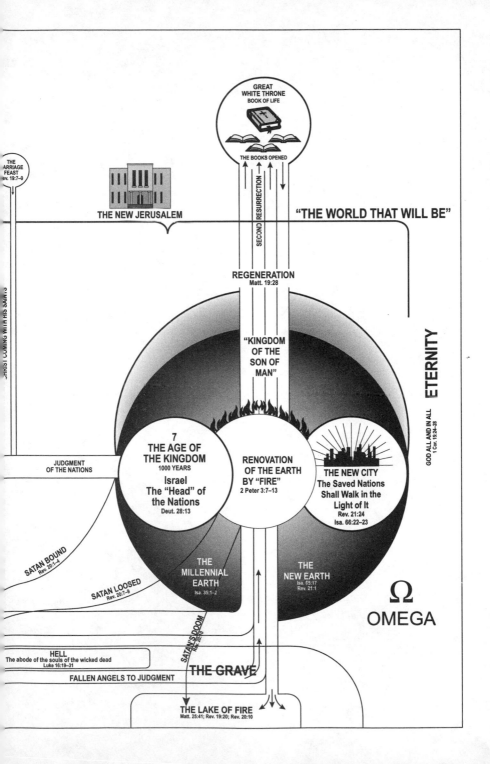

Journal, Page One

My name is Josias. You have never seen me, yet I
live, and to me has been given the task of recording a
testimony of the ages. I was among those who shouted for
joy at the creation of the present earth; I wept in a simple
overflow of feeling when God fashioned a lump of clay
into the man who became the father of your race.

But I existed long before those significant events. I
am one of a vast multitude of angels created by Him who
calls all things into being. By Him were all things created,
both in the heavens and on earth, visible and invisible,
whether thrones or dominions or rulers or authorities.

I have seen, child of Adam, things your human eye
could never record. I have heard music rare and celestial, I
have glimpsed glory and power and sorrow beyond human
imagining. I have bowed low in the presence of the Holy
One to whom belongs all power and glory forever. To me He
said, "Record the mysteries, and reveal the secrets of the
ages. Write what you have seen in eternity past, and write
of the things which will come to pass in eternity future."

And so, though I may falter with these earthly words and
this clumsy pen, I shall strive to show you God's yearning
through the continuum of time. He who is the same yesterday,
today, and forever bids me, and I rejoice to do His will.

After I came to be, God created the heavens and the
earth. The Word of God stretched out His hand and sent the
stars spinning out into the velvet darkness, and the fire of
His breath set the suns to burning. Tears from His eyes
formed the waters, for even then He knew . . . everything.

CHAPTER

THE WORLD
THAT WAS

Before the mountains were brought forth,
Or ever You had formed the earth and the world,
Even from everlasting to everlasting,
You are God.
—Ps. 90:2 NKJV

"In the beginning God created the heavens and the earth" (Gen. 1:1 NKJV).

The Hebrew word for *created*, *bara*, means "to create out of nothing." God brought the universe out of nothing by His own creative power. Hebrews 11:3 (NKJV) tells us, "By faith we understand that the worlds were framed by the word of God, so that the things which are seen were not made of things which are visible."

The Word of God framed the worlds, and John 1:1–3 (NKJV) explains that the Word of God is Jesus Christ: "In the beginning was the Word, and the Word was with God, and the Word was God. He was in the beginning with God. All things were made through Him, and without Him nothing was made that was made."

Make no mistake, my friend. If it were possible to have a picture of creation morning, you would see God the Father, Jesus Christ, and the Holy Spirit present and active at creation.

The first revelation of truth in Genesis is this: *God is a trinity!*

"In the beginning," says the Bible, "God created . . ." The word for *God* is *elohiym,* a plural form of the word. A picture of the Trinity appears again in Genesis 1:26 (NKJV): "Then God [*elohiym*] said, 'Let *Us* make man in *Our* image, according to *Our* likeness; let them have dominion over the fish of the sea, over the birds of the air, and over the cattle, over all the earth and over every creeping thing that creeps on the earth'" (italics added).

Other pictures of the Trinity appear throughout the Bible. Matthew tells us that when Jesus came up out of the water at His baptism, "Behold, the heavens were opened to Him, and He saw the Spirit of God descending like a dove and alighting upon Him. And suddenly a voice came from heaven, saying, 'This is My beloved Son, in whom I am well pleased'" (Matt. 3:16–17 NKJV).

Though the word *trinity* is not found in Scripture, Jesus Himself testified to the triune aspect of God. In Matthew 28:19 (NKJV), He told His disciples, "Go therefore and make disciples of all the nations, baptizing them in the name of the Father and of the Son and of the Holy Spirit."

The doctrine of the Trinity involves four propositions: first, that God is one, and that there is only one God.

Thus says the LORD, the King of Israel,
And his Redeemer, the LORD of hosts:
"I am the First and I am the Last;
Besides Me there is no God." (Isa. 44:6 NKJV)

Second, the doctrine of the Trinity states that the Father is a divine Person distinct from the Son and the Holy Spirit. Jesus said that the Father knew things He did not know (Mark 13:32, Acts 1:7), so He and His Father had to be separate and distinct.

Third, Jesus Christ is truly God, yet a Person distinct from the Father and the Holy Spirit.

Fourth and finally, the doctrine of the Trinity states that the Holy Spirit is also a distinct divine Person. Each member of the Trinity is eternal, holy, and true. The Father, Son, and Holy Spirit were present at creation.

Perhaps you find it difficult to understand how God could be three distinct persons and yet one. Consider water: In moderate temperatures, it flows freely as a liquid. In freezing weather, water forms a solid. In extremely hot temperatures, water becomes steam. In any state, the chemical structure of water is H_2O, yet it can appear in three distinct forms.

In the same way, God is one God, yet He is three-in-one. He is God the Spirit, who indwells believers and empowers them. He is God the Son, who possesses a human form and a divine nature. And He is God the Father, the eternal I AM.

EVOLUTION IS IMPOSSIBLE

Notice that the first verse of the Bible does not debate the existence of God; it *declares* His existence and power! We can learn a lesson from this forthright declaration. Don't spend your days debating God's existence; declare Him!

"In the beginning God created . . ." That simple statement completely refutes the theory of evolution. If you believe that billions of years ago light shone upon a stagnant pool of water, and somehow that light sparked life in a single cell, and that cell grew legs and crawled up out of the water, then climbed a tree and grew fingers and toes and finally evolved into a man—well, belief in that scenario requires far more faith than I have! I find it much more logical and sensible to believe that in the beginning God created the heavens and the earth.

Lately some unexpected voices have been supporting me in that belief. A few months ago, the Hubble space telescope sent infrared images to scientists here on earth. These photographs, of scenes that no human eye had ever glimpsed, revealed galaxies possibly more than twelve billion times six trillion miles away. After learning of these astounding pictures, columnist George Will wrote:

> Someday, if Congress thinks spaciously (thinks of things greater than ethanol subsidies), even better telescopes can peer into the remotest—what? edge?—of the universe and see galaxies being born. Looking deep into space is looking back in time. Hubble may have seen light emitted when the universe was 5 percent of its present age (it is approximately 13 billion years old), light cast by stars materializing in the formless dark that prevailed after the instant of bright light cast by the Big Bang.[1]

The Big Bang theory asserts that from a pinpoint of compressed potential, something sent a cosmos spiraling outward at unimaginable speed. Rather than refuting the existence of God, the Big Bang seems to point to Him. George Will explains:

> If the Big Bang had been slightly less violent, the expansion of the universe would have been less rapid, and would soon (in a few million years, or a few minutes—in any case, soon) have collapsed back on itself. If the explosion had been slightly more violent, the universe might have dispersed into a soup too thin to aggregate into stars. The odds against us were—this is just the right word—astronomical. The ratio of matter and energy to the volume of space at the Big Bang must have been within about one quadrillionth of 1 percent of ideal.

> This good news—that is the meaning of "gospel"—from science suggests . . . "a buoyant view of our being." Life is so improbable it must somehow be favored by something. By some First Cause, "to which," said Aquinas, "everyone gives the name of God."[2]

Kitty Ferguson, the biographer of Stephen Hawking and the author of two books on black holes, sees no conflict between her study of physics and her devout belief in God. "I believe there are things we have to attribute to God," she told a reporter for Britain's *Sunday Telegraph*. "People's personal experience of His love, for instance, or

The Revelation of Truth

our sense of beauty. Experience is richer than just the physical universe."[3]

Ferguson also reports that scientists today are more ready to admit they are religious than they were thirty years ago. "It's become known that more and more scientists believe in God. The more they admit their belief, the more others are encouraged to come forward. Religion is part of our experience: to deny part of our experience would be unscientific."[4]

Religious leaders are also reaching out to bridge the gap between science and religion. In November 1992, Pope John Paul II formally proclaimed that the Roman Catholic Church erred in the seventeenth century by condemning Galileo to house arrest for stating that the earth was not the center of the universe. Galileo had written that the Scriptures cannot err but are often misunderstood. This insight, said the pope, made the scientist a wiser theologian than the men who accused and condemned him for heresy.[5]

In that same year, 1992, *Time* magazine reported:

The year's most intriguing book about God was produced not by theologians but by 60 world-class scientists, 24 Nobel prizewinners among them. *Cosmos, Bios, Theos* gives their thoughts on the Deity and the origin of the universe and of life on earth. For instance, the co-editor, Yale physicist Henry Margenau, concludes that there is "only one convincing answer" for the intricate laws that exist in nature: creation by an omnipotent, omniscient God.[6]

Even more perplexing to scientists than the question of *how* the world began is *why* it began. Derek Parfit, a fellow at Oxford University, wrote, "No question is more sublime than why there is a universe: Why is there anything, rather than nothing?"[7]

John Haught, a writer for the *Washington Times*, reported that speculation about the origin of the universe has awakened theological curiosity among scientists. "Now that the big-bang theory has won the day," he wrote, "we can no longer assume that matter is eternal or that the universe has an infinite past. Science has brought home to us, in a startlingly fresh way, the radical 'contingency,' or non-necessity, of the cosmos." Haught continued:

> This vast world, it now seems, did not have to exist at all, nor did it have to possess the peculiar traits that allowed for the evolution of life and consciousness. But since there is no eternal necessity for this particular universe existing at all, it is not a bad question to ask why it does. Such "why" questions occur with surprising frequency in the writings of today's scientists, even though by the rules of their own game they should only be allowed to ask "how" things happen.[8]

Scripture clearly indicates the answer to "Why?" God created the universe because He wanted His creation to be inhabited with intelligent, free moral agents to whom He could reveal Himself and with whom He could fellowship. The Bible tells us the universe was created for habitation, and man was created to know God.

For thus says the LORD,
Who created the heavens,

Who is God,
Who formed the earth and made it,
Who has established it,
Who did not create it in vain,
Who formed it to be inhabited:
"I am the LORD, and there is no other." (Isa. 45:18 NKJV)

In Revelation 4:11 (NKJV), the apostle John recorded his vision in which he saw the elders chanting:

You are worthy, O Lord,
To receive glory and honor and power;
For You created all things,
And by Your will they exist and were created.

The word *created* in that passage comes from the Hebrew word *ktizo*, which means "to fabricate," and implies that the one who fabricates *owns* the thing he creates. Though God does own the universe, He has granted man the gift of free moral agency. We are not slaves. Those of us who love Him serve Him willingly.

God created the universe because He yearned for fellowship. Even then, He hungered to know you and to have you know Him.

HOW OLD IS THE UNIVERSE?

Some Christians get upset when they hear scientists claim that the universe has existed for millions of years. After all, since the creation of Adam occurred only about six thousand years ago, how could the universe be ancient?

We must not be like the church leaders who accused Galileo of heresy without carefully considering the facts and possibilities. Several ideas support the notion of an ancient universe. First, God could have created an *aged* universe—after all, Adam was created a mature man, not a child. Second, we must consider the endless span of time that stretched *before* the creation of Adam. When we hear the word *eternity*, we almost always think of the eternity to come. We tend to forget that the universe has known an eternity *past*. We do not know much about this mysterious span of history, but from Scripture we can glean certain clues about the origin of the universe.

Let's look first at Genesis 1:1 (NKJV): "In the beginning God created the heavens and the earth." The Hebrew word for *heavens, shamayim,* is plural. Scripture tells us there are three heavens—the sky, where the "fowls of the heaven" dwell (Gen. 2:19, 7:3; Ps. 8:8), the starry heavens (Deut. 17:3; Jer. 8:2; Matt. 24:29), and the "heaven of heavens" or the "third heaven," the place where the angels move and live (Deut. 10:14; 1 Kings 8:27; 2 Cor. 12:2).

In the first three verses of Genesis, we also find references to three distinct eras upon earth—the *original* earth, as it was created in the first verse of Genesis, the *chaotic* earth (Gen. 1:2), and the *present* earth (Gen. 1:3). Since the created world had become chaotic by verse 2, we can surmise that verse 1 stands for one period of time, and verse 2 represents a different time altogether.

How do we know a span of time existed between the first two verses of Genesis? This teaching, known as the Gap Theory, arises from a careful study of the original Hebrew language. The Hebrew word for *earth, erets,* means "dry land." So the first verse of Genesis tells us that in the beginning, God made the heavens and the dry land.

The concept behind the Gap Theory can be traced back in Christian writings as early as the fourth century A.D. Some theologians believe the concept became popular in the late nineteenth century only in order to counter evolutionists who were studying the fossil record, but the theory is more than an attempt by theologians to appease evolutionists. It results from a study of the Hebrew text of Genesis.

The words *in the beginning* refer to the dateless past and include only a part of the creative age, from the creation of the universe and the original earth with its dry land to the situation described in the second verse of Genesis (NKJV): "The earth was without form, and void; and darkness was on the face of the deep. And the Spirit of God was hovering over the face of the waters." By this time, the chaotic period, the original dry land had been flooded with water.

The word *was* in Genesis 1:2 is from the Hebrew verb *to become*, not *to be*. So the original earth *became* without form and void, or waste and empty. God had created a beautiful heaven and earth—for how could He create anything less?—but something ruined the original creation.

The earth existed in the second verse, as did *darkness* and *deep waters*. The Spirit of God was hovering over the surface of a flooded earth. This flood was more complete and devastating than Noah's flood, for it destroyed everything, even vegetation.

Many writers of Scripture refer to this dark period. Peter wrote:

> For this they willfully forget: that by the word of God the heavens were of old, and the earth standing out of water and in the water, by which the world that then existed perished, being flooded with water. But the heavens and the earth *which are now preserved* by the same word, are reserved for fire until the day of judgment and perdition of ungodly men. (2 Peter 3:5–7 NKJV, italics added)

What most people fail to realize is this: the earth was *created and flooded* before the six days of creation in which mankind appeared.

Notice what happened next: "Then God said, 'Let there be light'; and there was light . . . and God divided the light from the darkness" (Gen. 1:3–4 NKJV). Notice that God did not *create* the light at this time—He divided it. Isaiah 45:7 (NKJV) verifies this; God said, "I form the light." The Hebrew word for *form* is *yatsar*, which does not mean to create out of nothing, but "to mold," or squeeze into shape. God *shaped* the light; He pulled it out of darkness. Light, therefore, existed before the first day of creation.

God *created* the earth *in the beginning*, and afterward He *formed* the earth—He reshaped and redesigned what already existed.

Though we are confident that the age of the present earth is not much greater than six thousand years, the age of the original earth is unknown. But true science and Scripture always agree. Geologists who claim certain rocks and dinosaur skeletons are millions of years old may very well be right. God could have created an aged earth, or He could have formed this planet over the ages of eternity past. Dinosaurs and other prehistoric creatures may have lived before Adam's creation, or they may have lived during Adam's time and gradually become extinct.

How Do We Know the Present Creation Is Only Six Thousand Years Old?

Thomas R. Malthus, a population expert, has devised a formula that supports the theory of the relatively recent advent of mankind. Human populations tend to increase geometrically, says Malthus, doubling at equal increments of time. If the time for the population to double is referred to as "T," then, starting with an initial population of two people, after T years there would be four people, after two times T years the earth would hold eight people, and so on. This geometric doubling can be validated by the following known population figures:

1. At the time of Christ, the world population was around 300 million.
2. In A.D. 1650 it was 600 million.
3. In 1850 it was 1.2 billion.
4. In 1950 it was 2.4 billion.
5. In 1990 it was 4.8 billion.[9]

"Assuming the average life span to be seventy years and the average generation length to be thirty-five years," wrote Harold Willmington, "then starting with one family, the

present world population would result in about thirty doublings. These doublings would carry us back in history from
today to around 3500 B.C. This date is suggested by several
creation scientists to mark the time of Noah's flood!"[10]

HOW DID GOD CREATE
THE ORIGINAL EARTH?

We read in Hebrews 11:3 (NKJV) that "the worlds were
framed by the word of God," and I believe He was as careful, thoughtful, and wise in creating the original earth as He
was when He reshaped it to suit mankind. He called the
original earth into existence *out of nothing*, but in the six
days of creation, Scripture tells us He *formed* the present
earth with his hands.

The psalmist wrote:

When I consider Your heavens, the work of Your fingers,
The moon and the stars, which You have ordained,
What is man that You are mindful of him,
And the son of man that You visit him?
For You have made him a little lower than the angels,
And You have crowned him with glory and honor.
You have made him to have dominion over the works of
Your hands. (Ps. 8:3–6 NKJV)

"The great God who formed everything," wrote
Solomon, "gives the fool his hire and the transgressor his
wages" (Prov. 26:10 NKJV). Notice that Solomon used the
word *formed*, not *created*. Though God certainly did create
everything, the living things appearing during the six days

of creation were *formed* (Hebrew *chuwl*, not *bara* or *yatsar*) of material already in existence . . . including Adam, who was molded out of the dust of the earth.

How long was eternity past? We have no way of knowing how long God took to create the universe, but we could consider the creation of this present earth as a sort of measuring stick. Consider this: God took one day to divide the darkness and light, another day to divide the waters, another day to separate dry land from the water, another day to bring forth plant life, another day to synchronize the sun, moon, and stars with the restored planet, another day to make fish and fowl, and another day to make man and the animals.

God took six days to recreate the earth. How long might it have taken him to expend the same amount of care and attention upon the estimated forty *sextillion* stars in space? If God spent only six days on each, Finis Dake estimates that His creative work could have taken up to 4,164,383,561,643,836,164,383 earth years.[11]

WHY DID GOD CREATE A WORLD BEFORE THIS ONE?

Though I can't claim to fully understand the mind of God, I believe He created the original earth for the same reason He created this present world—He wanted to share Himself with free moral agents. In a manner of speaking, He created the universe for the same reason that we get married and have children—He yearned to love. Before the creation of this present earth, He yearned to fellowship with angelic beings.

During this time before time, God formed every angel, principality, and power out of nothing. He gave angels authority to rule the earth and other planets. The apostle Paul told us that God established a vast hierarchy in heavenly places, with the Son of God in a preeminent position over all:

> He [Jesus Christ] is the image of the invisible God, the firstborn over all creation. For by Him all things were created that are in heaven and that are on earth, visible and invisible, whether thrones or dominions or principalities or powers. All things were created through Him and for Him. (Col. 1:15–16 NKJV)

Let's consider Ephesians 3:8–11 (NKJV), where Paul wrote:

> To me, who am less than the least of all the saints, this grace was given, that I should preach among the Gentiles the unsearchable riches of Christ, and to make all see what is the fellowship of the mystery, which from the beginning of the ages has been hidden in God who created all things through Jesus Christ; to the intent that now the manifold wisdom of God might be made known by the church to the principalities and powers in the heavenly places, according to the eternal purpose which He accomplished in Christ Jesus our Lord.

From the beginning of the ages, God planned to draw His creation to Himself. But angels, like humans, have free will, and God's original creation fell prey to sin. The universe and the earth, beautiful and perfect, fell under the curse of rebellion . . . instigated by one cunning and crafty created being.

WHAT HAPPENED TO THE ORIGINAL EARTH?

During the time between the original creation and chaos, Lucifer ruled the earth in perfection. A dazzling and beautiful creation, he was known as "Son of the Morning" and "the anointed cherub who covers." His name, *Heylel* in Hebrew, comes from the Hebrew verb *halal*, "to shine."

Of Lucifer, the Bible says:

> You were the seal of perfection,
> Full of wisdom and perfect in beauty . . .
> You were the anointed cherub who covers;
> I established you;
> You were on the holy mountain of God;
> You walked back and forth in the midst of fiery stones.
> You were perfect in your ways from the day you were
>   created,
> Till iniquity was found in you . . .
> Your heart was lifted up because of your beauty;
> You corrupted your wisdom for the sake of your
>   splendor. (Ezek. 28:12, 14–15, 17 NKJV)

Bedazzled by his own beauty, Lucifer decided that he would overthrow God Himself. "I will ascend into heaven," Lucifer said. "I will exalt my throne above the stars of God." Lucifer's ambition provoked his downfall, and the Son of the Morning became Satan, the angel of light who deceives men to this day. We know that Satan and Lucifer are one and the same being because Satan is the only character in Scripture who has fallen from heaven, and he is the only ruler cast out of heaven with fallen angels.

The Bible further describes Lucifer's rebellion in Isaiah 14:12–15 (NKJV):

How you are fallen from heaven,
O Lucifer, son of the morning!
How you are cut down to the ground,
You who weakened the nations!
For you have said in your heart:
"I will ascend into heaven,
I will exalt my throne above the stars of God;
I will also sit on the mount of the congregation
On the farthest sides of the north;
I will ascend above the heights of the clouds;
I will be like the Most High."
Yet you shall be brought down to Sheol,
To the lowest depths of the Pit.

Lucifer rebelled against God's authority. He said, "I will replace God!" and God said, "No! You will be brought down to hell."

Satan led a revolt against God, and Jesus Himself witnessed Satan's defeat. He told His disciples, "I saw Satan fall like lightning from heaven" (Luke 10:18 NKJV).

Second Peter 2:4 (NKJV) tells us that the angels who followed Satan are bound and held in chains, awaiting judgment: "God did not spare the angels who sinned, but cast them down to hell and delivered them into chains of darkness, to be reserved for judgment." Jude 6 (NKJV) repeats this truth: "And the angels who did not keep their proper domain, but left their own abode, He has reserved in everlasting chains under darkness for the judgment of the great day."

Let me clarify an often misunderstood point: Fallen angels are not demon spirits. Angels are heavenly creatures who fly, and Scripture clearly indicates that the angels who rebelled with Satan are being held in chains. Demons, however, are earthbound. According to Matthew 12:43 (NKJV), "When an unclean spirit goes out of a man, he goes through dry places, seeking rest, and finds none."

While angels clearly live in their own bodies, demons wander the earth in search of a body to inhabit. That's why the demons in the demoniac from the region of the Gergesenes begged Jesus to cast them into the swine (Matt. 8:30–32). Demons crave a body so their perverse personalities can be manifested.

The Bible doesn't say where or how demons originated. We could speculate, of course, but their origin is not important. What is important is that through the authority of Jesus' name, believers have the power to bind and cast them out!

THE SIX DAYS OF CREATION

After Satan's revolt and ensuing destruction of the original earth, God literally reformed the earth.

> Then God said, "Let there be light"; and there was light. And God saw the light, that it was good; and God

divided the light from the darkness. God called the light
Day, and the darkness He called Night. So the evening
and the morning were the first day. (Gen. 1:3–5 NKJV).

The author of Genesis used the word *let* several times in
the first chapter, and not once does it imply an act of creation from nothing. The sense is to *make appear* or *make
visible*, expressing permission and purpose in connection
with already existing things.[12] The light of God had turned
away from the earth during Satan's rebellion, and without
light, the floodwaters covering the dry land could not evap-
orate or recede as they did in Noah's flood. But now, in
God's restoration, the light reappeared, and God separated
it from the darkness.

Then God said, "Let there be a firmament in the midst
of the waters, and let it divide the waters from the
waters." Thus God made the firmament, and divided
the waters which were under the firmament from the
waters which were above the firmament; and it was so.
And God called the firmament Heaven. So the evening
and the morning were the second day. (Gen. 1:6–8
NKJV)

On the second day of creation, God established the
three heavens we have already discussed. He divided the
waters in the clouds from the waters in the seas, with a blue
space of sky to separate the seas from the clouds.

Then God said, "Let the waters under the heavens be
gathered together into one place, and let the dry land

appear"; and it was so. And God called the dry land Earth, and the gathering together of the waters He called Seas. And God saw that it was good.

Then God said, "Let the earth bring forth grass, the herb that yields seed, and the fruit tree that yields fruit according to its kind, whose seed is in itself, on the earth"; and it was so. And the earth brought forth grass, the herb that yields seed according to its kind, and the tree that yields fruit, whose seed is in itself according to its kind. And God saw that it was good. So the evening and the morning were the third day. (Gen. 1:9–13 NKJV)

The color green appeared on the dry land of earth on God's third day of creation. Earth was restored. The flood-waters returned to the low places created for them, so dry land (*erets*) emerged once again.

Then God said, "Let there be lights in the firmament of the heavens to divide the day from the night; and let them be for signs and seasons, and for days and years; and let them be for lights in the firmament of the heavens to give light on the earth"; and it was so. Then God made two great lights: the greater light to rule the day, and the lesser light to rule the night. He made the stars also. God set them in the firmament of the heavens to give light on the earth, and to rule over the day and over the night, and to divide the light from the darkness. And God saw that it was good. So the evening and the morning were the fourth day. (Gen. 1:14–19 NKJV)

On the fourth day, God *made* (Hebrew *asah,* "to form," not *bara*) two great lights, one to rule the day, one to rule the night. Together they would regulate the length of man's days and define his months and years. They would provide heat for his crops and coolness for his rest.

This scriptural passage raises several interesting questions. First, how could God define the first three "evenings and mornings" without the sun and moon as guides? And how could the "morning stars sing for joy" at the earth's creation if God did not create them until the fourth day? The Bible tells us that the stars and angels watched as God fashioned the earth:

> Where were you when I laid the foundations of the earth?
> Tell Me, if you have understanding.
> Who determined its measurements?
> Surely you know!
> Or who stretched the line upon it?
> To what were its foundations fastened?
> Or who laid its cornerstone,
> When the morning stars sang together,
> And all the sons of God shouted for joy? (Job 38:4–7 NKJV)

We can only assume that God created the stars as part of the heavens *in the beginning,* before the fourth day, even though the Scripture mentions their creation alongside that of the moon and sun. The earth was already rotating on its axis. On day four, however, God formed the sun and moon to regulate the earth. These two lights were given to us in order to divide day and night, serve as signs for the seasons and years, and give light to the earth.

Then God said, "Let the waters abound with an abundance of living creatures, and let birds fly above the earth across the face of the firmament of the heavens." So God created great sea creatures and every living thing that moves, with which the waters abounded, according to their kind, and every winged bird according to its kind. And God saw that it was good. And God blessed them, saying, "Be fruitful and multiply, and fill the waters in the seas, and let birds multiply on the earth." So the evening and the morning were the fifth day. (Gen. 1:20–23 NKJV)

From nothing, God created (*bara*) animal life in the air and the waters. In the first four days of creation, He had fashioned things from materials already in existence, but on this fifth day, He brought life forth from nothing. If animals had lived prior to this time, they would have all been destroyed in the flood that covered the earth after Satan's revolt.

God saw the birds and sea creatures, He blessed them, and He pronounced them good.

Then God said, "Let the earth bring forth the living creature according to its kind: cattle and creeping thing and beast of the earth, each according to its kind"; and it was so. And God made the beast of the earth according to its kind, cattle according to its kind, and everything that creeps on the earth according to its kind. And God saw that it was good.

Then God said, "Let Us make man in Our image, according to Our likeness; let them have dominion over the fish of the sea, over the birds of the air, and over the cattle, over all the earth and over every creeping thing that creeps on the earth." So God created man in His own image; in the image of God He created him; male and female He created them. Then God blessed them, and God said to them, "Be fruitful and multiply; fill the earth and subdue it; have dominion over the fish of the sea, over the birds of the air, and over every living thing that moves on the earth."

And God said, "See, I have given you every herb that yields seed which is on the face of all the earth, and every tree whose fruit yields seed; to you it shall be for food. Also, to every beast of the earth, to every bird of the air, and to everything that creeps on the earth, in which there is life, I have given every green herb for food"; and it was so. Then God saw everything that He had made, and indeed it was very good. So the evening and the morning were the sixth day. (Gen. 1:24–31 NKJV)

On the sixth day, God combined the powers of formation and creation. Out of the ground He *formed* (*asah*) the bodies of animals and man from organic material (Gen. 2:19), but He *created* (*bara*) the spirit of life within them.

That is why, my friend, science will never be able to create life in a laboratory. Scientists can manipulate life and clone it, they can fashion and engineer DNA strands, but no one can or ever will call life into a nonliving organism. That creative power belongs to God alone.

The scientist who clones life from a cell or a strand of DNA is working with *already living* material. I'm always reminded of this principle when abortion proponents bring up the question of when life begins. "How can you say life begins at conception," they ask, "when a fetus cannot survive out-side the mother's womb in the first trimester of a pregnancy?"

My friend, life is not created at conception. The sperm and egg are alive before they ever join. Conception merely *passes* the gift of life from parents to a child.

Life began once, in the incredible and unique moment when "the Lord God formed man of the dust of the ground, and breathed into his nostrils the breath of life; and man became a living being" (Gen. 2:7 NKJV).

> And on the seventh day God ended His work which He had done, and He rested on the seventh day from all His work which He had done. Then God blessed the seventh day and sanctified it, because in it He rested from all His work which God had created and made. (Gen. 2:2–3 NKJV).

God rested on the seventh day, not because He was weary, but because He had completed His work. He had redeemed His creation and restored that which was lost. He had created man, an innocent and intelligent being with free will, in order to enjoy fellowship with Him.

God ordained seven days of the week—six days for labor, and a seventh day to enjoy the fruit of that labor. As we study the many revelations of truth in Scripture, you will notice that the God of heaven often deals in sevens. Seven golden candlesticks burn before the throne of God in heaven. God instituted seven holy feasts or festivals, which are detailed in my book *His Glory Revealed* (Thomas Nelson Publishers, 1999). In the Tribulation period God will send a series of judgments upon the earth: seven seal judgments, seven trumpet judgments, and seven vial, or bowl, judgments.

CREATION MARKS THE BEGINNING OF A
PERFECT SEVENFOLD PLAN

Gematria, the practice that associates Hebrew words or phrases with other words or phrases whose letters add up to the same numerical value, reinforces creation's perfection. Gematria is possible because each letter of the Hebrew alphabet stands for a unique number, and larger numbers are made up of combinations of letters. Thus, we may use gematria to interpret the biblical text and reveal information about people, places, and dates by each author's choice of words. To apply gematria to the creation account, let's look at Genesis 1:1—in this single verse, there are seven Hebrew words that have twenty-eight letters. Seven is the number of perfection, and the number of creation is four. Four multiplied by seven equals twenty-eight, demonstrating that God's creation was perfect in Genesis 1:1.

That perfect creation marked the beginning of God's master plan—seven ages, or dispensations, during which God gave a special revelation and commanded people to obey that specific revelation.[13] The book of Genesis details and depicts these seven ages, six to complete the work of God and the seventh to enjoy the fruit of His labor. The revelations of truth we will discover in this book are applicable to all seven God-ordained ages.

From the beginning, God had a plan to draw men to Himself. It began when He placed Adam and Eve in the perfect Garden of Eden. At this time mankind entered the Age of Innocence.

Journal, Page Two

I cannot begin to describe the holy hush that fell over the third heaven when God breathed life into the clay form He had created in His image. I felt my flesh prickle with anticipation as the man lifted his shaggy head, opened his eyes, and looked into the face of his Creator.

The Son smiled when Adam—for so the man is called—stood to his feet, then bowed his head. The garden burst forth into noisy life, as though the animals realized in that instant that another master had just been set above them. This one, this Adam, would walk among them. He would ride upon the strong ones, glean food with the nimble ones, and sing with the warbling creatures.

I perched on the branch of a towering tree as the animals came to meet their undershepherd. He gave them names, calling each one by a word that seemed apt, while the Son smiled in approval. How we laughed when the nimble ones—the man called them monkeys—clapped their hands with joy!

On and on the animals came, large and small, to hear what he would call them. The lion lifted his great head and roared in delight when the man said that he looked like a king of beasts, and the striped one—the tiger—made the ground rumble with his contented purring. I watched, fascinated, and wrote down every name as I had been commanded.

The one sad note of the occasion fell at the end of the naming, for of all the animals, none had been found worthy of the man's constant companionship. The dog volunteered to be his comrade, but since the dog could not stand and look the man in the eye, they seemed ill matched. One of the thick nimble ones—the man called it a gorilla—could look the man in the eye as an equal, but the man's intelligence blazed far brighter than the animal's. I personally thought the dolphin might have made a good associate for the man, if only God had given him feet instead of fins, for he was bright and articulate and of a goodly size . . .

But God had a better idea. As a cloud moved to block the bright light of Eden's sun, the man fell asleep. The finger of God parted the man's flesh and removed a rib, and from it the Creator fashioned a creature much like man, but rounder, and softer, and much more talkative.

And when the man awoke and saw the new creature sitting beside him, he called her woman, for she was taken out of man. And God said that it was good, for now man would not be alone. The Spirit moved through the Garden, the light of God trailing after him, binding the hearts of man and woman and God together.

Seeing all this, the Son smiled.

THE AGE
OF INNOCENCE

Innocence . . . the word brings sweet memories to mind, doesn't it? There's nothing quite like the innocence of a newborn baby, a two-year-old toddler running through the sprinkler in nothing but a diaper, or a young girl hugging a baby doll.

The earth knew an age of innocence. God created Adam and Eve and placed them in a perfect and glorious garden. For a time, however short, mankind enjoyed innocence and fellowship with God. Adam and Eve did not know what sin was. They had never encountered or conceived of it.

PERFECT INNOCENCE IN RELATIONSHIP

Before the Fall, Genesis 2:25 (NKJV) tells us that "they were both naked, the man and his wife, and were not ashamed." While Adam was sleeping, God had taken a rib from his side, and from that rib He fashioned a woman, a "perfect ten."

Husband, your wife is bone of your bone and flesh of

your flesh. She is your "missing rib." Together you are indivisible. God sees both of you or neither of you.

I hope you appreciate the value of a worthy wife. Solomon said that the price of a good wife is "far above rubies" (Prov. 31:10 NKJV). Just like a precious stone, in order for a wife to shine, she must be guarded, supported, and treasured. Paul wrote, "Husbands, love your wives, just as Christ also loved the church and gave Himself for her . . . Husbands ought to love their own wives as their own bodies; he who loves his wife loves himself" (Eph. 5:25, 28 NKJV).

I think God knew exactly what He was doing when He fashioned a woman from Adam's side. According to a familiar maxim, God did not take a bone from Adam's foot, that he might walk upon her, or a bone from his head, that she might lord over him. But God took a bone from the man's side, so the woman might be next to his heart and walk by his side as an equal in all things.

I love the way Mike Mason describes woman's creation in his book *The Mystery of Marriage*:

> The Lord God made woman out of part of man's side and closed up the place with flesh, but in marriage He reopens this empty, aching place in man and begins the process of putting the woman back again, if not literally *in* the side, then certainly *at* it: permanently there, intrusively there, a sudden lifelong resident of a space which until that point the man will have considered to be his own private territory, even his own body. But in marriage he will cleave to the woman, and the woman to him, the way his own flesh cleaves to his own bones.[1]

The idea that God created woman inferior to man is an incorrect assumption that preachers have supposed far too often. Some men have the idea that women were created only to be helpers for their husbands. If that's what you've been taught, it's time to reconsider your thinking.

First, notice what God said when He looked at Adam standing in the midst of creation. At the conclusion of each of the other days of creation, God had said, "It is good," but after man's creation, for the first time God found it necessary to say, "It is *not* good that man should be alone" (Gen. 2:18 NKJV, italics added).

Solomon, the wisest man who ever lived, knew that man should not be alone:

> Two are better than one,
> Because they have a good reward for their labor.
> For if they fall, one will lift up his companion.
> But woe to him who is alone when he falls,
> For he has no one to help him up.
> Again, if two lie down together, they will keep warm;
> But how can one be warm alone?
> Though one may be overpowered by another, two can
>   withstand him.
> And a threefold cord is not quickly broken. (Eccl. 4:9–12
>   NKJV)

God created woman to be man's companion, certainly. And many Bible translations use the word *helper* in Genesis 2:18 (NKJV): "And the LORD God said, 'It is not good that man should be alone; I will make him a helper comparable to him.'"

But the Hebrew word, *ezer,* does not exactly mean "helper." A more fitting translation is "strength" or "power." The authors of *Hard Sayings of the Bible* note that the noun *ezer* occurs twenty-one times in the Old Testament, and in many of the passages it is used to parallel words that clearly indicate strength or power.[2]

Therefore, I suggest that we translate Genesis 2:18 as "I will make a power or [strength] corresponding to man." Freedman even suggests, on the basis of later Hebrew, that the second word in the Hebrew expression found in this verse should be rendered "equal to him." If this is so, then God makes for the man a woman fully his equal and fully his match. In this way, the man's loneliness will be assuaged.[3]

When Adam woke up, God brought Eve to him down the grassy slopes of Eden . . . I'm sure you could almost hear "Here Comes the Bride" playing on celestial winds! Adam saw Eve—naked, beautiful, and perfectly designed—and he said, "Yes, Lord, Thy will be done!"

Know this, my friend—God is a matchmaker! If you are single, you can be sure of one thing: Just as God found a perfect mate for Adam by supernatural means, God can find a perfect mate for you. So quit looking for your future spouse in newspapers, computer date-a-mate programs, bars, and nightclubs. Looking for God's best in those places is like looking for a diamond in a sewer. Trust God to bring your perfect mate, and wait patiently for His answer! Just as God provided a perfect woman for Adam, He can provide a perfect mate if marriage is His will for you.

What a perfect marriage that first couple enjoyed! Adam didn't have to hear about all the guys she could have married, and Eve didn't have to hear about what a great cook his mother was.

When Eve asked Adam, "Do you love only me?" he responded, "Of course, honey. There's no one in the world for me but you."

Two People, Two Commands

After placing Adam and Eve in the Garden, God gave the first couple two commands: "Be fruitful and multiply; fill the earth and subdue it; have dominion over the fish of the sea, over the birds of the air, and over every living thing that moves on the earth" (Gen. 1:28 NKJV).

The first command, to be fruitful and multiply, meant that God wanted Adam and Eve to have children. Children have always been considered a sign of God's blessing. The psalmist wrote,

> Behold, children are a heritage from the LORD,
> The fruit of the womb is a reward.
> Like arrows in the hand of a warrior,
> So are the children of one's youth. (Ps. 127:3–4 NKJV)

Notice that the Bible compares children to "arrows," which are weapons used for defense. Children are a man's defense against old age! Your sons and daughters are God's social-security program. They are to take care of you in old age, just as you once took care of them!

I often tell my children, "When I get old, I'm coming to live with you. I'm going to do for you what you did for me—I'm going to eat you out of house and home, talk on the phone day and night, play loud music (so I can hear it without my hearing aid), and get in your new car and burn rubber for two hundred yards."

I'm sure they are looking forward to the day I move in!

GOD MADE CREATION FOR MAN

The second command God gave Adam and Eve was to "have dominion" over the fish, birds, and every living animal. Spotted owls, snail darters, blind beetles, and leopards were never meant to rule mankind. Humans are to have dominion over the animals—period!

I'm not antianimal. My family has loved domestic animals, and I appreciate the beauty and grace of God's wonderful animal kingdom. But when it comes down to a question of whose rights are more significant—man's or an animal's—I'll vote for man every time.

Pantheism, the ancient God-is-nature belief, is pure foolishness. America is drunk on the theology of pantheism today, but in the beginning *God created* the heavens and the earth. The heavens and the earth did not create themselves!

Drunk on nature worship, America's intellectuals are hugging trees instead of worshiping the true Creator. We have placed the rights of spotted owls above the rights and needs of human beings created in the image of God. If you think the Spirit of God dwells in a tree, my friend, go hug a ponderosa pine the next time you get sick, and see what happens.

Incidentally, have you heard about the PETA (People for the Ethical Treatment of Animals) campaign to discourage people from wearing fur? These animal-rights activists have ambushed people on city streets and thrown red paint over their fur coats. Just consider the logic! They say they are defending the rights of helpless, voiceless animals. If, however, I went around tossing buckets of red paint over women who stepped out of abortion clinics, would anyone accept the idea that I was defending the rights of helpless, voiceless babies? It's more likely I'd be tossed in jail and labeled a terrorist.

Too many writers, politicians, and media people are running into the woods, ripping off their shirts, and baying at the moon. They are worshiping "Mother Earth" and praying to "the goddess." They are saying it is more important for a yew tree to grow unmolested in the Pacific Northwest than for a woman with cancer to be cured with Taxol, a drug derived from the yew tree.

Hear me—there is no "Mother Earth." There is only Father God, the Creator of heaven and earth. We are to be good stewards of all God has given us—including the planet—but we are never to confuse the creation with the Creator!

THE PERFECT CREATION
RESTED UNDER GOD'S AUTHORITY

Adam and Eve knew their Creator, and they welcomed His leadership. In their innocence, they accepted the fact that happiness and joy come from living under a protective umbrella of authority. They did not question God's right to enforce His commands, expect obedience, and judge.

Before we examine what happened after Adam and Eve

stepped out from under that protective umbrella, let's look at four principles about authority:

1. *All authority comes from God.* The apostle Paul wrote, "Let every soul be subject to the governing authorities. For there is no authority except from God, and the authorities that exist are appointed by God" (Rom. 13:1 NKJV).

2. *Everything God does, He does by right of His spiritual authority.* He has authority over governments, churches, and even your home.

3. *Because God grants authority, a man cannot assume it without God's permission.*

4. *The Bible says that resistance to authority, or rebellion, is like the sin of witchcraft.*

EXAM DAY APPROACHES

Why couldn't Adam and Eve remain in the Garden for eternity? If the other fallen angels are being held in chains until the day of judgment, why didn't God bind Satan and hold him too? Why was he even allowed to *enter* the Garden of Eden?

The answer to those questions lies in man's free moral agency, his free will, and leads us to the second revelation of truth: *Every individual must be tested.* God created man with the freedom of choice, and choice is meaningless unless an individual is given at least two options.

Suppose you went to a fine Italian restaurant, studied the menu, and decided that you wanted penne pasta for dinner. While you're waiting for the waitress, your mouth is practically watering at the thought of those little noodles.

You love them, you want them, and the menu says this restaurant's penne pasta is the best in town.

So when your server comes to take your order, you eagerly order penne pasta.

Your heart sinks when the waitress shakes her head. "I'm sorry," she says, "but we're out of penne pasta."

Disappointed, you glance back at the menu. "Well, okay. I suppose I could enjoy lasagna."

"Sorry." She lowers her pencil. "We're out of lasagna."

"Okay." You swallow your disappointment. "Spaghetti?"

The waitress cracks her gum. "All we have is pizza. Actually, all we *ever* have is pizza."

In desperation, you slap the table. "But the sign outside says 'Italian Food.' If all you have is pizza, you should say so. I thought I'd have a choice!"

Do you see? One choice alone is no choice at all. So in order for Adam and Eve to have the freedom to choose *obedience* to God, they also had to be able to choose *disobedience*. That's why they were allowed to eat of any of the thousands of trees in the Garden *but* the tree of knowledge of good and evil.

Ironic, isn't it? That tree's name actually foretold its role in the drama. I don't know what kind of tree it was, but until Adam and Eve ate from it, they had no knowledge of evil. That dark awareness descended upon them immediately after their first bite.

SATAN IS A MONSTER

The Age of Innocence began with Adam and Eve living in perfection, enjoying fellowship with God, and accepting

His authority. They might have lived in Eden for eternity, but another being entered the picture, and that brings us to the third revelation of truth in Genesis: *Satan is a real being.*

Some people would have you believe that the devil is a fictional bogeyman invented just to keep people in line. Don't believe that falsehood!

A real Satan entered the Garden and seduced Adam and Eve.

A real Satan tempted Jesus in the wilderness.

A real Satan desires to rob and kill and destroy. He wants to wreck your marriage, your health, and your finances.

Like an expert photographer, God exposes Satan's disguises, methods, and monstrosity in the book of Genesis. First he is pictured as an angel of light. Remember his name? *Lucifer* means "shining." The anointed cherub who had been cast out of heaven and down to earth entered the idyllic Garden as a brilliant, radiant snake. Instantly, he attacked what God had said to Adam and Eve. Mixing truth with pride and accusation, he sidled up to Eve.

> Now the serpent was more cunning than any beast of the field which the LORD God had made. And he said to the woman, "Has God indeed said, 'You shall not eat of every tree of the Garden'?" (Gen. 3:1 NKJV)

Notice that Satan first began to work on Eve by attacking the Word of God. He asked a simple question, nothing terribly outlandish or designed to arouse her alarm. Eve answered truthfully, then she couldn't resist embellishing the truth a bit:

And the woman said to the serpent, "We may eat the fruit of the trees of the garden; but of the fruit of the tree which is in the midst of the garden, God has said, 'You shall not eat it, nor shall you touch it, lest you die.'" (Gen. 3:2–3 NKJV)

Eve hedged on her answer. Yes, God had told them not to eat of the tree in the midst of the Garden, but He had never forbidden them to touch it. What follows is the first lie recorded in Scripture:

Then the serpent said to the woman, "You will not surely die. For God knows that in the day you eat of it your eyes will be opened, and you will be like God, knowing good and evil." So when the woman saw that the tree was good for food, that it was pleasant to the eyes, and a tree desirable to make one wise, she took of its fruit and ate. She also gave to her husband with her, and he ate. (Gen. 3:4–6 NKJV)

Satan whispered in Eve's ear, and today, six thousand years later, he is still whispering in the ear of humanity. Perhaps you've heard his oily voice whispering one of the following phrases:

- "Has God indeed said His Word is true? *That* outdated book?"

- "Has God indeed said, 'Be sure your sins will find you out'? How fatalistic!"

- "Has God indeed said, 'The soul that sins shall surely die'? I don't see people dropping dead from sinning."

- "Has God indeed said, 'Remember the Sabbath day and keep it holy'? How old-fashioned!"

- "Has God indeed said, 'You shall have no other gods before me'? Rather intolerant of Him, isn't it?"

- "Has God indeed said, 'You shall not bear false witness'? How narrow-minded!"

- "Has God indeed said, 'You shall not commit adultery'? What is He, a cosmic spoilsport?"

- "Has God indeed said, 'Bring all the tithes into the storehouse'? What does He know about money?"

- "Has God indeed said, 'You must be born again'? What about the millions who aren't as fanatical as He is?"

Satan is a liar! Of the devil, Jesus said:

He was a murderer from the beginning, and does not stand in the truth, because there is no truth in him. When he speaks a lie, he speaks from his own resources, for he is a liar and the father of it. (John 8:44 NKJV)

Satan is a roaring lion, seeking those he may devour (1 Peter 5:8). On a beautiful day during the Age of Innocence, he devoured the innocence of Adam and Eve.

Adam and Eve failed the test of the Garden. God drove them from Paradise. Their failure was not only personal, but it also affected the entire world, plunging us all into the depravity of sin. "Therefore, just as through one man sin entered the world, and death through sin," Paul wrote, "and thus death spread to all men, because all sinned" (Rom. 5:12 NKJV).

THE PROGRESSION OF SIN

Look at the progression of sin in the Garden. First, sin was a *fascination.* "You shall be like God," Satan whispered. Eve stepped closer, fascinated by the possibility.

Next, sin became a *form.* "Eat this fruit . . ." Eve took the fruit, held it in her hand, and inhaled its scent.

Finally, the form became a *fact.* Adam and Eve ate the forbidden fruit, and with rueful sorrow they realized that Satan's truth contained a dark reality—they *did* learn the difference between good and evil, not because they ascended to holiness, like God, but because they descended to Satan's level of corruption, submerging their innocence in sin.

This progression is still Satan's modus operandi. Adultery does not begin with an immoral act in a hotel; first it is a mental fascination. The fascination takes form, then the form becomes a fact.

Lying begins with fascination—*I can escape the consequences of my conduct. I can lie and get out of trouble.*

Gossip is born in fascination—*How exciting to learn or share what is not common knowledge!*

Divorce springs from fascination—*Surely life would be better without my spouse!*

The apostle James wrote:

Let no one say when he is tempted, "I am tempted by God"; for God cannot be tempted by evil, nor does He Himself tempt anyone. But each one is tempted when he is drawn away by his own desires and enticed. Then, when desire has conceived, it gives birth to sin; and sin, when it is full-grown, brings forth death. Do not be deceived, my beloved brethren. (James 1:13–16 NKJV)

A wise man once said, "You can't stop a bird from flying over your head, but you *can* stop him from making a nest in your hair." Understand this: temptation is like the bird flying over your head. As long as we live in the world, we will be tempted, but by God's grace we have the power to overcome temptation.

Don't let temptation nest in your thoughts and actions. A temptation can result in a thought, which leads to a choice, which leads to an act, which leads to a habit, which leads to an addiction. A Christian cannot experience the victory and joy of the Christian life if he or she is addicted to sin.

THE RESULTS OF SIN

When sin entered the Garden of Innocence, "then the eyes of both of them were opened, and they knew that they were naked; and they sewed fig leaves together and made themselves coverings" (Gen. 3:7 NKJV).

After their act of sin, Adam and Eve were no longer God-conscious. They became self-conscious! When they turned their focus from the living God, they fell into sin. For their failure to obey God, they were expelled from the Garden of Eden.

What were the results of disobedience? Adam and Eve were cursed, as was creation itself. The curse of sin fell upon the ground:

> Both thorns and thistles it shall bring forth for you, and
> you shall eat the herb of the field. (Gen. 3:18 NKJV)

The sorrows of childbearing fell upon the woman.

> To the woman He said:
> "I will greatly multiply your sorrow and your conception;
> In pain you shall bring forth children;
> Your desire shall be for your husband,
> And he shall rule over you." (Gen. 3:16 NKJV)

Though children remain a blessing from God, the act of childbirth involves pain, and the process of child rearing in a sinful, fallen world will is fraught with danger and hazards. Furthermore, as a result of her sin, woman would turn away from her sole dependence on God and turn instead to her husband. God warned that the results will not always be pleasant.[4]

Adam, the first man, fell under the curse of sin.

> Then to Adam He said, "Because you have heeded the
> voice of your wife, and have eaten from the tree of which
> I commanded you, saying, 'You shall not eat of it':

Cursed is the ground for your sake;
In toil you shall eat of it
All the days of your life . . .
In the sweat of your face you shall eat bread
Till you return to the ground,
For out of it you were taken;
For dust you are,
And to dust you shall return." (Gen. 3:17, 19 NKJV)

Satan was cursed.

And I will put enmity
Between you and the woman,
And between your seed and her Seed;
He shall bruise your head,
And you shall bruise His heel. (Gen. 3:15 NKJV)

WHAT MAN LOST IN THE FALL

Not only was creation cursed as a result of man's fall, but Adam and Eve also lost blessings God had intended for them.

They lost spiritual and physical life. In Genesis 2:17 (NKJV), God had told them, "But of the tree of the knowledge of good and evil you shall not eat, for in the day that you eat of it, you shall surely die." He did not mean that the tree would poison them so that they would die immediately, but eating from the tree and their act of disobedience brought about immediate *spiritual* death. The phrase "in the day that you eat of it" doesn't mean that physical death would occur on the day they ate of the fruit. In the Hebrew, the phrase does not imply *immediate action*, but instead points to the *certainty of the predicted consequence*. And, just as God predicted, Adam and Eve did suffer physical death as a result of their banishment from Eden.[5]

They lost communion with God. After committing sin, the couple who had been privileged to walk with God in the cool of the day literally hid themselves from the presence of the Lord God. Sin still separates man from God. The prophet Isaiah wrote: "But your iniquities have separated you from your God; and your sins have hidden His face from you, so that He will not hear" (Isa. 59:2 NKJV).

They lost full dominion over all things. The psalmist wrote:

> For You have made [man] a little lower than the angels,
> And You have crowned him with glory and honor.
> You have made him to have dominion over the works of Your hands;
> You have put all things under his feet,
> All sheep and oxen—
> Even the beasts of the field,
> The birds of the air,
> And the fish of the sea
> That pass through the paths of the seas. (Ps. 8:5–8 NKJV)

God had planned for Adam to rule the earth, but sin thwarted that perfect plan.

They lost freedom from Satan. Writing to the Christians at Ephesus, the apostle Paul warned believers that they struggled against the evil ruler of this present world: "For we do not wrestle against flesh and blood, but against principalities, against powers, against the rulers of the darkness of this age, against spiritual hosts of wickedness in the heavenly places" (Eph. 6:12 NKJV). Having once surrendered to Satan's temptation, mankind would be susceptible to it for ages to come.

They lost the Garden of Eden.

> Then the LORD God said, "Behold, the man has become like one of Us, to know good and evil. And now, lest he put out his hand and take also of the tree of life, and eat, and live forever"—therefore the LORD God sent him out of the garden of Eden to till the ground from which he was taken. So He drove out the man; and He placed cherubim at the east of the garden of Eden, and a flaming sword which turned every way, to guard the way to the tree of life. (Gen. 3:22–24 NKJV)

They lost the right to eat of the tree of life. God had not forbidden Adam and Eve to eat from the tree of life, but they lost the opportunity to eat from this tree when they lost the Garden of Eden. We will not be able to eat from the tree of life until God allows us to stand before His throne in heaven.

> And he showed me a pure river of water of life, clear as crystal, proceeding from the throne of God and of the Lamb. In the middle of its street, and on either side of the river, was the tree of life, which bore twelve fruits, each tree yielding its fruit every month. The leaves of the tree were for the healing of the nations. (Rev. 22:1–2 NKJV)

They lost perfect health. Sickness and corruption could not dwell in Eden.

They lost all the benefits of perfect fellowship with God. Fortunately, these things will be restored to believers in heaven:

> And I heard a loud voice from heaven saying, "Behold, the tabernacle of God is with men, and He will dwell with them, and they shall be His people. God Himself will be with them and be their God. And God will wipe away every tear from their eyes; there shall be no more death, nor sorrow, nor crying. There shall be no more pain, for the former things have passed away."
>
> Then He who sat on the throne said, "Behold, I make all things new." And He said to me, "Write, for these words are true and faithful." And He said to me, "It is done! I am the Alpha and the Omega, the Beginning and the End. I will give of the fountain of the water of life freely to him who thirsts. He who overcomes shall inherit all things, and I will be his God and he shall be My son." (Rev. 21:3–7 NKJV)

GOD PROVIDES AN ANSWER

Adam and Eve were in a sorry condition after their sin, but there is another picture of Eden I'd like you to see. It points to yet the fourth revelation of truth in Genesis: *The work of salvation is accomplished through the shedding of blood.*

After Adam and Eve fell into sin, God himself clothed them with animal skins (Gen. 3:21). In clothing them, God preached the first gospel sermon, not with words, but with action. Innocent blood was shed to cover the guilty.

At Calvary, the Lamb of God was slain so that His blood could cover the stench of my sin. The Word of God tells us, "And according to the law almost all things are purified with blood, and without shedding of blood there is no remission [of sin]" (Heb. 9:22 NKJV).

I am not saved by the blood of goats and bulls, but by the precious blood of the Lamb of God, which takes away the sins of the world. I am not saved by the blood of rams and turtledoves, but the blood that flows from Emmanuel's veins. I am not saved by the blood of the church fathers slain for their testimony, but by the blood that washes whiter than snow!

In one of my previous books, *His Glory Revealed*, a study of the prophetic meaning attached to each of the seven major Jewish festivals, I discussed the sash attached to the scapegoat every year at the Feast of Atonement. According to Eddie Chumney, the *Mishnah,* the earliest surviving work of Rabbinic literature, mentions an interesting tradition about the scapegoat:

> A portion of the crimson sash was attached to the door of the Temple before the goat was sent into the wilderness. The sash would turn from red to white as the goat met its end, signaling to the people that God had accepted their sacrifices and their sins were forgiven . . . The *Mishnah* tells us that 40 years before the destruction of the Temple, the sash stopped turning white. This, of course, was when *Yeshua* [Jesus] was slain on the tree.[6]

Adam and Eve did nothing to be forgiven for their sin—God did all the work!

When the prodigal son came home—stinking like swine, ragged, and full of sin and shame—what did his father do? The father said to his servants, "Bring out the best robe and put it on him! Kill the fatted calf, and call our friends! We're going to have a celebration!"

The prodigal son did nothing to be forgiven . . . he only came home. His father accomplished the work of restoration.

So it is with you, my friend. You can do nothing to cover your sin and earn forgiveness. "For by grace you have been saved through faith," wrote Paul, "and that not of yourselves; it is the gift of God" (Eph. 2:8 NKJV). You can't earn this gift—but you can accept or reject it.

When Adam and Eve discovered they were naked, they wove fig leaves together to try and hide their shame. Rather than run to God, they hid from Him. They tried to cover their sin with the works of their hands, but soon they found the task impossible.

Self-manufactured aprons will not hide your sin. Religious ritual will not cover your shame. Professing Christ without possessing Him will not earn God's forgiveness. Paul wrote that the last days would bring people who have "a form of godliness" but deny its power (2 Tim. 3:5 NKJV). Those people, who may appear to be holy and religious, stand guilty and shamefaced before God.

All sinners are naked before God, and "all our righteousnesses are like filthy rags" (Isa. 64:6 NKJV). Nothing we can do will ever cover our sin, but when sinners realize their nakedness and turn to God, He clothes them in His own righteousness. As the prophet Isaiah wrote,

I will greatly rejoice in the LORD,
My soul shall be joyful in my God;
For He has clothed me with the garments of salvation,
He has covered me with the robe of righteousness,
As a bridegroom decks himself with ornaments,
And as a bride adorns herself with her jewels.

    (Isa. 61:10 NKJV)

FIG LEAVES THEN AND NOW

Does the image of a fig tree ring a bell in your memory? In Mark 11:13, we read about Jesus cursing a fig tree. This particular tree was full of leaves but had no fruit, for "the time for fruit had not yet come."

It might seem unfair for Jesus to curse a tree for having no fruit if it wasn't the season for figs, but fig trees bear fruit *before* they bring forth leaves. This particular tree had covered itself in glossy leaves before the appointed time, and when Jesus drew near, expecting to find fruit, He discovered that the tree was barren. It had a *form* of prosperity, it held the *promise* of much fruit, but it had nothing to offer the Son of God.

I believe God wants us to make the connection between the fig leaves on Adam and Eve and the barren fig tree. See the picture and the fifth revelation of truth: *No fig leaves, no good works, no church membership can hide your sin.* Your works, your memberships, your good intentions are under the curse of failure. The only thing that can grant forgiveness is the blood of God's slain holy Lamb.

THE SPIRIT OF REBELLION IS ALIVE AND WELL

Don't be too hard on Eve when you consider the loss of mankind's innocence. Just because you are a Christian does not mean the spirit of rebellion cannot influence you. Just because you are a child of God does not mean that your marriage, your life, your business, and your children will never suffer the storms of rebellion. Rebellion isn't pleasant; it is anything but peaceful. The Bible does not pull any punches—the Old Testament plainly tells us that "rebellion is as the sin of witchcraft, And stubbornness is as iniquity and idolatry" (1 Sam. 15:23 NKJV).

But, you may be thinking, *witchcraft involves darkness and demons and the occult! I would never dabble in anything like that!*

My friend, if there is one lesson we can learn from Lucifer's fall, it is this: Rebellion and Satan are like the sea and the shore—you can't have one without the other. Satan's pride led him to rebel against God, and every sin that man commits springs from rebellion against God or a God-ordained authority.

We have already seen that everything God does, He does through righteous authority. He established a righteous chain of command in government, in the home, and in the church.

The authority of the home is the father. When anyone in the home, be it wife, children, or mother-in-law, attempts to intimidate, manipulate, or disobey the father, that's rebellion not only against the father, but also against God.

The authority of the church is the pastor. If anyone in

the church—be it a deacon, an elder, or the pastor's wife—tries to threaten, intimidate, or falsely accuse the pastor, that's rebellion not only against the pastor, but also against God.

There are many authorities in our country. If anyone—be it the president, a congressman, or an ordinary citizen—breaks the laws of the land, that is rebellion not only against society, but also against God. The only exception is when the laws of a nation violate God's laws; in such cases we "ought to obey God rather than men" (Acts 5:29 NKJV).

MANIFESTATIONS OF REBELLION

The first major manifestation of rebellion is *manipulation.* A weaker person will often use manipulation to quietly rebel against his or her God-ordained authority. Satan tried to manipulate Eve when he suggested that God had not told her the entire truth about eating from the forbidden tree.

A wife might try to control her husband with sex. Inside the bounds of marriage, sex is wonderful—it's God's idea and He blessed it. But manipulation says, "If you'll allow me to have my way in this debate, tonight we'll have an exciting time in the bedroom. But if you don't, you'll find yourself sleeping on the sofa."

Husbands and wives can also be guilty of mood manipulation. Men, how many times have you been so upset you spent the afternoon pouting? Or perhaps you're the type who gets angry and yells because things didn't go the way you wanted. If so, you are demonstrating rebellion through your mood.

I've seen parents use guilt in an attempt to control their

adult children. A mother will sigh and tell her grown child, "I want you to always remember that I almost died giving birth to you. I slaved to feed you and took clothes off my own back to dress you. I worked twelve-hour days to put you through school. I begged and borrowed to give you a good wedding . . . So why won't you do what I want?"

Parent, those things may be true, but love keeps no record of offenses or wrongs. Love doesn't keep score, nor does it try to manipulate the ones it cares for. If you are manipulating your grown children in this way, you are rebelling against the God who brought them to adulthood. You didn't preserve their lives; God did! Trust Him with the future for your children and yourself!

Our churches are not immune to this kind of manipulation. Many times I've heard people say, "Well, we'd better give so-and-so what he wants, or he'll get on the phone and start a holy war." Well, my friend, if a church member is intent on war, turn him out and let him wage his battle in the world. When people become angry and threaten to leave the church, I always say, "God bless you, and I hope you find a place where you can be happy." People caught up in the spirit of rebellion, though, are never happy under authority. They need to confess their rebellion and repent.

Another manifestation of rebellion is *intimidation*. Husbands may try to intimidate their wives, or parents seek to rule their children, not through love or God-given authority, but through a spirit of intimidation. Husbands, don't bully your wives, but win them to your side through loving leadership. Children should obey not because parents are bigger or stronger, but because God has ordained Mom and Dad to be the authorities in the home. So do not scream and yell at your children when you discipline them! Speak clearly, and explain the reasons for your discipline by relying upon the principles of God's Word.

Parents who love their children establish rules. We tell our youngsters not to play in the street, and we tell our teenagers to be home by eleven o'clock on hot summer nights. We don't establish rules because we're craving power, but because we love our children. A child who violates those rules steps out from under the God-ordained umbrella of protection and may be hurt.

Satan often uses false prophecy to intimidate believers. If someone comes to you and says, "God showed me that something terrible is about to happen in your life" or "Look here! This ancient prophecy confirms that the Tribulation will begin while the church is still on the earth," don't you believe it. Don't let your faith be shaken. Don't let a false prophet manipulate the truth of God's Word. Paul wrote, "But he who prophesies speaks edification and exhortation and comfort to men" (1 Cor. 14:3 NKJV). Prophecy should edify and encourage and comfort, not terrify those who hear it. If some so-called prophet predicts anything that does not bring peace and comfort to believers, he is rebelling against the truth.

God never meant for us to resent authority. The people He places in positions of authority bear the weight of leadership in order to protect us.

Have you, like Adam and Eve, been tempted by the Prince of Darkness to disobey God? Have you fallen into sin? Have you eaten forbidden fruit? Is your mind pregnant with sinful fascination?

Just as Adam and Eve lived under a curse for their sin,

so will you, your children, and your children's children. Without repentance and confession, your life will be hell on earth. Yes, sin is exciting initially. It is fascinating. But Satan's poison will destroy your marriage, your mind, your health, your hopes, your wealth, your children, and your grandchildren!

God wants you to live in Paradise, and life can be heaven on earth. But you must confess your sin to be able to stay in Paradise.

Journal, Page Three

My spirit still quakes within me when I recall that black moment when Adam and Eve fled from their home in Paradise. The angel with the flaming sword, one of the mighty cherubim, kept his burning eyes upon them as the man and his weeping woman clutched each other and walked down a path the Son had cleared only a short time before. This was the path He walked to find the animals whose skins now covered the shivering couple . . .

Though that hour was the darkest we had known since the war in heaven, the light of love shone from the Father's eyes and gave us hope. "I am not done with man," His voice whispered on the wind. "I will make bare my holy arm in the eyes of all the nations; and all the ends of the earth shall see the salvation of the Son."

With the other angelic hosts, I watched as the man and woman settled in a pleasant part of the earth. 'Twas not Paradise, but God blessed them, and multiplied their crops as well as their lives. Two sons were born, Cain and Abel, and other children followed. And man began to multiply, and God preserved them, and blessed them, and sent the sunshine and cool mist upon those who honored Him as well as those who did not.

There was one particular man, Enoch, who so delighted the Father that He sent an angel host to bring the man bodily into heaven. I myself have spoken to this Enoch—he watches much and says little, but I sense that his heart is waiting for the Father to reveal His purpose. "For everything there is a season, and a time for every purpose under heaven" . . .

CHAPTER

THE AGE OF
CONSCIENCE

There is only one way to achieve happiness
on this terrestrial ball,
And that is to have either a clear conscience,
or none at all.[1]
—OGDEN NASH

A salesman was making his first visit to the uttermost reaches of his western territory. By this point in his travels, he had transferred to a train drawn by an antique engine on a shabby branch line. The train crept along, stopping at every little town. Finally, it halted in the middle of nowhere. By then the salesman was the only passenger aboard.

The conductor assured the salesman, "Nothing to worry about, sir. Just a cow on the track."

Sure enough, after a minute or two the train lurched forward, but after chugging along for a mile or two, it slowed and stopped again. "Just a temporary delay," the conductor said. "We'll be on our way shortly."

"What is it now?" the exasperated salesman asked. "Did we catch up to that cow again?"

Like that salesman, most people are impatient, and that makes it hard for us to understand how God could exercise patience with mankind through the ages. God is not only patient, He is longsuffering (2 Peter 3:9). People who misunderstand the longsuffering patience of God tend to make one of two false assumptions about Him: They either look at His judgments and conclude that He is an angry, vindictive tyrant, or they consider His patience and decide He is indifferent to evil in the world.

Neither of those conclusions is anywhere near the truth. The wickedness of our thoughts and actions pains God. He is deeply concerned about the cruelty of war and the strong's oppression of the weak. God's response to human sin has always been to provide a solution, then, with patient longsuffering, to call us back to Himself. Only after people reject God's grace and mercy over long periods of time do they find themselves facing His wrath.

In the Old Testament, the nations Israel destroyed had been decadent societies for centuries (Gen. 15:16). Israel and Judah went into exile only after laughing at God's prophets generation after generation (Isa. 65:2; Hos. 11:1–11). God wasn't looking for people to bully; He reluctantly released the consequences of sin.

God is not indifferent to evil in the world. He cares about ethnic violence, political repression, religious persecution, the abuse of children, and all kinds of exploitation. He suffers with His creatures and His creation. No one gets away with anything in terms of eternity, but everyone has many chances to respond to God's grace on earth.

God extended His grace and mercy to all who would accept it after Adam's expulsion from the Garden, but man's ears grew deaf to the voice of God. Finally, God had to act.

A New Age Dawns

The Age of Conscience is the antediluvian age, or the period of time between Adam's expulsion from the Garden and Noah's flood. During this period of 1,656 years, God waited to see if man would obey his conscience regarding right and wrong. This age is sometimes called the Age of Freedom, for man was free to do as he pleased. No laws governed his actions. God had not given the Ten Commandments. Only man's conscience restrained his actions.

According to *The American Heritage Dictionary of the English Language*, conscience is "the awareness of a moral or ethical aspect to one's conduct together with the urge to prefer right over wrong."[2] I'd like to take that definition a step further—conscience is the God-ordained watchdog of the soul. Conscience knows our acts and decisions, and approves or condemns them according to the principles of right and wrong.

The Judgment of Conscience

A guilty conscience produces fear. When Adam and Eve rebelled against God in the Garden of Eden, they hid themselves from God, saying, "We are afraid!"

Are you fearful? Are you afraid your past will be uncovered? Are you afraid your secret sins will be exposed? They will find you out if they are unconfessed! In Numbers 32:23 (NKJV), God reminds us: "Be sure your sin will find you out."

A clean conscience removes fear, but a guilty conscience produces remorse. When Adam and Eve left the Garden, they were filled with remorse. How many times did they go back to the gates of the Garden and beg the angels to let them return? They lost Paradise forever because they rejected conscience.

How many times I have seen church members trample their consciences, then live long, bitter lives of remorse! I've seen men and women turned out of the paradise of a happy home because they rejected the voice of conscience. I've seen men walk away from the paradise of a good marriage for one tempestuous fling. When conscience screamed, "Stop!" they refused. They traded paradise for remorse and repercussions that will last forever.

I've seen teenagers accept invitations from their friends. Just for one night, they decided to talk a walk on the wild side. While their consciences screamed, "Stop! Turn around, call home," the teens continued to follow their friends. One party, one snort of cocaine, one five-minute sexual fling, one short ride home in a car with a drunk driver . . . and their lives were forever ruined. Because they rejected the counsel of conscience, they forfeited the paradise path God had planned for them. Instead of fulfillment and joy, they drank from a cup of remorse, just like Adam and Eve.

How Much Spiritual Truth Did Man Have in the Age of Conscience?

With no laws, no Bible, and no churches, how could God expect people who lived prior to the Flood to live up to His expectations? Was it fair for Him to expect godly behavior of them?

Let's consider the Scriptures and see how much spiritual truth antediluvian man possessed:

1. *They had the witness of nature.* Romans 1:19–20 (NKJV) tells us that they knew enough to look at the world around them and realize Someone created it:

> What may be known of God is manifest in them, for God has shown it to them. For since the creation of the world His invisible attributes are clearly seen, being understood by the things that are made, even His eternal power and Godhead, so that they are without excuse.

2. *They had the witness of conscience.*

> For when Gentiles, who do not have the law, by nature do the things in the law, these, although not having the law, are a law to themselves, who show the work of the law written in their hearts, their conscience also bearing witness, and between themselves their thoughts accusing or else excusing them. (Rom. 2:14–15 NKJV)

3. *They had the promise of a Redeemer,* for God had promised to send One who would defeat Satan and sin.

And I will put enmity
Between you and the woman,
And between your seed and her Seed;
He shall bruise your head,
And you shall bruise His heel. (Gen. 3:15 NKJV)

4. *They knew the importance of sacrifice.* "Abel also brought of the firstborn of his flock and of their fat. And the LORD respected Abel and his offering" (Gen. 4:4 NKJV).

5. *They had prophets.*

Now Enoch, the seventh from Adam, prophesied about these men also, saying, "Behold, the Lord comes with ten thousands of His saints, to execute judgment on all, to convict all who are ungodly among them of all their ungodly deeds which they have committed in an ungodly way, and of all the harsh things which ungodly sinners have spoken against Him." (Jude 14–15 NKJV).

6. *They had preachers* such as "Noah, one of eight people, a preacher of righteousness, bringing in the flood on the world of the ungodly" (2 Peter 2:5 NKJV).

7. *They knew the difference between good and evil.* "Then the LORD God said, 'Behold, the man has become like one of Us, to know good and evil'" (Gen. 3:22). Cain knew the difference between good and evil when he became angry with his brother, Abel. When God accepted Abel's sacrifice and not Cain's, instead of correcting his improper offering, Cain burned with anger toward his brother.

So the LORD said to Cain, "Why are you angry? And why has your countenance fallen? If you do well, will you not be accepted? And if you do not do well, sin lies at the door. And its desire is for you, but you should rule over it." (Gen. 4:6–7 NKJV)

8. *They were acquainted with the ministry of the Holy Spirit.* "And the LORD said, 'My Spirit shall not strive with man forever, for he is indeed flesh; yet his days shall be one hundred and twenty years'" (Gen. 6:3 NKJV).[3]

Why did God establish the Age of Conscience? Since man knew good and evil, God wanted to teach man how to choose good. He wanted man to see that evil could only result in destruction, unhappiness, and death. Most of all, God wanted man to see that he was powerless in himself to resist evil, and only through God's help could he overcome. "Call out to me," God was saying. "I am your true friend, and you are my beloved. Only through me can you escape the curse of sin."

Though the Age of Conscience began favorably, with God blessing Adam and Eve with children, through the years man slipped further and further away from God. Without God-ordained or even man-made laws, people were free to do as they pleased, and they chose evil more often than they chose good. Satan celebrated as people repeatedly rejected God, and God grieved as He watched His creation move further away from the ideal of perfection He had designed. God allowed mankind to reach the full limit of wickedness before He acted.

But act He did.

Then the LORD saw that the wickedness of man was great in the earth, and that every intent of the thoughts of his heart was only evil continually. And the LORD was sorry that He had made man on the earth, and He was grieved in His heart. So the LORD said, "I will destroy man whom I have created from the face of the earth, both man and beast, creeping thing and birds of the air, for I am sorry that I have made them." (Gen. 6:5–7 NKJV)

This Scripture is remarkable—it says God regretted that He had made man. You will never find God regretting that He *redeemed* man, but this passage records how God wished that He could wipe man off the face of the earth in the same way you would wipe filth off a beautiful garment.

Judgment always comes to the man, the nation, and the world that tramples conscience and ignores God's authority. The Age of Conscience ended with the Flood of Noah. This judgment, one the world would never forget, was inescapable.

Geologists William Ryan and Walter Pitman, both of Columbia University, wrote *Noah's Flood*, a book that has received a surprising amount of publicity in recent months. The book—and the publicity—is remarkable because the authors assert there really was a world-ending flood, and its survivors were farmers.

According to the authors, the force of the water rushing from the Mediterranean into the Black Sea, then a freshwater lake, generated a roar that could have been heard sixty miles away. The Flood was unusually sudden, powerful, and deadly because sea waters were driven by the full force of the Mediterranean. By their calculations, the water would have rushed through the Bosporus Strait at fifty miles per hour with two hundred times more power than Niagara Falls.[4] One piece of proof discovered in the soil layers: Freshwater mollusks with smashed shells gave way to saltwater creatures with intact shells. Carbon-14 testing of the shell remains place this event at approximately 5600 B.C.[5]

I'm grateful that the book is causing people to dig out their Bibles and read about the biblical Flood, but I have to disagree with Ryan and Pitman's overall hypothesis. Noah's Flood was a divine act, not a natural phenomenon, and it was a worldwide flood, not a regional tragedy. The Bible specifically says, "In the six hundredth year of Noah's life, in the second month, the seventeenth day of the month, on that day all the fountains of the great deep were broken up, and the windows of heaven were opened" (Gen. 7:11 NKJV). The biblical Flood came from forty days and nights of rain *plus* water from the "fountains of the deep." I'm not saying the Mediterranean couldn't have rushed into the Black Sea during the Flood, but the event was not happenstance.

How do we know the floodwaters covered the entire earth? There is biblical, geological, and cultural evidence to prove that Noah's flood covered the planet.

If there was any safe place on earth, God could have sent Noah, his family, and the animals there. They would not have needed an ark.

Mankind was undoubtedly scattered far over the earth. "Even with the most literal interpretation of Scripture," wrote Harold Willmington, "that the Flood occurred just 10 generations after Adam, there would have been at least 10 million people on earth, and their nomadic ways could have taken them far beyond the Middle East."[6]

The Revelation of Truth

God promised not to send another deluge like Noah's
Flood. If Noah's Flood had been limited to only one area,
then God lied, for many local areas have been flooded since
Noah's time.[7]

Stories of a worldwide flood have been part of oral culture in nearly every part of the world. Marine fossils have
been discovered on mountaintops. How did they get there,
unless the mountains were once covered by floodwaters?[8]

Mark this down, friend: In the Flood of judgment, God
killed every living animal and man on the earth except those
who were on the ark. A recent television miniseries about
Noah and the ark depicted men and women in paddleboats
floating by the ark as it sailed to safety—that's sheer nonsense.
The only people who survived were Noah and his family.

The heavens opened with torrential rain, and the fountains of the deep began to rush forth. As the water rose
higher, people ran in panic toward the boat Noah had been
building for 120 years. They pounded the sides in terror,
but God had already shut the door. The ark began to groan
as the waters surrounded and lifted it. The weak drowned
immediately, the strong ran to the high mountains and the
tall trees, but no one could outrun the rushing waters. As
the water continued to rise, they swam; they treaded water
until exhaustion dragged them down to a watery grave.

Why would God inflict such a terrible judgment upon
the people He had created? Because the people of Noah's
day ignored the voice of God and defiled their consciences.
And today, as then, judgment looms on the horizon, but
with judgment comes redemption for the righteous. God
offered Noah and his family another chance to participate
in God's plan for mankind, and by preserving clean animals

tt

for sacrifice He emphasized that man would continue having faith in the coming Redeemer.

The writer of Hebrews told us:

> By faith Noah, being divinely warned of things not yet seen, moved with godly fear, prepared an ark for the saving of his household, by which he condemned the world and became heir of the righteousness which is according to faith. (Heb. 11:7 NKJV)

Why did God save Noah? The Bible tells us, "Noah was a just man, perfect in his generations. Noah walked with God" (Gen. 6:9 NKJV). The Hebrew word for *perfect* involves the idea of completeness, so we know Noah's life was complete, with no aspect missing.[9] Noah was not sinless, for no man is, but he accepted and applied God's standard to his life and actions. When all around him people were immersing themselves in evil and earning the wrath of God, Noah chose to follow God's standards. As a result, "Noah found grace in the eyes of the LORD" (Gen. 6:8 NKJV).

WHEN DID THE FLOOD BEGIN?

In his book *The Flood Reconsidered*, Frederick Filby gives us a fascinating picture of God's perfect timing:

> The Flood commenced on the seventeenth day of the second month, i.e., the month later known as Marcheswan. This month ran from a date (which could vary) in October to one in November. Taking the average date for the commencement of one of Noah's months as about the

middle of one of our months the Flood must have started early in November. When at last the Flood had completely receded and Noah emerged from the Ark, the date is recorded as the twenty-seventh day of the second month of the following year. Thus the old world perished in November and a year later a new era commenced in the same month. Both of these facts are indelibly enshrined in the memory of the human race. To many people around the world November brings the Day of the Dead. In a number of ancient and primitive calendars November also brings a New Year at a time which has neither solstice nor equinox nor astronomical event to justify it.

November 2 is All Soul's Day, the Day of the Dead. The Flood commenced and ended in November, lasting just over a year, but the recollection of it has never died out in the memory and the calendars of the descendants of that little group of survivors.

But these amazing facts lead us to something still more wonderful. We are specifically told that after 150 days the Ark rested on the seventeenth day of the seventh month. If the Flood started in November, the Ark rested in April. If it started in Marcheswan, the Ark rested in Nisan, the month which later became the new first month of the year. The Ark came safely to rest on Nisan 17. Centuries later the Israelites in Egypt took a lamb on Nisan 10, kept the Passover on Nisan 14 and then set out, pursued by the hosts of Pharaoh, but by the seventeenth everyone was safe across the Red Sea—a new nation, delivered from death and danger. And very many more centuries passed and Christ Himself kept that same Passover memorial and then went, not above, but down into the water of death to deliver, not eight souls, but an innumerable multitude and then rose triumphant over death itself on Nisan 17. With that Resurrection a new era began, a new creation was commenced. Thus Christ rose from the dead on the anniversary of the crossing of the Red Sea and the anniversary of the resting of the Ark on the mountains of Ararat. How wonderful indeed was Noah's calendar—or rather, God's![10]

REDEMPTION FROM JUDGMENT!

The portrait of truth in Genesis pertaining to the Age of Conscience is one of the most comforting pictures God has ever sketched. Look carefully at Noah and his family in the ark, and you will see the sixth revelation of truth: *Believers are secure; they will not have to face judgment.*

Dr. John Sailhamer, a professor of Hebrew Bible at Western Seminary, likens the story of Noah and the Flood to a Rembrandt painting. "There's a lot of darkness," he says, "but then you see these flashes of light. What was Rembrandt painting? He wasn't painting darkness. He was painting light."[11]

In Noah's flood, the judgment of God descended upon the earth and drowned all flesh—every man, woman, child, and animal. But the Bible tells us that the ark, which God designed, instituted, and sealed, saved Noah and his family.

"The whole theme of the Pentateuch and the Torah is that God is a God of salvation as well as judgment," Dr. Sailhamer told the *Dallas Morning News.* "Noah was not a perfect person, but he walked with God. He had fellowship with God, and God saved him." Sailhamer also notes that in the biblical narrative, God did not direct Noah's attention to the suffering and pain occurring *outside* the ark. "We don't see outside the window," he said. "God is outside judging the world, but we're inside with Noah. We're not to observe God's judgment. That's not our business. Our business is to be inside with Noah. We're only allowed to go out after it's all over. And there's the rainbow."[12]

Many preachers today are teaching that the church will go through the Tribulation, but the picture of judgment in the Age of Conscience refutes this. Not only will we not go through it, but we will not even *see* it.

In Genesis, God's hand snatched the righteous—Noah's family—from judgment and secured them safely. In another Genesis account, Lot and his family were led away from Sodom and Gomorrah before God sent judgment upon those two sinful cities. In the story of Sodom, the only person who saw God's judgment was Lot's wife, the woman who could not tear her heart or her eyes away from the sinful city (Gen. 19).

God's purpose for the Tribulation is to punish the ungodly who have rejected His Son, Jesus Christ. Why, then, would He want to punish believers? God will be true to the picture He painted in Genesis: first warning, then rescue, and then judgment. Jesus Himself reinforced this revelation of truth: "But as the days of Noah were," He told His disciples, "so also will the coming of the Son of Man be" (Matt. 24:37).

When hell breaks loose on earth during the Tribulation, I'll be gone from this planet. So, fellow believers, pray up, pack up, and look up. We're not going through the Tribulation; we're going up with the Lord!

HOW'S YOUR CONSCIENCE FARING?

Though the Age of Conscience is long past, it wouldn't hurt to take a moment and examine your own conscience. How sensitive is your conscience? Is it quick to hear the voice of God, or does He have to raise His voice to get your attention?

Recently I heard a story about three men sitting on the sidewalk of a major city. One man was blind, one deaf, and one had a bad back. Miraculously, Jesus appeared and touched the blind man. The man immediately jumped to his feet and said, "Praise God, I can see!"

Jesus then reached over and touched the deaf man. His eyes opened wide as he stood and cried out, "I'm healed! I can hear!"

Jesus then reached for the man with the bad back, but the fellow yelped and scrambled away. "Don't touch me," he cried, "I'm on workmen's comp!"

There is more truth in that little story than we would like to admit. Many men who consider themselves honest don't think twice about cheating their employers, the government, and their families. Their consciences have grown dull and past hearing. In fact, removing the conscience from some people would be only a minor operation!

Conscience, however, is the compass of the soul! Conscience is the voice of God saying, "*This* is the way—walk in it." Conscience is not only the voice of God, it is the *gift* of God.

The gift of conscience demands individual responsibility. You alone are responsible for the person you are and will become. You are responsible for your choices and the consequences of those choices. Secular humanists would have you believe conscience is nothing but a primitive, left-over feeling from a less enlightened time. They would have you be more "open-minded," willing to lower traditional moral standards and see perversion as merely "an alternate lifestyle." I have news for you, friend—most things that broaden the mind also narrow the conscience.

FOUR KINDS OF CONSCIENCE IN SCRIPTURE

The Bible describes four different kinds of conscience. The first kind, and the one we should all desire, is a *pure conscience*. Paul states that a pure conscience is one of the requirements a man must meet in order to serve in the church as a minister, an elder, board member, or any other leadership role (1 Tim. 3:9).

Do you have a pure conscience? Let's look at several areas that might provide telling clues: Are you the spiritual leader of your home? Do you have a prayer life? Do you study the Word of God to show yourself approved by Him? Are you a soul winner? Do you tithe? Do you pay your bills? Do you keep your promises? If you can't answer these questions with a resounding and confident "yes," you are not qualified for leadership in the Lord's church.

A wise man once said that conscience is what hurts when everything else feels good. If you still have an active, sensitive conscience, thank God for it. Remember this: When you have a fight with your conscience and get licked, you win.

A man with a pure conscience can sleep through a turbulent thunderstorm! A clear conscience is like a fortress in the day of battle! For some people, however, a clear conscience is nothing more than a poor memory. Thousands of people become hard of hearing when conscience speaks. Others have trained their consciences to roll over and play dead.

The second sort of conscience described in Scripture is *convicting conscience.* What made Adam and Eve hide from God in the Garden? Convicting conscience!

After King David sinned with Bathsheba, what made him cry out, "Have mercy on me, O God!"? Convicting conscience!

At Jesus' trial, what made Pilate's wife write her husband a note saying, "Have nothing to do with that just man"? Convicting conscience!

As he threw thirty pieces of silver to the Pharisees, what made Judas Iscariot scream, "I have betrayed innocent blood!"? Convicting conscience!

Before the invention of radar, sonar, or the compass, God provided every man with a built-in navigational device—convicting conscience. The pain of an agonized conscience is to the soul what suffering is to the body. When the body aches, we say, "I need a doctor to make this pain go away." When the conscience aches, we should say, "I am violating the laws of God, and I need to repent."

Is your conscience convicting you right now? If so, don't try to silence it. It's the voice of God trying to save your soul from remorse. You will not find peace or joy or prosperity until you ease the ache in your conscience. Stop eating the forbidden fruit; stop whatever sin you are committing. Go back to God and repent of your wrongdoing. Make your peace with God, and your conscience will stop troubling you.

Some people try to drown their consciences in a river of alcohol, but like a bloated corpse, conscience pops back up to the surface, demanding to be heard. Others try to sedate their consciences with tranquilizers. They dupe their consciences by searching for cowardly preachers whose "feel-good gospel" avoids even the *mention* of sin. Or they search for a counselor who will excuse their sin and blame it on the past.

My friend, if your conscience is convicting you, don't ignore it. Listen, repent, and turn back to the God who gave conscience to you. That's how you'll find peace.

The third kind of conscience described in the Bible is a *defiled conscience*: "To the pure all things are pure, but to those who are defiled and unbelieving nothing is pure; but even their mind and conscience are defiled" (Titus 1:15 NKJV). Many people with defiled consciences find a way to rationalize and excuse even vile actions, proving that a conscience is a safe guide only when God is the guide of the conscience.

The Bible says the way of transgressors is hard (Prov. 13:15). When a man's conscience goes one way and his conduct goes another, even if he is unbelieving, he will live in torment. There is nothing so painful as a stab of conscience, which is why so many people with defiled consciences quickly progress to a *seared conscience*. Writing to Timothy, Paul said:

Now the Spirit expressly says that in latter times some will depart from the faith, giving heed to deceiving spirits and doctrines of demons, speaking lies in hypocrisy, having their own conscience seared with a hot iron. (1 Tim. 4:1–2 NKJV)

People with seared consciences actually have had their consciences cauterized, as if with a blowtorch. The "nerve endings" of their consciences are dead, so they are beyond feeling. King Saul, who had ignored the voice of conscience far too many times, resorted to consultation with a witch because he could no longer hear the voice of God (1 Sam. 28).

It will literally take a miracle of God to heal and restore a seared conscience, but with God, anything is possible. Hebrews 9:14 (NKJV) tells us, "How much more shall the blood of Christ, who through the eternal Spirit offered Himself without spot to God, cleanse your conscience from dead works to serve the living God?"

THE WAY CONSCIENCE WORKS

The conscience God designed works from the inside out, while man works from the outside in. Several years ago I heard a story about a group of barbers who met in Chicago for the National Barbers' Convention. This particular group of fellows found a homeless man sleeping under a bridge, so they took him in and cleaned him up. They bought him a new suit, gave him a haircut, and shaved him. To promote their convention, they placed "before and after" pictures of the man in the newspaper above the caption, "Just look what your barber can do for you!"

Six weeks later, a curious newspaper reporter found the same man back under the bridge, a bottle in his hand, as unclean and unkempt as he had been before his miraculous conversion.

Why didn't he change for good? Because the barbers worked on him from the *outside*. They did nothing to change his heart.

Too many times, we try to change people by working on the outside. We send drug addicts to rehab programs; we send criminals to prisons in the hope they'll be rehabilitated. But any program that works on the outside of a man is doomed to fail. The United States government tries to solve America's social problems by working on the outside. Some politicians think they can change people by changing their environments. That's not only wrong, it's a foolish and wasteful approach!

Look around your community. Odds are, somewhere nearby you can see government-sponsored housing projects that were once beautiful, but now look like a war zone. Why? Because a new house won't do anything for a man who is unwilling to change his heart.

Man works from the outside in, but God and conscience work from the inside out. The prison programs that succeed in rehabilitation are those like Charles Colson's Prison Fellowship, which seeks to change a man through faith in Christ.

Perhaps you are familiar with Prison Fellowship. Former Nixon aide Chuck Colson founded Prison Fellowship Ministries in 1976, and it has broadened into a family of ministries that addresses each aspect of the crime problem. One noteworthy advance in prison ministry ensued from a request by the state of Texas. At a facility near Houston, Prison Fellowship launched the nation's first twenty-four-hours-a-day, seven-days-a-week Christian prison program. The program is called the InnerChange Freedom Initiative, and it consists of eighteen months of intense Bible teaching and discipleship. As they mature in their faith, prisoners are paired with a mentor and prepared for transition back into the community.

The Prison Fellowship Web page tells the story of James Peterson, a prisoner who spent seven months in the InnerChange program, then learned he was up for early parole. This posed a serious dilemma for Prison Fellowship leaders. Colson and his people couldn't really test the program unless inmates remained for the duration, but they didn't feel they could ask a man to remain in prison when he could go home. So they prayed.

Two weeks later, James Peterson asked the Texas Board of Pardons if he could turn down his early parole to finish his time at the InnerChange Freedom Initiative! Of Peterson's decision, Colson said, "I know firsthand what prison is like—and no matter how 'Christian' the prison is, no one wants to stay locked up for an extra ten months. Yet that is exactly what James Peterson is doing."

Peterson explained his decision:

> Believe me, there is nothing I want more than to be back in the outside world with my daughter Lucy—to play with her and take her to the zoo. But I see this as a small price to pay in comparison to the price that Jesus Christ paid on the cross for us when He took the sins of the world upon Himself.

Each day when I wake up here . . . inside the razor wire fences, I'll be crucifying my selfish wants and desires. I'll be saying to my brothers, here and on the outside, that I'm here because inner change is important to me. Maybe my decision to stay here will help others see that God is real—that He is the truth, and He changes people.[13]

Men like James Peterson are blessed because they recognize their need for change. The Pharisees who caught the woman taken in an act of adultery, however, thought they were perfectly righteous—and so they appeared to be, as long as you looked only on their outer appearance. They wore nice clothes; they kept every jot and tittle of the law; they participated in every religious festival.

As keepers of the law, they knew the punishment for adultery was death by stoning. But when Jesus stooped to write in the sand and refused to condemn the woman, the Holy Spirit of God pricked the Pharisees' consciences. They dropped the stones they gripped and slipped away. The apostle John told us why: "Then those who heard it, *being convicted by their conscience,* went out one by one, beginning with the oldest even to the last. And Jesus was left alone, and the woman standing in the midst" (John 8:9 NKJV, italics added).

Has the Holy Spirit pricked your conscience about something? If so, perhaps you've justified your actions by playing the "blame game" like Adam did in the Garden: "This woman You gave me made me eat the fruit!"

Or perhaps you've justified your actions with the "everyone else is doing it" refrain. Well, my friend, I don't care *who* else is doing it. The standards of righteousness God established in His Word will stand forever. I like what the playwright Lillian Hellman once said: "I cannot and will not cut my conscience to fit this year's fashions." Don't be swayed by society's shifting moral climate. Stand firm upon the absolutes of God's Word.

Too many Christians are like the church member who once prayed, "Oh, God, if there is any ungodly thing in my life, show me." Then, when the Holy Spirit touched His finger to an area of the man's life, he reared back and hollered, "I rebuke you, Devil!"

When a man won't listen to his conscience, it's usually because he doesn't want to accept advice from a stranger.

THE NATIONAL CONSCIENCE

We need a reawakening of conscience today, in our homes, our churches, and particularly in our nation. America needs a resurrection of conscience! When an able-bodied man who refuses to work accepts a welfare check, his conscience is defiled. He also defiles the consciences of his family, who, if they don't have the moral courage to rebuke him, must defend and justify his actions. The Word of God says, "If anyone will not work, neither shall he eat" (2 Thess. 3:10 NKJV). Nothing in your life will work until you do!

We need Americans who will tell their congressional representatives that conscience does not get its guidance from a Gallup poll. America's conscience is defiled because her values have been turned upside down. Only in America could a Vietnam veteran walk the streets sick and homeless while a draft dodger sleeps in the White House. We have made it illegal to even touch a bald eagle's egg, but we are killing our own unborn with impunity. We have reached the sad state of affairs described in Proverbs 17:15 (NKJV): "He who justifies the wicked, and he who condemns the just, both of them alike are an abomination to the LORD."

Abortion has defiled America's conscience. When more than three thousand babies are murdered every day in America's abortion mills, our national conscience is seared with a hot iron.[14] Only the most callous or most ignorant heart could excuse the killing of the most helpless and innocent souls. General Omar Bradley once said, "The world has achieved brilliance without conscience. Ours is a world of nuclear giants and ethical infants."

When public schools throw out the Ten Commandments and bring in condoms, when your child can obtain an abortion without your knowledge or approval, America's conscience is defiled! William F. Buckley once wrote, "A society that seduces the conscience by sweet reason is one thing, but ours is developing into a society that harpoons the conscience and tows it right into the maws of the mother vessel, there to be macerated and stuffed into a faceless can."

What is America's hope? We need a resurrection of conscience! We need a revival of righteousness, a revival of repentance! We Christians must lead the way by learning how to lead consistent Christian lives.

As a pastor, I am often asked how we can learn how to walk in the Spirit. The process is really simple—walking in the Spirit is as simple as learning how to respond to the voice of God through conscience. When that still, small voice speaks—obey it! It is the voice of the Spirit.

On Sunday morning, your spiritual man, your conscience, will shout, "Get up and go to church!" Your carnal man, your mind or emotions, will say, "Oh, but this bed feels so good . . . and I am really tired. Maybe this week I'll just stay here and sleep."

If you're walking in the Spirit, you'll get up and go to church. If you're walking in the flesh, you will ignore that quiet voice of conscience.

Beware of listening to the carnal man. Revelation 3:16 (NKJV) tells us that God has no use for a Christian who is lukewarm in his commitment to Christ: "So then, because you are lukewarm, and neither cold nor hot, I will vomit you out of My mouth."

THE BATTLEFIELD IN YOUR BRAIN

The mind will justify what conscience condemns. The carnal mind is at enmity with God, and carnal logic is at war with conscience. Your brain is a battlefield where the Holy Spirit fights the flesh. Let me illustrate: Suppose you go to the supermarket, go through the checkout line and pay for your purchases, and discover in the car that the cashier has given you three dollars too much change. What are you going to do?

Your mind and your conscience will have a minidebate:

MIND: "Three dollars isn't much. And how many times have you accidentally overpaid by a few cents? This is no big deal; everything will come out even in the end."

CONSCIENCE: "But that cashier will be three dollars short at the end of the day. She'll have to pay for this."

MIND: "Why shouldn't she have to pay for her mistake? You'll be teaching her a valuable lesson. After all, next week she could give somebody a hundred dollars too much, but today will teach her to be more careful."

CONSCIENCE: "It doesn't matter how much the amount is. And perhaps she could learn from seeing a testimony of honesty in action."

MIND: "She probably won't care. Or she'll think you're a fool for returning three bucks. After all, people cheat every day, and about things a lot more important than three measly dollars."

CONSCIENCE: "Right is right, and wrong is wrong. Take the money back."

MIND: "Right is right, sure, but life is filled with gray areas. This is one of them."

To which voice would you listen? At what point would you tell conscience to back off and keep quiet? Conscience is well-mannered; it will soon stop talking to those who don't wish to hear it.

If the Holy Spirit controls you, you will obey the voice of your conscience and return those three dollars. If you are a carnal Christian, ruled by your mind, you will keep the money and justify your actions. And later, at night, you'll lie awake in bed and wonder why you can't fall asleep.

When faced with a moral dilemma, cowardice will ask, "Is it safe?" Practicality will ask, "Is it useful?" Vanity will ask, "Is it popular?" But conscience will ask, "Is it right?"

A wise man once said, "Conscience is condensed character." If you are listening to the voice of God as He speaks through conscience, you will exhibit a godly character.

What Can I Learn from My Conscience?

In the fourteenth century, Dan Michel of Northgate in England wrote a treatise on the seven deadly sins. He entitled it *Ayenbite of Inwyt*. Translated from Middle English, the title is *The Remorse of Conscience*. If you look at the ancient words you will see that conscience is an inward wit (*inwyt*) that bites again and again (*ayenbite*) to remind by its nip that we have violated moral standards.

In the New Testament, the Greek word translated "conscience" is *suneidesis*. The root of this word comes from a verb "to know," and the prefix *sun* means "with," implying that a second party shares knowledge with you. The earliest classical Greek usages of this word referred to two eyewitnesses who agreed on what they saw.

The New Testament use of *suneidesis* depends on an Old Testament understanding of guilty feelings. Whether it was Cain regretting his murder of Abel, Jacob's older sons ruing their treatment of Joseph, or David mourning his sin with Bathsheba, the decisive element that prompted guilt was God's expectation about human behavior. Old Testament characters judged themselves by much more than subjective feelings. In the Old Testament, the concept of conscience was always negative. It judged and condemned.

The New Testament builds on the idea that the Word of God is the second party with which a person's inward voice should agree, but a conscience can be a good conscience as well as a bad one (1 Tim. 1:19). In one passage, Peter directly connected *suneidesis* and God. "For this is commendable, if because of conscience toward God one endures grief, suffering wrongfully" (1 Peter 2:19 NKJV). Much of 1 Peter concerns learning to suffer as Jesus did. Peter's point is that when our conscience tells us to do the same thing Christ's conscience told Him to do in the face of suffering, then we have a pure conscience toward God.

Is God's voice the second voice that speaks with your conscience? Or have you been listening to the voices of the world? If you listen too long, your conscience will become defiled and finally seared. You will become insensitive to the things of God.

Conscience is like an old spring-driven alarm clock. We can pay attention to its alarm and rouse our godly behavior, or we can give it a good swat and go back to sleep. The alarm clock is a machine; it'll be back on the job tomorrow morning. But we need to respond regularly to it or soon we'll become oblivious to its alarm. So it is with conscience.

I'd like to close this chapter with a portion of an article from the Philippine edition of *Business Daily*:

> Your conscience never makes its own laws; it simply acts upon the laws it knows. It passes judgment based on the knowledge it has previously received . . . It's God's supreme court in your heart, which passes moral and spiritual judgment based on the knowledge you possess.
>
> Psychiatrists of the 20th century have attempted to deny the effects of conscience. They may convince a man it's

all right to try to still the voice of conscience, but they cannot remove the guilt of conscience. Christ alone can do that, because of the blood He shed at Calvary.

He personally identified Himself with our guilt and made it possible for us to be identified with his righteousness. The Savior is loving and compassionate. To Him we can pour out the deepest feelings of our hearts and find a refuge. Hebrews exhorts, "Let us draw near with a sincere heart in full assurance of faith, having our hearts sprinkled clean from an evil conscience."[15]

Amen!

Journal, Page Four

God has made everything beautiful in its time, but I think I have never seen anything as delightful as the sunlight He sprinkled over the mount called Ararat. The wooden ark came gently to rest upon a slope of the mountain, and the animals spilled forth in gleeful abandon. Noah and his family stood by the doorway and watched, their eyes filling with wonder as the creatures woke—for many of them had slept the months away— and scampered out across the rocks. The continents were one undivided landmass at this time, for the dry land divided later, during Peleg's lifetime.

Unaccustomed to the feel of solidity beneath his feet, Noah rocked from side to side as he traversed the wooden gangway, then he fell to the dark earth and pressed his face to it as if he would breathe in the scents of mud and grass and stone. His sons followed, and the women, then they lifted their hands in praise to God for the dry land, for green life, for the salvation that the Father had offered.

And while Noah busied himself with preparing an offering for sacrifice, the Spirit brought the blue of the sky, the pink from a baby's cheek, the gold of reflected starlight, the violet from a deepening twilight, and every hue in between. The Son mixed His hand in the colors and swept His fingers across the sky. Then the Father said, "This is the sign of the covenant which I have established between me and all flesh on the earth. With every cloud that darkens the sky, I will also provide a rainbow, that man may know that I will never again bring a flood to destroy the earth."

And as Noah and his children bowed their heads in silent agreement, I marveled that God would exhibit such patience with His creation. Surely His love was greater far than even men could comprehend. Now, every time I see a rainbow shining through the clouds beneath the third heaven, I am reminded that God's promises are certain . . . and I chuckle at the memory of Noah's first teetering steps down the walkway that returned mankind to dry land.

CHAPTER

THE AGE OF
HUMAN GOVERNMENT

I once heard a story about a little boy named Barney. Though he seemed to be a bright toddler, Barney's parents were concerned because he hadn't begun to talk by his first birthday. After two years passed without a word, Barney's parents took him to the pediatrician. The doctor examined the boy, then told his parents not to worry. "He's fine," the doctor said. "Just be patient, and he'll talk when he's ready."

The silence prevailed through many more weeks and months. Finally, just after the little boy's fourth birthday, Barney looked up from his breakfast bowl and announced, "This oatmeal is too lumpy!"

His parents were thrilled and amazed. "Barney," said his mother, "why haven't you talked before?"

The boy shrugged. "Up until now," he said, "everything has been great!"

God allowed man to live by his conscience until conscience failed. Then God had to speak. Because He had to implement laws, mankind moved from the Age of Conscience into the Age of Human Government.

After passing through the terrible Flood, Noah, his wife, his three sons, and their wives—eight people—constituted the world's population. Noah must have wondered whether his family and the animals from the ark could survive on an empty earth. God made a covenant with Noah that assured him that people and animals would endure.

> Then Noah built an altar to the LORD, and took of every clean animal and of every clean bird, and offered burnt offerings on the altar. And the LORD smelled a soothing aroma. Then the LORD said in His heart, "I will never again curse the ground for man's sake, although the imagination of man's heart is evil from his youth; nor will I again destroy every living thing as I have done." (Gen. 8:20–21 NKJV)

All living humans descended from Noah's line, and it's safe to assume that each of Noah's sons—Shem, Ham, and Japheth—knew that God hated sin. They had survived the Flood, their godly father had set a good example for them, and they were well-acquainted with conscience. Surely Noah hoped that they would teach their children to revere, worship, and obey God.

But conscience was obviously not enough to guide mankind. The third age, or dispensation, is known as the Age of Human Government because after the Flood, God instituted laws to regulate man's life through human government. Because He could not trust man to live by the law of his conscience, God gave Noah certain laws by which the human race could rule themselves. Man would be held responsible for self-government.

Operating in the principle of sevens, God gave Noah seven laws that would pertain not only to him and his family, but to every member of mankind:

1. *Be fruitful, multiply, and replenish the earth* (Gen. 9:1, 7). This was the same command God gave to Adam and Eve, but now the danger of death, natural and violent, existed. These things had not disturbed the human race prior to the Fall.

2. *Rule over the animals.* God told Noah:

And the fear of you and the dread of you shall be on every beast of the earth, on every bird of the air, on all that move on the earth, and on all the fish of the sea. They are given into your hand. (Gen. 9:2 NKJV)

Noah may have feared that the wild animals from the ark would prove a threat to his family. God covenanted with him that the wild animals of every type would fear and avoid humans. God promised Noah and his descendants that they would still exercise dominion over the birds, animals, and fish.

3. *Eat animal food instead of only grains, herbs, and vegetables.* "Every moving thing that lives shall be food for you. I have given you all things, even as the green herbs" (Gen. 9:3 NKJV). By the terms of the Edenic Covenant, human diet had been vegetarian (Gen. 1:29, 2:16). God's covenant with Noah introduced meat to the human diet. In some way this reflects further alienation within God's creation after the Fall: Animals now lived in terror of humans who might kill and eat them.

4. *Do not eat the blood of animals.* "But you shall not

eat flesh with its life, that is, its blood" (Gen. 9:4 NKJV). Even though people could eat animals, they needed to respect the principle of life represented by the blood of animals. They could not eat the blood.

5. *Do not commit murder.* "Murder is forbidden" (Gen. 9:5 NLT). Human blood holds a higher value than animal blood, for human blood is the life symbol of a person bearing the image of God.

6. *Execute men who commit murder.* God said:

Animals that kill people must die, and any person who murders must be killed. Yes, you must execute anyone who murders another person, for to kill a person is to kill a living being made in God's image. (Gen. 9:5–6 NLT)

Violence had been a primary cause of the Flood (Gen. 6:11), so God introduced the principle of capital punishment as a deterrent to the repetition of wholesale bloodshed.

7. *Keep God's covenant eternally.*

Then God spoke to Noah and to his sons with him, saying: "And as for Me, behold, I establish My covenant with you and with your descendants after you, and with every living creature that is with you: the birds, the cattle, and every beast of the earth with you, of all that go out of the ark, every beast of the earth. Thus I establish My covenant with you: Never again shall all flesh be cut off by the waters of the flood; never again shall there be a flood to destroy the earth."

And God said: "This is the sign of the covenant which I make between Me and you, and every living creature that is with you, for perpetual generations: I set My rainbow in the cloud, and it shall be for the sign of the covenant between Me and the earth. It shall be, when I bring a cloud over the earth, that the rainbow shall be seen in the cloud; and I will remember My covenant which is between Me and you and every living creature of all flesh; the waters shall never again become a flood to destroy all flesh. The rainbow shall be in the cloud, and I will look on it to remember the everlasting covenant between God and every living creature of all flesh that is on the earth." (Gen. 9:8–16 NKJV)

Some of the terms of this covenant hark back to the original arrangement God made with Adam and Eve when sin had not corrupted creation. The covenant with Noah, however, adapted the Edenic Covenant to a world in which sin, violence, and death were terrible realities. Notice that God created the rainbow to be a sign, a visible reminder of God's promise that He would never again destroy the earth by flood. He will destroy it by fire at the end of the Millennium, but not by flood.

GOVERNMENT AND GOD ARE INSEPARABLY LINKED

Several of these seven laws have formed the basis for human laws for all ages since the Flood. Notice that this passage of Scripture records the birth of capital punishment—it is God's idea! When a criminal murders someone, he not only attacks his victim, but the victim's family, society at large, and God Himself, for men are created in the image of God.

The authors of *Hard Sayings of the Bible* stress the importance of this concept:

> But if a society persists in refusing to take the life of those conclusively proven to have deliberately and violently taken others' lives, then that society will stand under God's judgment and the value, worth, dignity and respect for persons in that society and nation will diminish accordingly. It is self-defeating to argue on the one hand for civil and women's rights and to turn around on the other and deny them to the one struck down by a murderous blow.[1]

Scripture tells us it is imperative that we punish criminals, both as individuals and nations. God Himself sanctions law enforcement, and sometimes war, as unpleasant as it is, is necessary and justifiable. When nations become criminal, they must be called to account for their actions.

Writing in *USA Today*, Chuck Colson explained how Christian tradition has shaped Western views on the morally permissible use of force. The Just War Theory, which Saint Augustine first formulated in the fifth century and Thomas Aquinas expanded in the thirteenth, gives us several criteria to help judge whether a nation is right to wage war.

- A just war is one aimed at repelling or deterring aggression.

- A just war must be authorized by legitimate authority with genuine intentions.

- War must be a last resort, with all peaceful alternatives exhausted.

- The probability of success must be sufficiently clear to justify the costs.

- The damage inflicted must be proportionate to its objectives.

- Noncombatants must not be targeted.[2]

The next time an American president decides to drop bombs on another nation, consider these principles to judge whether or not military action is justified.

As he wrote to the church at Rome, Paul explained the relationship between government and God:

> Let every soul be subject to the governing authorities. For there is no authority except from God, and the authorities that exist are appointed by God. Therefore whoever resists the authority resists the ordinance of God, and those who resist will bring judgment on themselves. For rulers are not a terror to good works, but to evil. Do you want to be unafraid of the authority? Do what is good, and you will have praise from the same. For he is God's minister to you for good. But if you do evil, be afraid; for he does not bear the sword in vain; for he is God's minister, an avenger to execute wrath on him who practices evil. Therefore you must be subject, not only because of wrath but also for conscience' sake. For because of this you also pay taxes, for they are God's ministers attending continually to this very thing. (Rom. 13:1–6 NKJV)

Human government is intended to promote the highest good for all members of society. Only those who break the law need fear it. All citizens, therefore, have a responsibility to take an active part in government by supporting it and complying with the laws of the land. The next time you're tempted to disobey a traffic sign or hedge on your income tax, remember that God ordained the authorities who rule your life!

THE AGE OF GOVERNMENT'S GODLY BEGINNING

The Age of Human Government lasted from the end of Noah's flood to the call of seventy-five-year-old Abram—a total of 427 years. During this age, men were to live according to the seven laws God established, punish those who strayed, and worship the God who had saved them from destruction.

Noah's descendants possessed a godly heritage, a cleansed earth, and seven laws that would enable them to live peacefully . . . but they also possessed fallen natures and were prone to sin. This period of time had a glorious beginning, for Noah and his sons were a righteous family, but they were certainly not perfect. And sin, being what it is, soon began to spoil mankind's new beginning upon the earth.

The seventh revelation of truth in Genesis is this: *God will honor the man or woman who honors authority—even when that authority is wrong.* Let's look more closely at the story of what happened to Noah and his sons after the Flood.

And Noah began to be a farmer, and he planted a vineyard. Then he drank of the wine and was drunk, and became uncovered in his tent. And Ham, the father of Canaan, saw the nakedness of his father, and told his two brothers outside. But Shem and Japheth took a garment, laid it on both their shoulders, and went backward and covered the nakedness of their father. Their faces were turned away, and they did not see their father's nakedness.

So Noah awoke from his wine, and knew what his younger son had done to him. Then he said:

"Cursed be Canaan;
A servant of servants
He shall be to his brethren."

And he said:

"Blessed be the LORD,
the God of Shem,
and may Canaan be his servant.
May God enlarge Japheth,
and may he dwell in the tents of Shem;
and may Canaan be his servant." (Gen. 9:20–27 NKJV)

God allowed Noah to curse Canaan, Ham's son, because Ham mocked Noah's spiritual authority. Though drunk and naked, Noah still deserved respect as the head of the family, but Ham treated him with scorn and derision. Shem and Japheth, acting in honor, covered their father's nakedness and restored Noah's dignity.

For years this passage was used to justify slavery of dark-skinned people, but nothing could be more incorrect. Genesis 10:6 lists the genealogy of Noah's descendants, and Canaan settled in the area of Palestine, not Africa.

Why did Noah curse Canaan, the son, and not Ham? Several Bible scholars believe that Noah could not curse Ham because he had been the beneficiary of God's blessing as recorded in Genesis 9:1. Balaam later learned that you cannot reverse God's blessing with a curse (Num. 22–24). So Canaan, who may well have demonstrated his father's scornful attitude, bore the curse. And years later, when Joshua led the children of Israel into Canaan, the people of that land were either totally destroyed or became slaves to the tribes of Israel.

Notice the importance of *respect* in the story of Noah and his sons. A few months ago I was thrilled to read that the state of Louisiana has passed legislation requiring public school students to address teachers and other school employees as "sir" and "ma'am."[3] America is slowly realizing that we have neglected several important virtues, and respect is only one of them. Throughout the country, school systems are beginning to insist that parents or students sign codes of discipline. Some states, including Arkansas and Georgia, require "character education," which teaches honesty, fairness, and respect for others.[4]

Satan Is Still Alive and Well on the Planet

The Flood destroyed an entire population of godless individuals, but it did not touch Satan. That wily being was still traveling to and fro upon the earth, and the Flood did not weaken his intention to devastate God's creation. He purposed in his heart to lie and kill and destroy yet again, and he began with the first of the seven laws God had ordained: *Be fruitful, multiply, and replenish the earth.*

God clearly intended for humanity to disperse and subjugate the untamed planet. But faced with the threat of wild animals, rough weather, and the perils of the unknown, Noah's descendants decided to huddle together. Instead of placing their faith in God, they trusted in the strength of numbers. Instead of venturing into the wilderness to subdue it, they clung to the land they knew and built cities.

Now the whole earth had one language and one speech. And it came to pass, as they journeyed from the east, that they found a plain in the land of Shinar, and they dwelt there. Then they said to one another, "Come, let us make bricks and bake them thoroughly." They had brick for stone, and they had asphalt for mortar. And they said, "Come, let us build ourselves a city, and a tower whose top is in the heavens; let us make a name for ourselves, lest we be scattered abroad over the face of the whole earth."

But the LORD came down to see the city and the tower which the sons of men had built. And the LORD said, "Indeed the people are one and they all have one language, and this is what they begin to do; now nothing that they propose to do will be withheld from them. Come, let Us go down and there confuse their language, that they may not understand one another's speech."

So the LORD scattered them abroad from there over the face of all the earth, and they ceased building the city. Therefore its name is called Babel, because there the LORD confused the language of all the earth; and from there the LORD scattered them abroad over the face of all the earth. (Gen. 11:1–9 NKJV)

Jewish tradition asserts that the builders' purpose was to take heaven by storm, defeat God, and set up idols in his place. "They knew that God had control over water," wrote Alan Unterman, "for He had brought the Flood, but they thought that they could shelter in a high tower from any future deluge."[5]

Bible scholar Harold Willmington points out that the builders did not intend for their tower, or ziggurat, to actually reach into outer space. If they were truly seeking *altitude*, they would have built the tower upon a mountaintop instead of a flat plain. They intended to build a tower "whose top was in heaven," and they were successful.[6]

In his *Annotated Reference Bible,* Finis Jennings Dake notes:

A Babylonian description of the tower of Babel discovered in 1876 indicates there was a grand court 900 x 1156 feet and a smaller one, 450 x 1056 feet, inside of which was a platform with walls about it, having four gates on each side. In the center stood the tower with many small shrines at the base dedicated to various gods. The tower itself was 300 feet high with decreased width in stages from the lowest to the highest point. Each was square. On the top platform, measuring 60 x 80 feet, was a sanctuary for the god Bel-Merodach and signs of the Zodiac. The builders evidently finished the tower, for the work was stopped on the city only. One ancient Babylonian tablet reads, "The building of this illustrious tower offended the gods. In a night they threw down what they had built. They scattered them abroad and made strange their speech. Their progress was impeded. They wept hot tears for Babylon."[7]

God was merciful—He stopped the building before the condition of man descended to the level of corruption that had existed before the Flood. He scattered humanity instead of destroying it, a mild chastisement compared to the ferocity of the Flood of a previous generation.

Though they were not as depraved as the people of Noah's generation, notice how completely the builders of Babel seemed to have forgotten about God! In their declaration of purpose, their talk was full of *us*—let *us* build a city, and let *us* make *us* a name. They made lofty plans for their one-world religion and one-world government, but God had other ideas! As the psalmist wrote, "The LORD brings the counsel of the nations to nothing; He makes the plans of the peoples of no effect" (Ps. 33:10 NKJV).

And here, amid the confusion and arrogance of Babel, is the eighth revelation of truth God wants us to see: *Babel and its founder, a man called Nimrod, are pictures of the coming Antichrist and his empire.*

BABEL AND BABYLON
ARE ONE AND THE SAME

Nimrod, whom Scripture describes as a hunter and a mighty man, was a ruthless conqueror with ambitious political aspirations.[8] His very name meant "revolt." The Jewish Talmud describes him as a "hunter of the souls of men."

Bible scholar Charles Dyer says that Nimrod's mighty skills as a hunter added to his standing in society and rocketed him into a position of leadership. "Nimrod directed his God-given skills and natural abilities toward conquest and subjugation," wrote Dyer. "And this was the beginning of Babylon."[9] And Babel.

Nimrod's Tower of Babel was the first worldwide empire in open revolt against God. The tower of his kingdom was to reach high enough over the plain so travelers could see it for miles. He wanted to build a new world order, to unite all people into one mass. His followers—and everyone followed him—intentionally disobeyed God's command to go into the world and replenish it.

Another man, much like Nimrod, will be coming to the world stage very soon. Like Nimrod, he will institute a one-world religion and a one-world government. Like Nimrod, he will be a killer. Like Nimrod, he will be a hunter of the souls of men. He will hunt down every man, woman, and child who refuses to take his mark on the hand or forehead—and execute them by decapitation (Rev. 20:4).

Nimrod was a king, with a kingdom called Babel on the plain of Shinar . . . very near present-day Babylon in Iraq. In Daniel 11:36 (NKJV), the Antichrist is also called "the king":

> Then the king shall do according to his own will: he shall
> exalt and magnify himself above every god, shall speak

blasphemies against the God of gods, and shall prosper till the wrath has been accomplished; for what has been determined shall be done.

Notice that Isaiah 14:4 (NKJV) calls the Antichrist "the king of Babylon": "Take up this proverb against the king of Babylon, and say: 'How the oppressor has ceased, The golden city ceased!'"

The demon spirit that drove Nimrod was the spirit of pride. More than anything, he wanted to make a name for himself. The Antichrist will be like his father, Satan, the prince of pride. Pride caused Satan to be cast out of heaven, and the Antichrist will suffer the same spiritual affliction. Paul wrote that the Antichrist will "exalt himself and defy every god there is and tear down every object of adoration and worship. He will position himself in the temple of God, claiming that he himself is God" (2 Thess. 2:4 NLT).

Let's look more closely at Nimrod's kingdom. The city's name, *Babel*, is translated "gateway to a god." Nimrod's worldwide government was occultic! The builders' plans for the city, discovered in the nineteenth century, confirm that the citizens of Babel worshiped idols, foreign gods, and the stars themselves!

The kingdom of Nimrod enjoyed the power of united speech. They knew nothing else, for they had spoken the same tongue since coming off the ark, but God knew exactly how to confound them. Every time humanity has been able to communicate in one language, their efforts result in revolt against God.

Adam and Eve talked together and rebelled against

God. Nimrod and his followers did the same thing at the Tower of Babel. And now computers have made it possible for the nations of the world to communicate in one language.

In May 1999 Senator Bob Bennett compared the year 2000 computer bug to the biblical Tower of Babel. "The world speaks a common language called digital code," Bennett told a meeting at the Software Technology Conference sponsored by the Department of Defense. "If the connection gets broken, we're back to the Tower of Babel where we cannot talk to each other. We can't trade securities. We can't change currency. We can't exchange information. Everything shuts down."[10]

By the time you read this book, the year 2000 will have arrived. Whatever problems arose are being solved, and mankind is steadily working to keep the lines of communication open. We may not all speak the same tongue, but computers have opened the doors of communication to all. The word *globalization* has replaced the term *new world order*. But know this, friend: Mankind is still trying to unite so it can dismiss God.

After World War I, in relentless pursuit of a one-world government, President Woodrow Wilson established the League of Nations. It failed.

Adolf Hitler told the German people he would produce in Europe "a new order" that would last a thousand years. He failed!

The communists pledged "a new world order." Their atheistic, God-hating empire collapsed like a house of cards. They tried to cast God out of the earth, and, just like Nimrod at Babel, they failed!

BABEL IS THE BIRTHPLACE
OF ORGANIZED IDOLATRY

Babel introduced the first organized, idolatrous religious system in the history of the world. That's why John calls Babylon "the mother of harlots" (Rev. 17:5 NKJV). Since Babylon was the birthplace of spiritual adultery, the apostasy of the end times is called by the name *Babylon*, the mother of harlots.

What was Babylon's idolatrous system? Among other aspects of astrology and idol worship, Babylon (the former city of Babel) included a cult that followed Semiramis, wife of Marduk, whom most scholars identify with Nimrod. We know that Semiramis and Marduk/Nimrod were the ancient god and goddess of Babylon. Their son (whom Semiramis claimed was virgin born) was known to the Babylonians as Dammuzi, to the Hebrews as Tammuz, and to the Greeks as Adonis. The cult spread throughout the ancient world like a grass fire. The divine mother and child appeared in Egypt as Isis and Horus, and in Greece as Venus and Adonis. According to Hislop's "The Two Babylons," the ancient cult Nimrod and Semiramis started spread among all nations when the people of Babel scattered throughout the world.[11]

When God called Abraham out of Ur, He called him from a region devoted to the worship of false gods, including the "queen of heaven," the mother figure of the mother-child cult. Joshua 24:2 (NKJV) tells us:

> Thus says the LORD God of Israel: "Your fathers, including Terah, the father of Abraham and the father of

Nahor, dwelt on the other side of the River in old times; and they served other gods."

The cult continued to spread unabated through the years. Generations after Babel, the rebellious people of Israel told God why they preferred to make offerings and sacrifices to the "queen of heaven" instead of to Him:

> But we will certainly do whatever has gone out of our own mouth, to burn incense to the queen of heaven and pour out drink offerings to her, as we have done, we and our fathers, our kings and our princes, in the cities of Judah and in the streets of Jerusalem. For then we had plenty of food, were well off, and saw no trouble. (Jer. 44:17 NKJV)

In the eighth chapter of Ezekiel, God told the prophet to do a little eavesdropping. Ezekiel was to go to the Temple set apart for the worship of Jehovah God and observe:

> So He brought me to the door of the court; and when I looked, there was a hole in the wall. Then He said to me, "Son of man, dig into the wall"; and when I dug into the wall, there was a door. And He said to me, "Go in, and see the wicked abominations which they are doing there." So I went in and saw, and there—every sort of creeping thing, abominable beasts, and all the idols of the house of Israel, portrayed all around on the walls. (Ezek. 8:7–10 NKJV)

What did Ezekiel see? Idols to the queen of heaven! The mother-child cult had taken over the sanctuary of Jehovah

God in Jerusalem. The picture, however, grew worse. As Ezekiel continued to look around the city, the Spirit of God took him "to the door of the north gate of the LORD's house; and to my dismay, women were sitting there weeping for Tammuz" (Ezek. 8:14 NKJV).

These were the temple virgins, weeping for Tammuz, Semiramis's son who had been slain by a wild boar.

Fast-forward to a few years before Christ's birth. In 63 B.C. Julius Caesar was named Pontifex Maximus, or head of the state religion, which was the heathen mother-child cult. By 12 B.C., when Augustus received the title, the role of Roman high priest was automatically conferred upon the emperors of Rome. In A.D. 306, the emperor Constantine became a Christian and declared that Christianity was the religion of the Roman Empire. But what kind of Christianity was it?

The people went to the same temple, worshiped the same trinity of mother-child-God, and followed the same rituals. But now their rituals and religion were called "Christian." Not until A.D. 376 did an emperor realize that the Roman church was not truly Christian. The emperor Gratian refused the title of Pontifex Maximus because he recognized that Babylonianism was idolatrous. As a result, two years later Demasus, bishop of the Christian church at Rome, was elected to the position and from that time Babylonianism and organized Christianity merged. The rites of Babylon—complete with the veneration of images and relics, penances, pilgrimages, and other pagan rites and festivals—became part of Christian worship.

Thousands of people followed, trusting the rituals, the worship, and the acts of self-denial to save them from hell.

The introduction of Babylonianism, an ancient and false mother-child cult, into the church of Jesus Christ was a satanic stroke of genius. Satan knew God's prophesied plan for his own destruction, and in this cult we can see the devil's clever attempt to falsely foreshadow the authentic virgin birth of Jesus Christ.

Satan is an imitator, my friend, and he loves to imitate Christ! Jesus said, "I am the light of the world" (John 9:5 NKJV). Satan disguises himself as an angel of light (2 Cor. 11:14). He spreads a false illumination upon the Word of God, resulting in false doctrine that leads people astray.

Christ is the Lion of Judah (Rev. 5:5), while Satan is a roaring lion, seeking whom he may devour (1 Peter 5:8).

God sent a Messiah, Jesus Christ. Satan will send a messiah too—the Antichrist.

God will send His son to earth on a white horse (Rev. 19:11). Satan will send *his* son, the son of perdition, on a white horse (Rev. 6:2). The devil is a master of deception!

BABEL IS A PICTURE OF MYSTERY BABYLON

God wants you to understand the things that will come to pass in His prophetic plan. In the story of Babel, we can see another prophetic picture and the ninth revelation of truth: *Babel represents Mystery Babylon, which God will judge during the great Tribulation.*

After the Rapture of the true church, or believers in Christ, a church will still exist on the earth, but she will be an *apostate* church. Revelation 17:1 (NKJV) labels this heretic church as "the great harlot who sits on many waters." A harlot is one who is unfaithful to her marriage partner. This is a religious order that claims to be married to Christ, but is in fact an unfaithful harlot. In this religion you will find ritual without righteousness, ceremony without change, and a form of godliness that denies the power of God.

The great harlot's sphere of influence is worldwide. An angel told John to interpret the term *many waters* as "peoples, multitudes, nations, and tongues" (Rev. 17:15 NKJV). This is a worldwide false religious system. In verse 2 (NKJV) we discover that this "great harlot" has seduced "the kings of the earth," not just the general population. The kings of the earth "were made drunk with the wine of her fornication." Not only common people have dealt with her, but kings, queens, presidents, and prime ministers have bowed their knee to this worldwide religious system built on Babylonian paganism.

Where is this rich and powerful worldwide religious system headquartered? John gave us an obvious clue: "Here is the mind which has wisdom: The seven heads are seven mountains on which the woman sits" (Rev. 17:9 NKJV). The only city in the world built on seven mountains is Rome!

John further wrote, "So he carried me away in the Spirit into the wilderness. And I saw a woman [the great harlot] sitting on a scarlet beast which was full of names of blasphemy, having seven heads and ten horns" (Rev. 17:3 NKJV). Revelation 13:1 (NKJV) reads, "Then I stood on the sand of the sea [the world]. And I saw a beast rising up out of the sea, having seven heads and ten horns." What we see in Revelation 17:3 and 13:1 is the same, so the beast the great harlot sits upon is the revived Roman Empire under the control of the Antichrist. John described a world where the apostate church and the Antichrist have joined forces to rule the world.

THE HARLOT IS BEAUTIFUL BUT DEADLY

In Revelation 17:4 (NKJV), John described the apparel of the great harlot: "The woman was arrayed in purple and scarlet, and adorned with gold and precious stones and pearls." She has the outward appearance of royalty; she is wearing gold and an array of jewels, meaning she has unlimited wealth. In her hand is "a golden cup full of abominations and the filthiness of her fornication." To the outward appearance, the great harlot is beautiful, but the contents of her cup are poison to the nations of the world.

In Revelation 17:5 (NKJV) John identified the great harlot by saying, "And on her forehead a name was written: MYSTERY, BABYLON THE GREAT, THE MOTHER OF HARLOTS AND OF THE ABOMINATIONS OF THE EARTH." The word *mystery* in the New Testament does not refer to something mysterious, but to some truth God has not previously made known to men. The mystery God is revealing is that in the last days there will be a worldwide apostate church that will reject Christ, dishonor God, and join forces with the Antichrist.

What will be the end of Mystery Babylon, the great whore? In the middle of the Tribulation, members of the European confederation that arises from the old Roman Empire will realize they are mere puppets of the great harlot. Let's look to Revelation: "And the ten horns which you saw on the beast, these will hate the harlot, make her desolate and naked, eat her flesh and burn her with fire" (Rev. 17:16 NKJV).

The ten horns of the Beast, which are ten European nations affiliated with the Antichrist, will hate the harlot because they are under her control. They will utterly destroy her, "for God has put it into their hearts to fulfill His purpose, to be of one mind, and to give their kingdom to the beast, until the words of God are fulfilled" (Rev. 17:17 NKJV).

The Antichrist, who rules over the confederation, will be content to share his power with her for a while; then he will turn on her and destroy her with a vengeance. By eliminating the false church, the Antichrist will clear the way for his own cult and his own worship.

But God will not remain silent for long. Each dispensational age brings its own test and judgment.

THE POWER OF THE TONGUE

Imagine the confusion, irritation, and belligerence that must have resulted when God struck the inhabitants of Babel with different tongues. Can you picture the chaos that must have erupted when Nimrod's chief foreman couldn't communicate with his masons and brick bakers? The remaining work on the city had to stop, for they couldn't understand each other at all. God used the power of diverse tongues to halt production on mankind's city and its "stairway to heaven."

Now notice yet another picture God wants us to see: When God sent the Holy Spirit to the believers at Pentecost, He used the power of diverse tongues to proclaim His "stairway to heaven," the only way man could truly reach God. By sending His Son and the Spirit, God defeated

Satan, the author of evil! This "gateway to God" was not accomplished by the sweat of slaves or man's determination, but by the blood of a Servant and Christ's willingness.

At Babel, God confused the tongues of men to alienate them.

At Pentecost, God gave tongues of fire to unite His church. Cloven tongues of fire sat upon the heads of the 120 disciples in that upper room, and they spoke with unknown tongues, "as the Spirit gave them utterance" (Acts 2:4 NKJV).

At Babel, the power of the tongue separated ungodly men and scattered them across the world. Scripture tells us that the continents, which had been one undivided landmass, divided around this time. "To Eber were born two sons: the name of one was Peleg, for in his days the earth [*erets*, or "dry land"] was divided" (Gen. 10:25 NKJV).

At Pentecost, the power of the tongue united the spirits of men and broke the language barrier. The first missionaries were instantly created, and they carried the gospel of Jesus Christ throughout the known world. God even gave them a head start, for Pentecost was a Jewish festival, and the city of Jerusalem was filled to overflowing with men and women from foreign lands. The power of God reversed at Pentecost the international scattering that took place at Babel!

And there were dwelling in Jerusalem Jews, devout men, from every nation under heaven. And when this sound occurred, the multitude came together, and were confused, because everyone heard them speak in his own language. Then they were all amazed and marveled, saying to one another, "Look, are not all these who speak

Galileans? And how is it that we hear, each in our own language in which we were born? Parthians and Medes and Elamites, those dwelling in Mesopotamia, Judea and Cappadocia, Pontus and Asia, Phrygia and Pamphylia, Egypt and the parts of Libya adjoining Cyrene, visitors from Rome, both Jews and proselytes, Cretans and Arabs—we hear them speaking in our own tongues the wonderful works of God." (Acts 2:5–11 NKJV)

DON'T UNDERESTIMATE THE POWER OF THE TONGUE

Never forget that the tongue is a supernatural instrument. The Bible tells us that "death and life are in the power of the tongue" (Prov. 18:21). The spoken word of God created the sun, moon, stars, and dry land. God created Adam from a handful of dirt and breathed into him the breath of life. That's power, my friend.

The spoken word of God conquered the winds and waves on the storm-tossed Sea of Galilee. "Then [Jesus] arose and rebuked the wind, and said to the sea, 'Peace, be still!' And the wind ceased and there was a great calm" (Mark 4:39 NKJV).

God's spoken word raised Lazarus from the dead. "[Jesus] cried with a loud voice, 'Lazarus, come forth!' And he who had died came out bound hand and foot with grave-clothes" (John 11:43–44 NKJV).

God's spoken word conquered disease and demon powers. The psalmist wrote, "He sent His word and healed them, and delivered them from their destructions" (Ps. 107:20 NKJV).

Can any man command nature into obedience? Can the most powerful man on earth break the bonds of death or disease with a *word*? No. God is God, and no one can take His rightful place.

Mankind has imagined a thousand ways to reach God, but not one of those man-made spiritual paths will lead you to heaven and save you from a dark eternity apart from Jesus Christ. Luke wrote, "Nor is there salvation in any other, for there is no other name under heaven given among men by which we must be saved" (Acts 4:12 NKJV).

The mysticism of the New Age movement will not save you. Eastern philosophies cannot save you. Abraham cannot save you. Mohammed cannot save you. The Virgin Mary cannot save you. Education, intellect, wealth, and power cannot save you.

Only Jesus Christ can save you.

Journal, Page Five

With all the other hosts of heaven, I watched mankind spread across the earth. Silence reigned in the throne room of God, and though I felt a distant anxiety about man's fate, the Father showed no sign of wavering. He would still pursue man; He would still redeem the fallen ones, though I could not see how He could possibly accomplish His goal. Of all the men on earth, not one turned his attention or his thoughts toward the One who had created him.

Then one morning, as the sun rose over the eastern shores of the river called Euphrates, God spoke to a man called Abram. This man's heart, though as sinful as any other, yearned for the Righteous One, and God honored his heart's desire. He spoke to Abram, and the man gathered his family and set out with a caravan, traveling westward toward the Great Sea.

"I will make of this man a great nation," God told the assembled heavenly host. "I will give him a land forever, and through this man of tender heart I shall bring forth a Redeemer."

The Son leaned closer to the balcony of heaven, to peer down at the motley assortment of mortals who would be His earthly forefathers. Something in Abram's disheveled and dusty appearance must have pleased Him, for He straightened and gave the Father a smile brimming with confidence and gratitude.

"May his descendants be as the dust of the earth," He said, settling back upon His throne. "And through him may all nations of the earth be blessed."

Curious, I descended through the heavens and sat upon the plain, to watch and wait for the arrival of this extraordinary man. I wondered why he was so different. And how could one man possibly influence the entire earth?

I had no idea how the Father would work, but the endeavor would certainly provide an interesting way to while away eternal hours . . .

THE AGE
OF PROMISE

The Age of Promise began with the call of Abram, later called Abraham, and lasted 430 years, until the Hebrews' exodus from Egypt. During this period of time, God began to emphasize the coming of the promised Seed of the woman through a particular branch of the human race— Abraham's lineage. Not only did God promise that the Messiah would come from Abraham's line, but He also stated that He would give the Promised Land eternally to Abraham's descendants, the Jewish people.

The test of this period was for Abraham and his descendants to have faith in God, obey Him, remain separate from all other nations, and evangelize the world. God intended to use Abraham and his offspring as moral, spiritual, and financial examples to all men. He wanted to demonstrate how the blessings of the one true God could benefit mankind. And in the Hebrews' program of sacrifices, God painted a clear picture of how the Messiah would one day redeem the world from sin.

After the judgment of mankind at Babel, God sought

an individual through whom He might build a nation of people who would separate themselves unto him. He had tested the human race through conscience and human government, and mankind had completely failed both tests. Only Noah escaped God's fierce judgment at the conclusion of the Age of Conscience, and the Bible does not record the name of even one righteous man living during the Age of Human Government. But after Babel, as God searched the land called Ur of the Chaldees, He saw something special in a seventy-five-year-old man named Abram.

God then made a decision that would shake the world—"I will choose a special people who will keep my commandments, covenants, and statutes." God chose Abram to be the father of these people.

THE MAN FROM UR OF THE CHALDEANS

Ten generations from Noah and descended from the line of Shem, Abram was born in 2165 B.C. We know almost nothing of his early life or what it was that caused God to look upon him with favor. Scripture tells us that his family worshiped idols. Regardless of Abram's past, everything changed when the God of glory appeared to him while he lived in Mesopotamia (Acts 7:2).

In Abram's day, Ur was a prosperous commercial center and seaport at the mouth of the Euphrates River on the Persian Gulf. A ziggurat similar to the infamous Tower of Babel dominated the city's skyline.[1] Into this heathen setting the God of glory appeared, spoke to Abram, and made him three promises:

I will make you a great nation;
I will bless you
And make your name great;
And you shall be a blessing.
I will bless those who bless you,
And I will curse him who curses you;
And in you all the families of the earth shall be blessed.
(Gen. 12:2–3 NKJV)

Notice that the promises are *personal* ("I will bless you and make your name great"), *national* ("I will make you a great nation"), and *universal* ("in you all the families of the earth shall be blessed"). This Abrahamic Covenant was an important link between all God had already done, what He intended to do through Abram, and what He will continue to do until the end of the age.

ABRAHAM'S CALL TO SEPARATE

The tenth revelation of truth, pictured for us in the Age of Promise, is this: *We are to be separated from the world!*

When God called Abraham, then called Abram, He didn't say, "Stay here in Ur, live in the shadow of that ziggurat, and work among those who are worshiping the stars above and the pagan queen of heaven." No—God told Abram to leave that sinful city. He said,

Get out of your country,
From your family
And from your father's house,
To a land that I will show you. (Gen. 12:1 NKJV)

Notice that this was a threefold separation—Abram had to leave his country, his extended family, and his father's house. He had to cut all ties to the past. Amos 3:3 (NKJV) asked, "Can two walk together, unless they are agreed?" Abram's idolatrous past would be at odds with his God-ordained future. He had to remove himself from all influences of the past.

Americans today are marching to a mantra of tolerance and inclusion, but God's command is separation. Moses was not tolerant. He told the children of Israel, "Whoever is on the LORD's side—come to me!" (Ex. 32:26 NKJV). Paul was not tolerant. He wrote, "Come out from among them and be separate, says the Lord" (2 Cor. 6:17 NKJV). Jesus was not tolerant. He said, "He who is not with Me is against Me" (Matt. 12:30 NKJV).

Hear me, friend: The collapse of character begins with moral compromise, and moral compromise begins when we begin to tolerate sin in order to gain the world's acceptance.

God had commanded Abraham to leave all . . . but Abraham clung to his family. He did leave his country, but he took his father, Terah, and his nephew, Lot, to Haran. Note this: *Terah* means "delay." *Haran*, the name of the city, means "parched." And *Lot* means "veil." Translation? Until you totally separate from the world, your place of blessing will be delayed. You'll live in a parched place until you separate from the world. It wasn't until Abraham separated from Lot that he received his inheritance and the fullness of God's blessing.

God gave Abraham three commands: Leave your country, your kindred, and your father. In return, God gave Abraham three blessings:

1. *He promised to make Abraham a great nation.* Abraham left his country, so God gave him a nation. Christian, if you give up this world, God will give you the New Jerusalem!

2. *He promised to bless Abraham with covenant blessings.* He blessed Abraham with health, wealth, and peace that passes understanding. Abraham gave up his extended family, but God became a friend that sticks closer than a brother.

3. *He promised to make Abraham's name great.* Abram left his father, the source of his name, and God not only gave Abram a new name, but He made that new name great!

Abraham was not only separated to obey God, but he was separated to worship. Genesis 12:8 (NKJV) tells us:

> And he moved from there to the mountain east of Bethel, and he pitched his tent with Bethel on the west and Ai on the east; there he built an altar to the LORD and called on the name of the LORD.

Abraham recognized the God who led him, and he separated himself to worship God and God alone. We are not to touch the gods of this world. The ancient Chaldeans worshiped the sun and stars and moon, while modern man kneels at the temples of humanism, paganism, and hedonism. While the people of Abraham's day bowed and sacrificed their children to idols, the people of our day bow to convenience and sacrifice the unborn.

Modern men and women bow to pleasure and sacrifice morality while they indulge in pornography. They bow to the sun, moon, and stars as they consult their astrological charts and entrust their futures to the charlatans who operate psychic hot lines. They bow to human intellect and immerse their minds in Eastern philosophies that blind the heart, mind, and spirit to the things of the Creator.

"Do not be unequally yoked together with unbelievers. For what fellowship has righteousness with lawlessness? And what communion has light with darkness?" asked the apostle Paul (2 Cor. 6:14 NKJV).

God is not looking for politically correct followers. He's looking for men and women without spot or wrinkle. He's not looking for comfortable Christians—he's looking for Christians who are willing to conquer sin in Jesus' name!

James said:

> Adulterers and adulteresses! Do you not know that friendship with the world is enmity with God? Whoever therefore wants to be a friend of the world makes himself an enemy of God. (James 4:4 NKJV)

Hear me, friend. A wishbone will never take the place of a backbone. The church of Jesus Christ is not a retirement center for religious fat cats; it's a recruiting center for the army of the living God! We are salt and light, and we must act like it! We are *in* the world, but we must not be *of* it. We are not to be *isolated* from sinful men and women, but if you want to preserve the sanctity of your testimony, you must be *insulated* from sin.

THE COVENANT WITH ABRAHAM

Covenant is the most important word in the Bible. It is not just another topic; it is the foundation of Christianity.

Covenant is the soil in which every flower of God blooms. It is the key that ties together the Old and New Testaments. Covenant is the secret of divine revelation.

Mark this: God made a covenant with Abraham and his descendants to demonstrate His power to provide for His children. In effect, God was saying to the world, "Let's compare the blessings of serving the living God to those of serving dead idols!"

The psalmist wrote: "The secret of the LORD is with those who fear Him, and He will show them His covenant" (Ps. 25:14 NKJV).

Do you want to know God's secrets? Do you want to understand divine revelation? Then learn how to enter into covenant relationships!

WHAT IS COVENANT?

Research about the concept of covenant has revolutionized recent decades of Old Testament studies. Many scholars maintain that Old Testament theology must be constructed and understood around the organizing principle of covenant. In the Near Eastern world of the second millennium before Christ, formal covenants were the primary way people who were not blood relatives related to one another.

People in ancient Mesopotamia, Asia Minor, and Palestine depended on covenants to regulate personal affairs, business deals, and international relations, and to appease the gods. All kinds of covenants existed—between equal partners, between greater and lesser partners, and between absolute sovereigns and abject servants. People often memorialized their covenants with stone pillars, or *stellae,* as in the example of Jacob and Laban (Gen. 31:44–47). A ceremonial meal between the parties involved signified the harmonious nature of the new relationship. A marriage between two families might seal the compact, as in the case of the royal dynasties of Israel and Egypt (1 Kings 9:16, 24). In every case, the gods of all parties involved were called to witness and guarantee the agreement, contract, vow, or treaty.

Fortunately for biblical scholars, the people of the ancient Near East went out of their way to write down all kinds of covenants. All during the twentieth century archaeologists dug up, dusted off, and deciphered clay tablets and stone monuments that recorded countless covenants regulating the commercial, political, and religious life of nation after nation. Many of the most significant covenants for Old Testament studies turned up in the archives of the Hittite monarchs, which were discovered in 1906 among the ruins of Boghaz-koi in Turkey.

THE COVENANT FORM

Several scholars have demonstrated that the structure of the Hittite treaties between these oriental monarchs and their abject vassals parallels in close detail the covenant format between Jehovah and Israel found in Exodus 20–23, the book of Deuteronomy, and Joshua 24. When the one, true, living God initiated a relationship with the descendants of Abraham, He used a covenant style universally understood at the time:

- A preamble identifying the absolute sovereign.

- A brief history of relations between the absolute sovereign and the subject people.

- The benefits for and obligations of the subject people.

- An oath of allegiance and its accompanying blessings for obedience and curses for disobedience.

- A list of witnesses and directions for keeping the covenant. Sometimes instructions for periodic renewal of the covenant followed.

The Bible is divided into an Old Testament and a New Testament. *Testament* was a synonym for *covenant* in the English of the era of King James I. All of God's Word concerns an old and a new form of the way in which He provides for a personal, mutually committed relationship between Himself and those whom He calls and who respond in faith to Him.

The covenant in Eden (Gen. 2:15–17), the covenant with Adam (3:14–19), and the covenant with Noah (9:1–17) were God's general provisions for the entire human race in their existence on earth. The covenant with Abraham is the first of God's promises to establish a spiritual relationship with a called, believing people. The covenant with Abraham and those that follow are called "theocratic" covenants because they pertain to the rule of God. He always relates to believers as the Sovereign, gracious and

merciful though He may be, and they submit to His lord-
ship.

A covenant, simply speaking, is a contract or agreement
between two parties. In the Old Testament the Hebrew
word translated "covenant" is *berith*, which comes from a
root that means "to cut." There are three kinds of
covenants in the Bible: the shoe covenant (Ruth 4:7), the
salt covenant (Num. 18:19), and the blood covenant (Gen.
15:7–21). Of these three, the blood covenant was the most
serious and somber, for it involved the shedding of blood
and the giving of life.

When God made His covenant with Abraham, Abraham
split the carcasses of a heifer, a she-goat, a ram, a turtle-
dove, and a pigeon. He then arranged the pieces of the animals into two lines. Usually, if the transaction or agreement
was between two people, they would join hands and walk
together in the space between the split carcasses. By this act,
they were pledging, in the presence of blood and suffering
and death, to keep the terms of the contract.[2]

Because this particular contract was between
Abraham and God, however, God put Abraham into a
deep sleep. As he slept, God's presence passed through the
bloody pieces alone, thus indicating that the promises of
Jehovah concerning Abraham's salvation and his posses-
sion of Palestine were both unconditional, with no heavenly strings attached whatsoever![3]

God's covenant with Abraham depended solely upon
God, who obligated himself in grace. God's "I will" decla-
rations in the Abrahamic Covenant indicate its unconditional character—there are no corresponding "you must"
demands on Abraham. God gave this covenant in broad

outline in Genesis 12:1–3 and later confirmed it to Abraham at various times in greater detail (Gen. 13:14–17, 15:1–7, 18–21; 17:1–8).

THE ABRAHAMIC COVENANT INCLUDES A PROMISE OF LAND

Israel is the only nation in world history to be created and endowed by a sovereign act of God. Part of God's covenant with Abraham included the promise of a land that would belong to the Jewish people forever.

> On the same day the LORD made a covenant with Abram, saying: "To your descendants I have given this land, from the river of Egypt to the great river, the River Euphrates—the Kenites, the Kenezzites, the Kadmonites, the Hittites, the Perizzites, the Rephaim, the Amorites, the Canaanites, the Girgashites, and the Jebusites." (Gen. 15:18–21 NKJV)

> And the LORD said to Abram, after Lot had separated from him: "Lift your eyes now and look from the place where you are—northward, southward, eastward, and westward; for all the land which you see I give to you and your descendants forever." (Gen. 13:14–15 NKJV)

Forever means forever! God ratified that promise of a title deed to the Promised Land with a blood covenant. Scripture details the exact borders of Israel just as our heavenly Father dictated them. The divine Surveyor drove the original stakes into Judean soil and decreed that no one should ever change these property lines. The real estate contract and land covenants were signed in blood and stand to this very hour. Jews have the absolute right as mandated by God to the land of Israel.

By what right did God grant this land to Abraham and his descendants? God could give the land to the Jewish people because it belonged to Him.

In Exodus 9:29 (NKJV), Moses told Pharaoh, "As soon as I have gone out of the city, I will spread out my hands to the LORD; the thunder will cease, and there will be no more hail, that you may know that the earth is the LORD's." Deuteronomy 10:14 (NKJV) repeats the principle: "Indeed heaven and the highest heavens belong to the LORD your God, also the earth with all that is in it."

You don't need a doctorate in theology to understand that this land belongs to the Jewish people alone. It does not belong to Yasser Arafat, the Roman Church, the Crusaders, or the Turks. For as long as the sun shines and the moon glows at night, the Promised Land belongs to the seed of Abraham, Isaac, and Jacob!

COVENANT BREAKERS IN THE LAST DAYS

A covenant is a binding promise, but Scripture tells us:

> In the last days perilous times will come: For men will be lovers of themselves, lovers of money, boasters, proud, blasphemers, disobedient to parents, unthankful, unholy, unloving, unforgiving, slanderers, without self-control, brutal, despisers of good, traitors, headstrong, haughty, lovers of pleasure rather than lovers of God, having a

form of godliness but denying its power. And from such people turn away! (2 Tim. 3:1–5 NKJV)

These people, who lack the integrity to keep their promises to wives and husbands and children, are faithless and ruthless. Look around our world today, and you can find a half dozen examples of men like this in the headlines of your morning paper.

Lying and deception have become a way of life in politics. A man's word is no longer his bond. If a man is caught in a lie, he will hire a lawyer to debate the meaning of the word *is*.

Covenant keeping requires faithfulness! If you are to keep your covenants, you must keep your word.

Let's look at the Age of the Law for an example of the kind of covenant keeping that God expects. The ninth chapter of Joshua tells the story. As the children of Israel moved into the Promised Land, they were attacking and destroying every city in their path. They were about to enter the land of the Gibeonites, and, as you might expect, the Gibeonites were terrified by the destruction headed their way. In order to save themselves from certain annihilation, they entered into a conspiracy of lies. The people put on old clothing, tattered shoes, and stuffed their baskets with molded bread. They mounted donkeys and camels and went to pay a call on the Israelites, who were camped a few miles away.

After staggering, apparently exhausted, into the Israelites' camp, the leaders of the Gibeonites told Joshua that they were from a far country. "Your God is great," they said, "and we want to make a covenant with you."

Without investigating their story, Joshua agreed. And it was only after he had entered into a blood covenant with the Gibeonites that he learned that the Gibeonite leaders had lied. They weren't from a far country at all—they were next on Joshua's "to be whipped" list!

Understand this: The Gibeonites lied in order to enter into a covenant with Israel. God had sent Joshua to wipe out every tribe in the land of Canaan, but he had just promised to protect and defend the Gibeonites, a pack of liars.

The plot thickened as time passed. Five kings of the Amorites decided to attack the people of Gibeon, and the leaders of that land sent an emergency SOS to Joshua:

> And the men of Gibeon sent to Joshua at the camp at Gilgal, saying, "Do not forsake your servants; come up to us quickly, save us and help us, for all the kings of the Amorites who dwell in the mountains have gathered together against us." (Josh. 10:6 NKJV)

What did Joshua do? What would you have done?

Joshua consulted the Lord, who had never broken a single covenant with man. God wasn't about to allow His people to break covenant, not even with a pack of liars. "And the LORD said to Joshua, 'Do not fear [the kings coming against Gibeon], for I have delivered them into your hand; not a man of them shall stand before you'" (Josh. 10:8 NKJV).

God then commenced to work one of the greatest miracles in the Old Testament on behalf of Joshua and the Gibeonites. The sun actually *stood still* in order to provide light so the children of Israel could utterly defeat the kings who had come against Gibeon (Josh. 10:13).

God will perform mighty miracles for people who keep covenant! He doesn't break His covenants . . . and neither do His people!

THE SECRET OF SUCCESSFUL COVENANT KEEPING

Remember this: Every covenant consists of a solemn oath in which two wills die and one unified will is born. When you take marriage vows, your will and your spouse's become one. When you enter into a business arrangement, your will and that of your partner die so that they can become one.

If you break your wedding vows—your covenant with your spouse—God considers you a faithless covenant breaker. If you give your word in a business deal and then break your word, whether or not you had a written contract, you are a covenant breaker. Every broken covenant is the result of a war of wills, a conflict between self-centered people who insist upon getting their own way.

The secret to successful covenant keeping is this: Let your will die. This principle will work in marriage, in business, and in the church. Every Christian is born into the body of Christ by the blood covenant of Calvary. We are one in the Lord. We are brothers and sisters in Christ. It is not possible for us to be separated by race, wealth, power, or position.

CHRISTIANS ARE BOUND BY COVENANT

When darkness covered Calvary's hill, God the Father and Jesus the Son were walking in the blood of Calvary reciting the contents of the new covenant. The Father asked, "What are the stipulations of the covenant?"

The Son answered, "Father, let their sins be blotted out, buried in the deepest sea, never to be remembered again. Though their sins be as scarlet, let them be as white as snow.

"Let the veil of the temple be torn down, so men can come boldly into the presence of God in my name.

"Let them be members of the royal family . . . kings and priests unto God.

"Let them receive the keys to death, hell, and the grave. Let them have power over the world, the flesh, and the devil, over disease and demons, over principalities and powers in high places.

"Let Gentiles be adopted into the blessings of Abraham. Let them no longer be without hope and cut off, but graft them into the olive tree as full partners with descendants of Abraham, Isaac, and Jacob.

"Give them eternal life for death, and health and healing for sickness and disease. Father, give them my name, and let them be known as my people. Let them be a covenant people, faithful, loyal, and true."

The Father said to the Son, "Is that all?"

"Yes!"

And in the darkness of Calvary, the Father agreed, and the Son cried out, "It is finished!"

The covenant was consummated, and the slaves to sin and Satan were freed. And those the Son sets free are free indeed!

I believe that all the scars of Jesus healed except the scars in His hands—because in biblical history, some blood covenants were sealed when two men would cut their right palms and then shake hands. In the handshake, their blood would mingle, effectively sealing the covenant. God speaks of this gesture in Isaiah 49:16 (NKJV): "See, I have inscribed you on the palms of My hands."

Remember the two disciples on the road to Emmaus? They did not recognize Jesus . . . until they saw the scars in His hands. When Jesus returns to earth, the prophet Zechariah tells us, "[The children of Israel] will look on [Jesus] whom they pierced" (Zech. 12:10 NKJV). The covenant scars in His palms will still be there!

Friend, becoming a Christian is entering into a covenant with Jesus Christ. We take His name, *Christian*, we are sealed with His blood, we surrender our lives and our wills, and He promises us a life more abundant and a home in heaven. Then we share a covenant meal—the Lord's Supper! When you take communion, you are saying, "I am bound by blood to Christ and His church and to the people in this church." If you can't say that when you pass the cup and the bread, then don't take communion!

God takes this covenant meal very seriously. Paul dealt with a problem in the Corinthian church regarding communion—some people were overindulging and actually becoming drunk with the communion wine. Because they forgot the spiritual significance of the covenant meal, Paul wrote, "For this reason many are weak and sick among you, and many sleep [are dead]" (1 Cor. 11:30 NKJV). It's a fact—God destroys covenant breakers!

Though communion is a serious matter, it doesn't have to be solemn. I can scarcely keep from shouting "Hallelujah!" when I think about all Christ did for me at Calvary. Through the covenant of His blood, He defeated the prince of darkness, He gave me an undeserved inheritance, and He made me a joint heir with Him, the King of kings. So you'll never catch me mumbling into the communion cup! I rejoice to lift it to my lips, because I am a child of the King.

United as we are in covenant with Christ, it's a shame we Christians aren't more united in purpose and harmony on earth. In John 17:21 (NKJV), Jesus prayed for us, the church, "that they all may be one, as You, Father, are in Me, and I in You; that they also may be one in Us, that the world may believe that You sent Me."

A divided, bickering church testifies to the world that Jesus is a fraud! A united church, however, in which men and women walk in covenant relationships, testifies that Jesus Christ is Lord.

How in the name of God can some people say they are Christians, bound by blood covenant to other believers, if they can't be civil to their fellow church members? The answer is simple: Either they were never saved, or they are covenant breakers. Many people who sing "Amazing Grace" at the top of their voices on Sunday morning are worthless in the kingdom of God.

Hear this: Every disciple is a Christian . . . but not every Christian is a disciple. Disciples do what Jesus did. He lived in covenant relationships.

THE COVENANT IN AMERICAN HISTORY

America was born in covenant! The Mayflower Compact, authored by the emigrants who sailed from England in 1620 to establish the first colony in New England, states:

In the name of God, Amen. We, whose names are underwritten, the Loyal Subjects of our dread Sovereign Lord, King James, by the Grace of God, of Great Britain, France and Ireland, King, Defender of the Faith, &c. Having undertaken for the Glory of God, and Advancement of the Christian Faith, and the Honor of our King and Country, a voyage to plant the first colony in the northern Parts of Virginia; do by these presents, solemnly and mutually in the Presence of God and one of another, covenant and combine ourselves together into a civil Body Politick, for our better Ordering and Preservation, and Furtherance of the Ends aforesaid; And by Virtue hereof to enact, constitute, and frame, such just and equal Laws, Ordinances, Acts, Constitutions and Offices, from time to time, as shall be thought most meet and convenient for the General good of the Colony; unto which we promise all due Submission and Obedience. IN WITNESS whereof we have hereunto subscribed our names at Cape Cod the eleventh of November, in the Reign of our Sovereign Lord, King James of England, France and Ireland, the eighteenth, and of Scotland the fifty-fourth. Anno Domini, 1620.[4]

This nation was born in covenant with God! As long as we kept the covenant with Him, God poured out His blessings upon this country, making it the envy of the world.

Are we keeping covenant with God today? How can we, when the Supreme Court rules that the Ten Commandments have no place in our public schools? How can we, when our president allows homosexuals to remain in the military? How can we, when the government recognizes the occult

The Revelation of Truth

and the CIA hires psychics to guide military intelligence? How can we, when Harvard University, which was founded in order to teach men how to preach the gospel, allows students to chant occult rituals on the campus grounds? How can our nation walk with agreement with God when our government spends our tax dollars on art that blasphemes the Son of God?

The color red in the American flag represents the spilled blood of our men. As a nation, we are bound together by the blood of those who have died in the battle for freedom. Americans—black, white, brown, red, and everything in between—must come together and be bound by loyalty. We must look back to our forefathers, to the principles they held dear. They died for those principles and cherished beliefs. We must reclaim them.

ABRAHAM TOOK GOD AT HIS WORD

Think of the miracle—God appeared to an aging man in a pagan country, called him to an unknown land, and promised him a son and a nation, a permanent soil, and a Savior, three unimaginable gifts. Now notice this: *Abraham believed God*. The Word of God tells us, "And [Abraham] believed in the LORD, and He accounted it to him for righteousness" (Gen. 15:6 NKJV).

The eleventh revelation of truth in Genesis is this: *We are justified by faith*. Abraham believed God—not *loved* God, or *served* God—but *believed* God, and God credited him with righteousness. Belief, or faith, is powerful!

Mark 9:23 (NKJV): "Jesus said to him, 'If you can believe, all things are possible to him who believes.'"

136

Mark 16:17–18 (NKJV): "And these signs will follow those who believe: In My name they will cast out demons; they will speak with new tongues; they will take up serpents; and if they drink anything deadly, it will by no means hurt them; they will lay hands on the sick, and they will recover."

Acts 16:31 (NKJV): "So they said, 'Believe on the Lord Jesus Christ, and you will be saved, you and your household.'"

Do you need a miracle? Only believe! Faith can move mountains and calm the troubled sea. Faith can produce streams in the desert. Faith packs a bag and begins the journey before the traveler knows where the road will lead.

THE SON DELIVERED FROM DEATH

In Genesis we can find two pictures of Abraham as a faith traveler. The first picture shows him setting out from Ur for an unknown promised land. The second picture, that of Abraham trudging up Mount Moriah to sacrifice his beloved son, Isaac, would tug at the heart of any loving parent. But look at the revelation of truth revealed in that second picture: *The promised Son will be delivered from death!*

The story behind this latter portrait of Abraham is straightforward: God had long before promised the aging Abraham a son, and through that son, a nation. After an agonizingly long wait, at age ninety, Sarah finally gave birth to Isaac, the child of promise.

Then God put Abraham's devotion and faith to the ultimate test. He commanded Abraham to take his boy to a nearby mountaintop and sacrifice him there. It was a shocking request, the kind of instruction that surely left Abraham feeling weak-kneed and nauseous. Nevertheless, Abraham somehow summoned the courage and strength to obey, trusting, if in nothing else, the power of God to bring his dead son back to life.

> By faith Abraham, when he was tested, offered up Isaac, and he who had received the promises offered up his only begotten son, of whom it was said, "In Isaac your seed shall be called," concluding that God was able to raise him up, even from the dead, from which he also received him in a figurative sense. (Heb. 11:17–19 NKJV)

At a bleak moment in the story, Isaac, who surely was no fool, realized that though they carried a weapon and wood, they had not brought an animal for the sacrifice. He innocently asked his father, "Where is the lamb?"

Abraham answered, "God will provide a lamb, my son."

As time passed, did Abraham question his own assertion? We don't know, but we do know that Abraham proceeded, even binding Isaac and placing the boy upon the altar. As Abraham raised the knife to slay his son, the angel of the Lord called out to him, "Do not lay your hand on the lad, or do anything to him; for now I know that you fear God, since you have not withheld your son, your only son, from Me" (Gen. 22:12 NKJV).

That is the surface picture. The revelation of truth within points to a portrait of the future salvation of the world through Jesus Christ.

The similarities between the two pictures are obvious.

Isaac was Abraham's only legitimate son, and Christ is the only Son of God. Abraham loved God so much that he was willing to sacrifice his son; God loved the world so much that He was willing to sacrifice *His* Son. Isaac did not resist the will of his father; Christ did not resist the will of *His* Father. Isaac carried the wood for the sacrifice on Mount Moriah; Christ, at least until He became weary, carried His cross up to Golgotha. Even the site of Abraham's sacrifice is near the site where Jesus was crucified. The author of Chronicles identifies Mount Moriah as the mountain where the temple in Jerusalem was built (2 Chron. 3:1).

However, there is another amazing parallel—notice that God provided Abraham with a substitute sacrifice. After laying aside his blade, Abraham spied a ram tangled in a nearby thicket. "So Abraham went and took the ram, and offered it up for a burnt offering instead of his son" (Gen. 22:13 NKJV). God has done the same for us! He has provided not a ram, but the Lamb. Christ, through His death on the cross, has become our substitute. He died so that we might live.

Some Bible scholars have supposed that God instructed Abraham to take Isaac to Mount Moriah to demonstrate how He planned to use Abraham's lineage to bless the entire world. God wanted to teach Abraham through an experience, or picture, what He had already explained in words. In John 8:56 (NKJV), Jesus Himself reinforced this idea when He said: "Your father Abraham rejoiced to see My day, and he saw it and was glad." Jesus' Jewish audience was astounded at His statement, for they understood His use of the word *see* in a very literal sense. But, as the authors of *Hard Sayings of the Bible* point out:

Our Lord does not correct them in this notion. But it must be noticed that it was not he himself that Christ asserted that Abraham rejoiced to see, but his day, by which he meant the circumstances of his life which was of the greatest importance . . . Nothing in the Old Testament says in so many words that Abraham saw the death of Messiah as the Savior of the world. It is possible, however, that what our Lord is referring to is the transaction in Genesis 22 when Abraham was asked to sacrifice his only son on Mount Moriah. In offering his son, Abraham would have had a lively figure of the future offering of the Son of God as a sacrifice for the sins of the world.[5]

THE BRIDE AND BRIDEGROOM

As wonderful as the picture of salvation upon Mount Moriah is, there is another, equally delightful, portrait in the Age of Promise. Abraham's beloved son, Isaac, grew to manhood and needed a wife. In Genesis 24 Abraham sent his trusted servant, probably his steward Eliezer, back to his home country in order to find a worthy bride for his son. In Mesopotamia, the servant asked God for a sign regarding the right choice of a bride, and, at the perfect moment, Rebekah entered the scene. Once the servant had explained his errand to the bride-to-be and her family, Rebekah agreed to journey with him to Canaan.

Here's the thirteenth revelation of truth, painted within a beautiful wedding picture: *The church is the bride of Christ.* Harold Willmington has done a wonderful job of explaining the typology in the story of Isaac and Rebekah:

Abraham is a type, or picture, of the heavenly Father, who is planning a marriage for His beloved Son (Matt. 22:2).

Isaac is a picture of Christ, who was offered up as a sacrifice and seeks His bride. Like Isaac, Christ dearly loves His bride (Gen. 24:67; Eph. 5:25).

The servant is a picture of the Holy Spirit. He journeyed to Mesopotamia for one reason alone—to find a bride for the father's son. The Holy Spirit came at Pentecost for only one purpose—to gather a bride for the Son. The servant gave honor to the father and son. Today the Holy Spirit gives honor to the Father and Son (John 15:26).

Rebekah is a picture of the church. Before anyone can be a part of Christ's bride, he or she must answer the same question Rebekah answered: "Are you willing to go with this man?" (Gen. 24:58).[6]

SEVEN PROPHECIES TO ABRAHAM

In Genesis 15:12–21, God gave Abraham seven prophecies, all of which were fulfilled in the Age of Promise:

1. His descendants would be strangers in a foreign land (Gen. 46:2–7).

2. They would be servants in that land (Ex. 1:7–14).

3. They would not settle in the Promised Land until four hundred years had passed (Ex. 12:40).

4. God would judge the nation that had enslaved them (Ex. 7–12).

5. Abraham would be spared from the coming sorrow (Gen. 25:7–8).

6. After four generations, Israel would return to Canaan (Ex. 6:16–20).

7. Israel would come out of Egypt with great wealth (Ex. 12:35–36; Ps. 105:37).

JUDGMENT UPON EGYPT

As we saw earlier in this chapter, as part of the Abrahamic Covenant, God made the following promise to Abraham and his descendants:

> I will make you a great nation;
> I will bless you
> And make your name great;
> And you shall be a blessing.
> I will bless those who bless you,
> And I will curse him who curses you;
> And in you all the families of the earth shall be blessed.
> (Gen. 12:2–3 NKJV)

It is historical fact—those who have blessed the Jewish people have prospered, while those who have cursed the Jews have earned the wrath of God. Consider Egypt—one Pharaoh honored Joseph and gave the Jews the land of Goshen to dwell in during the famine. Because God enabled Joseph to interpret Pharaoh's dream, Egypt prospered during the time of famine, becoming the richest kingdom in the world! Pharaoh personally prospered, for it was during this time that the king became owner of all the land. The Bible tells us that the people surrendered to Pharaoh their gold, then their livestock, then their land. When they had nothing else to give, Joseph decreed that the people should give 20 percent of their income to Pharaoh, a system that remained in place for several dynasties (Gen. 47:13–24).

The Age of Promise is filled with many wonderful and thrilling pictures that are part of God's revelation of truth, but this age is not without God's judgment. After Joseph's death the growing population of Hebrews fell into disfavor with the Egyptians, and the time of their "affliction" (Gen. 15:13) began. They were severely oppressed, but they continued to increase in number. Remembering His promise to Abraham, God looked down from heaven and kept a careful account of the Egyptians' sins against Israel.

The Bible also tells us that another Pharaoh rose to power, one "who did not know Joseph" (Ex. 1:8 NKJV). This king oppressed the children of Israel even more brutally than his predecessors, resorting even to infanticide, and as a result God sent a deliverer, Moses. As part of His divine plan, God sent ten plagues of judgment, the last and most terrible bringing death to the firstborn in every Egyptian home.

The Egyptians were chief among the idol-worshiping nations, with a god for everything from childbirth to the afterlife. Included among the pantheon of their gods was the god/goddess/divine child trio, known as Osiris, Isis, and Horus. Isis was known by many names, among them "Mother of God, Lady of Heaven." Pharaoh was seen as

Horus, the incarnation of God in human form, until he died and became Osiris. Interestingly enough, the Egyptians insisted upon believing that Pharaoh was directly descended from God and of divine birth. He was also the divine victim, the one who had to sacrifice his life to appease the gods if the land suffered through a famine.[7]

Because the land of Egypt had so thoroughly fallen under the influence of Satan's counterfeits, each divine plague of judgment specifically attacked one of Egypt's gods. The first plague, which turned the water to blood, mocked the authority of Hapi, the god of the Nile. The Egyptians depended upon the Nile and its annual flood to bring water and fertility to their land. When the waters turned to blood, God demonstrated that Hapi had no power. While Moses stood firm, the Egyptian priests begged Hapi to return the waters to their pure state, but Hapi could not answer.

God leveled the second plague, the plague of the frogs, against the frog goddess, Heket. To the Egyptians, Heket controlled fertility and regeneration and protected women in childbirth. By flooding the land with frogs, God seemed to be saying, "You want a god of fertility? Let me demonstrate my powers of reproduction!"

Through the third plague, when lice literally swarmed from the earth to invade the flesh and clothing of men, God mocked the authority of Geb, the ancient earth god. Geb was known as the Great Cackler in some eras and was depicted as a man with a goose on his head to signify that he laid the first cosmic egg of creation.[8]

The fifth plague, flies, dared to attack Isis, the wife of Osiris and the mother of Horus. Isis was one of the great mother goddesses, known as a protector of the living and the dead. The word translated as "flies" in the Exodus account is the Hebrew *arob,* and is not the same word translated as "flies" in Ecclesiastes 10:1. Bible scholars believe the fifth plague included swarms of mosquitoes, flies, and beetles. The ancient Egyptians believed that beetles, which were often depicted in scarab amulets, were associated with rebirth and the afterlife.

The sixth plague, boils that brought intense pain and inflamed the flesh, struck at an obscure god called Setekh, whose worship included human sacrifice. Setekh was identified as an animal with a long curving snout like that of a crocodile. The Greeks called him Typhon, a name that connects him with the whirling pillars of scorching sand that often raced across the dry Egyptian fields in summertime.[9]

The seventh plague, hail and fire, was leveled against Shu, the ancient Egyptian god of the air who separated earth and the sky.

The eighth plague, locusts, seems to have been directed against Wadjet, the cobra goddess who was viewed as a protectress of Egypt. Depicted as a woman with a cobra head about to strike at the nation's enemies, she could do nothing to stop the swarm of locusts that covered the land like a cloud.

The ninth plague, thick, impenetrable darkness, was a direct slap at the sun god, Re, reported to be the father of the kings of Egypt. Since the Egyptians believed that Re's journey across the sky in his golden chariot accounted for the rising and setting of the sun, when Moses stretched out his hand and darkness settled upon Egypt, the Israelites' God appeared to have bound Re and kept him from his daily journey through the heavens.

The tenth and final plague, the death of the firstborn, revealed the weakness of Osiris, the god whose myth included the story of his own murder and resurrection. Osiris was the god of the dead, and dead pharaohs were considered to be embodiments of Osiris, having been equated with Horus, Isis's son, while on the throne.[10] With the advent of the angel of death, God struck at the Osiris cult by striking not only the supposed "son" of Horus, Pharaoh's firstborn, but also the firstborn of every Egyptian family. Osiris was powerless to prevent God's terrible judgment.

The death angel crept through the darkness, reaching out his cold hand to stop the heart of a son here, a daughter there, until he had struck the firstborn of all Egypt. When he passed through the streets where the Hebrews lived, however, he paused at the threshold of every door, noticed the blood smeared on the doorposts, and turned away. The next morning, when the sun finally rose, weeping and wailing filled the homes of the Egyptians, but the Hebrews knew joy and confident peace.

The message of the plagues to Egypt? Protection is found only in the God of Abraham, Isaac, and Jacob! Protection is found only in the blood of the Lamb of God!

THE POWER OF PRAYER

Can't you just see the children of Israel as they tiptoed out of their homes on their morning of freedom? God had heard their prayers and groanings, and He had sent a miraculous deliverance. Not only would they leave Egypt, but they would leave with great wealth, just wages for their years of enslavement.

See the fourteenth revelation of truth in the picture of liberation: *Prayer has real power*.

Abraham prayed for a son, and God sent Isaac, whose name literally means "son of laughter."

Abraham's servant, Eliezer, prayed for God to direct him to the perfect wife for Isaac, and God sent the beautiful Rebekah.

The children of Israel prayed for a deliverer, and God sent Moses.

Why should we pray? Because God answers prayer! "Call to Me," says the Lord, "and I will answer you, and show you great and mighty things, which you do not know" (Jer. 33:3 NKJV).

Why pray? Because Jesus Christ did not teach His disciples how to raise money, how to preach, or how to counsel religious neurotics. He taught them how to pray (Luke 11:1–13).

Why pray? Because prayerlessness is sin! First Samuel 12:23 (NKJV) says, "Moreover, as for me, far be it from me that I should sin against the LORD in ceasing to pray for you."

Why pray? Because a prayerless Christian is a powerless Christian. As powerful as God is, He cannot answer prayer until you pray.

The Bible teaches us four principles of prayer:

1. *We should pray in Jesus' name.* "If you ask anything in My name, I will do it" (John 14:14 NKJV).

2. *We should pray in faith.* "And whatever things you ask in prayer, believing, you will receive" (Matt. 21:22 NKJV).

3. *We should pray specifically and from the heart, not using repetitious words.* Jesus said:

> And when you pray, do not use vain repetitions as the heathen do. For they think that they will be heard for their many words. Therefore do not be like them. For your Father knows the things you have need of before you ask Him. (Matt. 6:7–8 NKJV)

4. *We should pray according to the Word of God.* The Bible says:

> Now this is the confidence that we have in Him, that if we ask anything according to His will, He hears us. And if we know that He hears us, whatever we ask, we know that we have the petitions that we have asked of Him. (1 John 5:14–15 NKJV)

Is your marriage failing? Pray! Are your finances a mess? Pray! Is your son or daughter addicted to alcohol or drugs? Pray! God answers prayer!

As the Age of Promise drew to a close and the children of Abraham marched out of Egypt and its bondage, they carried with them the promise of the Redeemer. The examples of animal sacrifice demonstrated how redemption would be accomplished, and the miracle of the Passover had just reaffirmed that lesson. The Passover Lamb, innocent and without fault, was a perfect picture of the coming Lamb of God who would take away the sin of the world.

The apostle Paul wrote:

And the Scripture, foreseeing that God would justify the Gentiles by faith, preached the gospel to Abraham beforehand, saying, "In you all the nations shall be blessed." (Gal. 3:8 NKJV)

The promise the Israelites carried with them was not exclusive to the Jewish people—it also belongs to you and me. Through Abraham's seed, we have all been blessed!

THE GREAT SHEPHERD IS STILL SEEKING THE LOST

The fifteenth revelation of truth in Genesis is this: *God, the great Shepherd, is still seeking the lost!* In the Age of Promise, He sought out Abram, an idolater, to make him "the father of all who believe." That's unbelievable!

God has a seeker's heart. He sought Jacob at Bethel, when he was fleeing the consequences of his sin and the fury of his cheated brother. God looked down from the throne room of heaven and said, "See that aggressive, pushy hustler who just stole his brother's birthright? I want him! I'll use him!"

God sought Moses while he was a fugitive in Midian. As He touched His finger to the bush that would soon burn and draw Moses near, God said, "See that murderer hiding out in the wilderness? I want him!"

Jesus Christ sought the twelve disciples while they were going about their daily work. He chose fishermen, a physician, and a hated tax collector. "You have not chosen Me," He told them, "but I have chosen you." He would use this group of ordinary men to change the world.

Jesus did not come to earth because He needed us. He came to earth because we needed Him. The shepherd seeks the lost sheep. And, once found, we understand the truth of the Scripture that says, "We love Him because He first loved us" (1 John 4:19 NKJV).

How I thank God for the day the Chief Shepherd, Jesus Christ, came searching for me! He saw me sitting on the back pew of my father's church in Houston, Texas. "I want that one," he said. "I'll take him and shape him into something useful."

Thank God for the night He came by the hellhole where you were serving Satan. "I want that one," He said, then He lifted you out of the miry clay and set your feet on a rock to stay. He put a song in your heart, just as He did in mine.

Perhaps you have not yet responded to the Shepherd's call. Are you hiding from God? He sees you, He knows you, and He wants you. If you will answer His call, He will make something beautiful of your life.

Journal, Page Six

Great shouts of celebration echoed in the halls of heaven on the day Moses led the children of Israel out of Egypt. I flew to the precipice of a stony Egyptian cliff to watch the mighty exodus, and my heart thrilled with delight to see these beloved children fulfill the Father's desire. How He had longed for them! How He still longed to fellowship with His creation!

I do not know what the coming days will bring, but there has been much activity before the throne. I've heard rumors that God Himself will descend to speak with Moses, and that He will share His heart with this man. Sometimes I wonder what the Father sees in this wild-eyed man from the desert, but He looks upon the human heart, a place I cannot see. And Moses' heart, as troubled as it may sometimes be, is courageous and strong. The years in the desert have tempered His hot temper, and the trials of the journey will calm His fears.

After seeing all God has done for them in Egypt, how could any of Abraham's children doubt His love for them?

THE AGE
OF THE LAW

My mother, who had a bachelor's degree in theology before she was married, told her four sons, "If God made the children of Israel live under the Law of Moses for two thousand years, it's good enough for the boys of the Hagee household!"

We didn't live under grace in our home—my mother said we weren't ready to understand it. So when my brother hit me, I got to hit him back! If some kid bit me, well—you get the picture. Turning the other cheek certainly has its merits for a mature person, but as a child, I loved and understood the law of God as given to Moses!

The Age of the Law began with the Exodus from Egypt and continued to the preaching of John the Baptist, or from Moses to Christ—a period of more than 1,718 years. During that span of time, Israel settled in the Promised Land, sought a king, received a king, and enjoyed glory days under King David and King Solomon. After the days of glory, when Solomon's heart departed from the Lord and the people also began to fall away, the nation of Israel endured several periods of servitude, civil war, famine, siege, and failure.

The Age of the Law, however, began favorably. With their own eyes the children of Israel saw the power of God in signs and wonders in Egypt. In the wilderness, they heard the voice of God thundering from Mount Sinai. Just look at the supernatural power God demonstrated:

- He spoke the Law in an audible voice (Deut. 5:22–24).

- He was visible in the pillar of fire by night and the cloud by day (Ex. 13:21).

- He caused fresh bread, or manna, to rain from heaven six days a week (Ex. 16:14–15, 26).

- For forty years, the Israelites' clothing did not wear out (Deut. 8:4).

- God caused water enough for two million people and their livestock to gush out of a rock (Ex. 17:6)!

- Because they had been unpaid slaves for four generations, He gave them the riches of Egypt (Ex. 12:35–36).

- He gave them supernatural victories over the giants living in their promised land!

- He gave them a land flowing with milk and honey.

- He gave them a code of laws, the Ten Commandments, which were the blueprint for a perfect and orderly society.

- He made covenants with them and gave them a complete code of laws for spiritual and physical health.

The test of this age? To see if the children of Abraham would obey the Law He had ordained. God wanted to establish a system of worship that would picture the coming redemption and give Israel His revelation for the entire human race. He wanted to fulfill His promise to Abraham and make the Jews a blessing to all nations. God also intended to set Israel in the Promised Land and bless them, so that as a nation they would publicly demonstrate the benefits of serving the one true God.

Another of God's purposes in giving the law was "that every mouth may be stopped, and all the world may become guilty before God. Therefore by the deeds of the law no flesh will be justified in His sight, for by the law is the knowledge of sin" (Rom. 3:19–20 NKJV).

Though it was added as a result of sin, the law pictured good things to come. God intended to use it only until the arrival of the Messiah. "The law and the prophets were until John," wrote Luke. "Since that time the kingdom of God has been preached, and everyone is pressing into it" (Luke 16:16 NKJV).

Jesus Himself said:

Do not think that I came to destroy the Law or the Prophets. I did not come to destroy but to fulfill. For assuredly, I say to you, till heaven and earth pass away, one jot or one tittle will by no means pass from the law till all is fulfilled. (Matt. 5:17–18 NKJV)

JUDGMENT AT THE END OF THE AGE

Like the ages preceding it, the Age of the Law proved that man could not measure up to the standards God demands. The Israelites failed in the wilderness—murmuring, rebelling, and worshiping a golden calf even while Moses was receiving the stone tablets inscribed by the finger of God. The Israelites failed to obey God under Joshua, under the judges permitted to rule over them, and under a series of kings. After the kingdom divided, the people entered such apostasy that God allowed the nation to be taken into slavery and exile in Babylon. Even after their restoration, when they returned to Jerusalem and the Promised Land, they continued to follow false gods. Finally, they failed by rejecting their own Messiah and the gospel.

God's judgment at the conclusion of this age was twofold: First, His judgment of the entire world resulted in the cross of Jesus Christ. "Now is the judgment of this world; now the ruler of this world will be cast out," said Jesus. "And I, if I am lifted up from the earth, will draw all peoples to Myself" (John 12:31–32 NKJV).

Second, as judgment upon Israel, the kingdom of God was temporarily taken from them. In Matthew 21:33–46 (NKJV), Jesus explained in the form of a parable:

> There was a certain landowner who planted a vineyard and set a hedge around it, dug a winepress in it and built a tower. And he leased it to vinedressers and went into a far country. Now when vintage-time drew near, he sent his servants to the vinedressers, that they might receive its fruit. And the vinedressers took his servants, beat

one, killed one, and stoned another. Again he sent other servants, more than the first, and they did likewise to them. Then last of all he sent his son to them, saying, "They will respect my son." But when the vinedressers saw the son, they said among themselves, "This is the heir. Come, let us kill him and seize his inheritance." So they took him and cast him out of the vineyard and killed him. Therefore, when the owner of the vineyard comes, what will he do to those vinedressers?

They said to Him, "He will destroy those wicked men miserably, and lease his vineyard to other vinedressers who will render to him the fruits in their seasons."

Jesus said to them, "Have you never read in the Scriptures:

'The stone which the builders rejected
Has become the chief cornerstone.
This was the LORD's doing,
And it is marvelous in our eyes'?

"Therefore I say to you, the kingdom of God will be taken from you and given to a nation bearing the fruits of it. And whoever falls on this stone will be broken; but on whomever it falls, it will grind him to powder."

Now when the chief priests and Pharisees heard His parables, they perceived that He was speaking of them. But when they sought to lay hands on Him, they feared the multitudes, because they took Him for a prophet.

This second judgment upon Israel resulted in the destruction of Jerusalem in A.D. 70, with the survivors of the massacre being scattered among the other nations until 1948, when Israel was miraculously reborn as a nation.

ANOTHER WEDDING PORTRAIT

Do you remember how Isaac's wedding to Rebekah pictured the coming marriage between Christ and His church? Notice the sixteenth revelation of truth: *The arranged marriage between Isaac and Rebekah is also a picture of God's betrothal to the nation of Israel.*

The image of a wedding occurs frequently in Scripture. Typically, an ancient Hebrew wedding took place in two stages: The first stage was the betrothal, during which the bride and groom were legally joined, though they did not live together. The written betrothal contract was called a *ketubah*, and it could not be broken without a legal divorce, a *get*.

You may recall from the Christmas story that Mary and Joseph were betrothed when she became pregnant with Jesus. Alarmed by the possibility that his bride-to-be was carrying another man's child, Joseph was tempted to quietly obtain a divorce until an angel spoke to him in a dream and told him that Mary carried the Son of God.

The second stage of a Hebrew wedding is the consummation of the marriage. The groom prepares a place for his bride, then journeys to her father's house to get her. Amid great rejoicing, the groom returns with his bride, calls his friends, and arranges for a festive wedding supper.

Jeremiah 2:2–3 (NKJV) tells us that God betrothed Himself to Israel at Mount Sinai:

I remember you,
The kindness of your youth,
The love of your betrothal,
When you went after Me in the wilderness,
In a land not sown.
Israel was holiness to the LORD,
The firstfruits of His increase.

The Torah, or *teaching*, that God gave to Israel at Mount Sinai was a betrothal contract. Just as marriage is a covenant between two people, even so the words of the Law formed a marriage covenant between God and Israel:

> And Moses wrote all the words of the LORD. And he rose early in the morning, and built an altar at the foot of the mountain, and twelve pillars according to the twelve tribes of Israel . . . Then he took the Book of the Covenant and read in the hearing of the people. And they said, "All that the LORD has said we will do, and be obedient." And Moses took the blood, sprinkled it on the people, and said, "This is the blood of the covenant which the LORD has made with you according to all these words." (Ex. 24:4, 7–8 NKJV)

God established another blood covenant with Israel, to reinforce the blood covenant He had established with Abraham. The people were ready, even eager, to accept God's teaching, so Moses went back up the mountain to receive further instruction from the Lord. When Moses came down from the mountain many days later, the newly betrothed nation of Israel had already forsaken her first love. Her leaders were dancing around the image of a golden calf; her love had already eroded to unfaithfulness. In a fit of righteous anger, Moses threw down the stone tablets which God Himself had inscribed, breaking the record of a covenant with Israel (Ex. 32:15–19).

God did renew the covenant with Israel (Ex. 34:10–28), but Moses, not God, wrote upon the second set of stones. The bride's fickle heart interrupted the "wedding rehearsal," but God's love is an enduring love. He loved the children of Abraham then, and He loves them still.

LOVE MADE VISIBLE THROUGH LAW

The best-known covenant in the Bible is the one God made with Moses on Mount Sinai. This is the second of the theocratic covenants (after the covenant with Abraham) that elaborate on how God relates to His people as their sovereign Lord. Unlike the Abrahamic Covenant, God's covenant with Moses was conditional: "If you will indeed obey My voice . . . then you shall be a special treasure" (Ex. 19:5 NKJV). God's covenant with Moses did not deal with how to enter a relationship with the Lord. The Abrahamic Covenant had already established who the chosen people were. The Mosaic Covenant, the Law, spelled out terms for fellowship with God.

You may not know that the Law was much more than the Ten Commandments. The Law, in fact, is contained in the books of Exodus and Leviticus and later expanded upon in Deuteronomy. In the Law God gave Israel explicit instructions about how they were to relate to each other and to God.

The Law was divided into three major sections. First was

the *moral code,* or the Ten Commandments (Ex. 20). The second division was the *spiritual code,* which dealt with special ordinances that were a picture of the coming Christ and His redemption. This section included instructions for the seven religious festivals and five offerings (Ex. 35–40; Lev.). The third division was the *social code,* which included rules governing Israel's diet, sanitation, quarantine, soil conservation, taxation, military service, marriage, childbirth, divorce, and other issues (Ex. 21–34; Lev.).[1] It is interesting to note that God's laws about sanitation kept Israel healthy and safe years before mankind ever discovered microscopic germs and the danger of unsanitary conditions!

God did not give the Law for salvation; keeping the law does not save. Rather, the law keeps and prepares a person for salvation by faith. Paul wrote, "Therefore the law was our tutor to bring us to Christ, that we might be justified by faith" (Gal. 3:24 NKJV).

THE BEST BASIS FOR SOCIETY

God intended that His Law be the blueprint for a great society. The cornerstone of the Law was the Ten Commandments, and Jesus said the Ten Commandments could be summed up in two:

> Then one of the scribes came, and having heard them reasoning together, perceiving that He had answered them well, asked Him, "Which is the first commandment of all?"

> Jesus answered him, "The first of all the commandments is: 'Hear, O Israel, the LORD our God, the LORD is one.

161

And you shall love the LORD your God with all your heart, with all your soul, with all your mind, and with all your strength.' This is the first commandment. And the second, like it, is this: 'You shall love your neighbor as yourself.' There is no other commandment greater than these." (Mark 12:28–31 NKJV)

Paul, writing to the church at Galatia, said love summed up the duties of the law: "For all the law is fulfilled in one word, even in this: 'You shall love your neighbor as yourself'" (Gal. 5:14 NKJV).

Love is the basis for the Ten Commandments and the entire Law. Love God, and love your neighbor. If you can do those two things, you will not have to worry about breaking any of the Ten Commandments.

But let's be realistic—we don't live in a perfect world, and we don't always feel like loving our neighbor—especially when he or she doesn't love us. So God gave us the Ten Commandments, the keys to personal, social, and national greatness.

Are the commandments still valid today? Absolutely! Jesus said, "Whoever therefore breaks one of the least of these commandments, and teaches men so, shall be called least in the kingdom of heaven; but whoever does and teaches them, he shall be called great in the kingdom of heaven" (Matt. 5:19 NKJV).

Though the average American may not be aware of it, the Ten Commandments are woven into the fabric of American society. Moses' two tablets are prominently displayed on state legislative and courtroom walls, on the bronze doors of the Supreme Court, and in the frescoes above the Supreme Court justices' bench. Thomas Jefferson's Declaration of Independence refers to the Creator as the ultimate legislator ("the laws of Nature's God"), executive ("Divine Providence"), and judge ("Supreme Judge of the world"). In 1997 the House of Representatives overwhelmingly endorsed a sense of Congress resolution that the public display of the Ten Commandments should be permitted, even in government offices and courthouses.[2]

Yet resistance to the Ten Commandments grows stronger each day. United States Representative Bob Aderholt of Alabama introduced the Ten Commandments Defense Act in Congress in 1997, but it never got out of committee. In the case of *Stone v. Graham* in 1980, the Supreme Court ruled that posting the Ten Commandments in schools was unconstitutional. Fortunately, while I was writing this book, the House of Representatives voted to permit the Ten Commandments to be posted in schools and state public facilities. The vote had no sooner been tallied than Democratic presidential hopeful Bill Bradley spoke up to say that the legislative amendment may be unconstitutional. But Republican candidate Steve Forbes called the House's approval "a positive thing. The Ten Commandments, we need to understand and adhere to. The more we see them, the better off we'll be."[3]

In Colorado, the Freedom from Religion Foundation tried to remove a three-foot-by-four-foot granite monument in Lincoln Park that the Fraternal Order of Eagles of Colorado had erected in the mid-1950s. The stone, which was engraved with the Ten Commandments and the words *I am the Lord thy God,* also depicted two stars of David, an American flag, and a bald eagle.[4]

The United States Supreme Court allowed Colorado to keep its monument, but the Freedom from Religion Foundation wasted no time before again attempting to undermine the Ten Commandments' message. They petitioned for permission to place next to the monument a granite slab inscribed with these words: "There are no gods. No devils. No angels. No heaven or hell. There is only our natural world. Religion is but myth and superstition that hardens hearts and enslaves minds." Proponents of the monument said it is designed to celebrate our constitutional freedoms.[5] Fortunately, the State of Colorado denied permission to erect such a monument to man's foolishness.

Two years ago, the *Dallas Morning News* reported that two judges, one in Alabama and another in Houston, were under fire for displays of the Ten Commandments in their courtrooms. Over his jury box, Houston's District Judge John Devine has also placed pictures of Abraham Lincoln and George Washington kneeling in prayer.[6]

Judge Devine said the items on his courtroom walls celebrate "Texas history, U.S. history, and Western civilization." The judge rightfully acknowledges that Christianity has played an important role in American history and is therefore appropriate to acknowledge in his courtroom. He quotes James Madison's call to Americans to govern, control, and sustain themselves "according to the Ten Commandments of God."[7]

Rita Woltz, an attorney for the Virginia-based Rutherford Institute, told the *Dallas Morning News* that many of our nation's laws are based on the Ten Commandments. "The fact that this case is even an issue shows just how awry our jurisprudence has gone," she said. And Dr. Peter

Riga, one of the lawyers arguing against Judge Devine, acknowledges that most people entering Judge Devine's courtroom may not even know enough to be influenced or offended by the Ten Commandments. He pointed to a recent national poll that asked the question, "Who received the Ten Commandments from God?" Several people answered, "Jesus."[8]

We cannot allow this woeful ignorance to continue. Our nation needs the message implicit in the Ten Commandments!

An Alabama jurist agrees. Judge Roy S. Moore, a West Point graduate and a Vietnam veteran, carved his own plaque commemorating the Ten Commandments and said that he believes his judgeship is a divine appointment. "I believe that God has placed me in this job to do my job and do a good job. And of course, I would like to acknowledge Him in doing this job."[9]

Bobby Segall is the ACLU attorney who in 1997 led a successful drive to force Judge Moore to remove the Ten Commandments from his courtroom. When asked by ABC's *20/20* reporter Tom Jarriel why he thought the Ten Commandments should not be in a courtroom, Segall replied, "Well . . . it's pretty tough when you're accused of robbery, for example, or stealing, and right up there is God's word about that."[10]

So what's wrong with that picture?

Judge Moore said, "This God of the Holy Scriptures is a basic foundation of this country. And . . . we have a duty to uphold the Constitution, which is to uphold and support its foundation. And, indeed, that's what I'm doing, and there can be nothing wrong with that."[11]

In the introduction to *The Ten Commandments: The Significance of God's Laws in Everyday Life*, Dr. Laura Schlessinger explains why God's commandments are personally significant to her life:

In life, a higher idealism and a more profound, just, and consistent morality is only found through the commandments. My life has focus, purpose, and meaning. I feel a part of something more important than my daily experience might indicate; that is, that my actions and being have significance past my personal joy and/or pain. I don't feel so alone anymore. I feel as if I am part of a bigger picture—even if I don't always "see it" or "get it." I feel more able, actually, to help folks who call in or listen to my radio program, where I "preach, teach, and nag!" I can offer them a plan, God's purpose; a way, God's commandments; and a goal, God's holiness. My family life has a focus above and beyond creature comforts, needs, and desires. I have some deeper friendships because of shared, though different, religious interests and involvements. I have a more fair, just, and consistent framework upon which to make moral decisions. I have discovered the inherent peace in that acceptance.[12]

WE NEED THE TEN COMMANDMENTS
NOW MORE THAN EVER

What would happen in America if we lived by the Ten Commandments? Let's consider just a few of the implications.

"You shall have no other gods before Me" (Ex. 20:3 NKJV). Our country would see the end of paganism, secular humanism, Satanism, and hedonism. We would revere God as the one true God. We would no longer see neopagans hugging trees and jabbering about Mother Earth. We would be reminded of the truth that is written on our money: "In God we trust." We would acknowledge that God is our Creator and the source of universal, unalienable rights and absolute moral standards.

"You shall not make for yourself a carved image—any likeness of anything that is in heaven above, or that is in the earth beneath, or that is in the water under the earth; you shall not bow down to them nor serve them. For I, the LORD your God, am a jealous God" (Ex. 20:4–5 NKJV). If America obeyed the Ten Commandments, we would not see people bowing down to status symbols, the television, or the cult of celebrity. We would realize that *things* are just *things*, and that the only real power comes from God.

"You shall not take the name of the LORD your God in vain, for the LORD will not hold him guiltless who takes His name in vain" (Ex. 20:7 NKJV). We would see the end of profanity. Listen, my friend—when you use God's name in vain, you damn your soul. Dr. Laura Schlessinger and Rabbi Stewart Vogel explain:

> Cursing God; profaning God's name; misrepresenting God; pretending a special relationship to God for personal gain; using God's name to manipulate; invoking God's name while engaged in evil (remember the Crusaders raping and murdering with the sign of the cross embroidered on their chests and banners); making vows, oaths, or promises you don't really intend to honor—all these defy the third commandment.

The care that believers take not to misuse God's name is a sign of love. We take care not to curse at a spouse, parent, or child, because every time we do, it diminishes the status in which we hold that person. Likewise, every time we misuse the name of God we risk estranging ourselves further from God.[13]

Look at God's command concerning Sunday:

Remember the Sabbath day, to keep it holy. Six days you shall labor and do all your work, but the seventh day is the Sabbath of the LORD your God. In it you shall do no work: you, nor your son, nor your daughter, nor your male servant, nor your female servant, nor your cattle, nor your stranger who is within your gates. For in six days the LORD made the heavens and the earth, the sea, and all that is in them, and rested the seventh day. Therefore the LORD blessed the Sabbath day and hallowed it. (Ex. 20:8–11 NKJV)

If we followed this commandment, churches would be packed on Sunday as we remember the Lord's Day and keep it holy. We would also see the end of welfare, for all men would be laboring six days a week.

"Honor your father and your mother, that your days may be long upon the land which the LORD your God is giving you" (Ex. 20:12 NKJV). We'd see the end of juvenile delinquency as children respect and revere their parents. There would be no gangs in the street. America's little hellions would be home saying, "Yes, sir" and "No, ma'am."

"You shall not murder" and "You shall not steal" (Ex.

20:13, 15 NKJV). No more crime waves! We'd save billions of tax dollars as we turned penitentiaries and prisons into schools. Families would save hundreds of dollars each year as they retired their security systems. Our police departments, instead of begging for more staff, would be cutting back!

"You shall not commit adultery" (Ex. 20:14 NKJV). The divorce rate would drop to zero as couples recommitted themselves to one another. We would see the end of AIDS, other sexually transmitted diseases, and abortion. American homes would become a little bit of heaven on earth as men and women recommitted themselves to one another and determined to make their marriages work.

"You shall not bear false witness against your neighbor" (Ex. 20:16 NKJV). The judicial system could once again bring equal justice under the law. Under the Ten Commandments, truth would be truth.

"You shall not covet your neighbor's house; you shall not covet your neighbor's wife, nor his male servant, nor his female servant, nor his ox, nor his donkey, nor anything that is your neighbor's" (Ex. 20:17 NKJV). Our nation would no longer be divided by materialism. Each man would be content to live with the blessings God has given him.

America is hungry for the Ten Commandments. Judge Judy, of television fame, is about a hundred pounds of pure dynamite. In her court of law, she dispenses no-nonsense answers based on the Ten Commandments, and America loves her.

In another medium, Dr. Laura, America's number one radio talk-show host, answers her calls with advice straight from the Ten Commandments. She doesn't pull punches or sugarcoat; and she doesn't hesitate to call sin by its rightful name. America can't get enough of her.

Why are these two women so successful? Because America is hungering for someone with enough moral courage to say, "A lie is still a lie. Wrong is still wrong, and truth is still truth. There is a God, and He is almighty, all-knowing, and all-powerful."

The Last Is As Crucial As the First

Notice the ordained order of the Ten Commandments. The first four commandments relate to our actions toward God; the next five pertain to our actions toward other men. The last commandment, and perhaps the most difficult to obey, relates to our thoughts: *You shall not covet.*

What is coveting? To covet is to passionately crave something—and it's sinful to crave something that belongs to someone else. The first nine commandments forbid specific actions—you shall not steal, lie, murder, worship other gods, and so on. The last commandment, however, forbids a state of mind. God demands that you control your thought life.

Look at the text—you shall not covet your neighbor's house or his wife, his male or female servant, his animals, or anything that is his. We are not to touch, not even to *think about,* acquiring something that belongs to someone else.

I always laugh at the Pepsi television commercial featuring Shaquille O'Neal and a little boy. In the commercial, O'Neal, a seven-foot, 315-pound center for the L.A. Lakers, walks onto a playground. He's hot and sweaty, and the sun is beating down on him. He looks into an ice chest for a cold Pepsi, but the chest is empty. He then turns to a little boy standing nearby, and his eyes widen at the sight of an ice-cold can of Pepsi in the boy's grip. The little kid looks up at the mountain-sized man, narrows his eyes, and says, "Don't even *think* about it!"

That's what God is saying in the tenth commandment. Don't even *think* about your neighbor's wife, his house, his car, his Rolex, or his Arnold Palmer golf clubs.

Covetousness—which is strongly related to the love of money—is the root of all sin! Covetousness withers the bloom and beauty of life, replacing love with hatred and suspicion. Covetousness consumes peace and spews forth torment and worry. Covetousness rapes goodness and gives birth to misery and heartache.

In Luke 12:15 (NKJV), Jesus told His disciples, "Take heed and beware of covetousness, for one's life does not consist in the abundance of the things he possesses." And in Mark 7:21–23 (NKJV), we read:

> For from within, out of the heart of men, proceed evil thoughts, adulteries, fornications, murders, thefts, covetousness, wickedness, deceit, lewdness, an evil eye, blasphemy, pride, foolishness. All these evil things come from within and defile a man.

Do you see? Covetousness is among the sins that destroy a man from *within*.

Paul warned the church at Ephesus about covetousness: "For this you know, that no fornicator, unclean person, nor covetous man, who is an idolater, has any inheritance in the kingdom of Christ and God" (Eph. 5:5 NKJV).

171

From Scripture, we learn the following things about the sin of covetousness:

- Covetous people are the saddest people on earth. They are never satisfied, for they always want more possessions.

- A covetous person will never enter the gates of heaven.

- A covetous person is an idolater! Why? Because he worships the god of materialism!

- Covetousness will destroy you emotionally, spiritually, and physically.

Leo Tolstoy's award-winning short story "How Much Land Does a Man Need?" is a picture of covetousness. The story begins when a peasant, Thomas, learns of fertile lands that can be obtained for a pittance from the far-off nomadic people known as the "Baskers." Eager to become rich, Thomas travels to this distant country. When he arrives, he finds a land beyond his wildest dreams. The soil is lush, black, and fruitful, carpeted with thick green grass that would be perfect for grazing cattle. As far as Thomas can see, lakes, meadows, and thick forest adorn the horizon.

Thomas turns to the chief of the Baskers and asks, "What is the price of this land?"

The chief answers, "One thousand rubles a day."

"One thousand rubles a day?" Thomas gapes at the man. "What do you mean?"

"For one thousand rubles you can have all the land you

can run around in one day," the chief explains. "But there is one condition—you have to come back to the same spot from where you started on that same day, or you lose all your money."

That night, Thomas can hardly sleep. He envisions himself running around thousands of acres, claiming pristine lakes, verdant meadows, and thickly wooded forest. He will be far richer than anyone he has known in his life.

At daylight the next morning, Thomas gives one thousand rubles to the chief of the Baskers, then begins running. With every step he takes, the ground beneath his feet seems more beautiful and luxuriant. He runs past a flowering meadow, past a deep lake that glitters, diamondlike, in the sun. He turns toward a fragrant stand of pine, knowing he has to claim that area too. Driven by his ambition, he runs faster and farther as the sun climbs overhead.

At noon, he is farther from his starting point than he had intended to be. Regretfully, he turns to run back toward the Baskers' village. His legs begin to drag. His lungs begin to burn. His chest rises and falls like a blacksmith's bellows, while his heart beats like a trip-hammer. His anxiety increases as the sun sets, so he urges his heavy legs to run faster.

Finally he can see his starting point, where a group of Baskers are cheering him on. "Run!" they shout. "Soon it will all be yours!"

Just as the sun disappears beneath the horizon, Thomas lunges for the finish line. His hands fly back, his neck strains, and he falls forward, gasping . . . and takes his last breath. The effort has killed him.

The chief shakes his head, then picks up a shovel and

digs a trench long enough for Thomas's body. He buries Thomas in a long row of other graves, each earthen mound inhabited by another man who killed himself trying to get "just a bit more."

HOW MUCH IS ENOUGH?

How much land does a man need? About six feet, or whatever the measurement from his head to his heels. That's all.

Are you running like a madman from dawn till dark, killing yourself for "just a bit more"? Are you compulsively sacrificing your marriage, your health, your relationship with your children, and your fellowship with God because the cancer of covetousness has consumed you?

The apostle Paul gave us the cure for the disease of covetousness: "Godliness with contentment is great gain" (1 Tim. 6:6 NKJV). There's a difference, my friend, between making a living . . . and making a life. Happiness comes not from having what you want, but wanting what you have.

In 1 John 2:15–16 (NKJV), John wrote:

Do not love the world or the things in the world. If anyone loves the world, the love of the Father is not in him. For all that is in the world—the lust of the flesh, the lust of the eyes, and the pride of life—is not of the Father but is of the world.

This world will pass away, but the man who does the will of God will live forever.

Consider Elvis Presley. The rock 'n' roll star attained godlike stature in America, with millions of devout fans.

He owned three jets, a Rolls Royce, Cadillacs, Lincolns, a touring bus, and fast motorcycles. The top of his Cadillac was painted with forty coats of special paint that included crushed diamonds. The car's trim was plated with eighteen-karat gold. In his house were two gold-flaked telephones, a gold electric razor, gold nail clippers, and a gold-plated television.

But with all he possessed, Elvis Presley was not happy. I met him once at a private reception, and I've never met a more lonely person. He died alone, unhappy, and all too early.

Listen again to the Master's words: "Take heed and beware of covetousness, for one's life does not consist in the abundance of the things he possesses" (Luke 12:15 NKJV).

Christina Onassis was one of the world's richest women. Though she was raised in fairy-tale luxury—Dior dressed her dolls, and Saudi Arabian King Ibn Saud presented her with ponies—she was reportedly a sad, lonely child who shuttled between family homes in Paris, Athens, Antibes, and Skorpios. Later, when her father died and Christina found herself his only heir, she said, "I am all alone in the world now."[14] When her favorite drink, Coca-Cola, was available only in the United States, she sent a jet to America to pick up a case of "the real thing." She enjoyed sailing and swimming, but she died miserable.

Listen to the words of Solomon, the wisest man who ever lived: "He who loves silver will not be satisfied with silver; nor he who loves abundance, with increase" (Eccl. 5:10 NKJV).

Just because a man is wealthy, however, does not mean he is guilty of covetousness. A man driving a '52 VW Bug can have more covetousness in his heart than a man driving a Rolls Royce. Money itself is not the root of all evil . . . the *love* of money is the source of sin.

WHAT ENTICES COVETOUSNESS?

What do we covet?

Sometimes we covet *people. If only I had that family,* you may have thought. Or *If only I had been born a Rockefeller, what a life I would have!*

It's a fact: To dislike the unchangeable aspects of who you are is to criticize the wisdom of God. He put you where you are for a purpose. He gave you your parents for a reason. Find that reason, find your purpose, and then fulfill it. No one would have thought the son of a poor Jewish carpenter living in a small village under Roman oppression would accomplish much, but Jesus of Nazareth changed the entire world!

King David coveted a person. One afternoon he saw Bathsheba, a beautiful woman, and coveted her. He took her into his bed, got her pregnant, and then murdered her husband to cover up his sinful liaison. But God saw everything David did. He sent the prophet Nathan, who pointed his bony finger at David and said, "You are the man!"

Even though David confessed, repented, and paid a dear price, pain, poison, and perversion never left David's household. Bathsheba's baby died. David's handsome son, Absalom, became a murderous rebel. Another son raped one of David's daughters. Why did David suffer so much sorrow? Because he coveted and took what belonged to another man, and God settled the account.

We not only covet people, but *possessions*. After journeying to Canaan with his uncle, Abraham, Lot coveted the best land and ended up in Sodom. Notice how his covetousness progressed from a fancy to a fascination to a fact:

- First, Lot looked longingly at Sodom (Gen. 13:10).

- He then chose the area of ground near Sodom (Gen. 13:11).

- He then pitched his tent near Sodom (Gen. 13:12).

- He then moved into the city (Gen. 14:12).

- He then became a leader in the city, and even offered his virgin daughters to the sinful men of Sodom (Gen. 19:1–11).

- Finally, almost reluctantly, Lot left the city as his friends were cremated by fire and brimstone from the hand of God (Gen. 19:15–16).

But Lot is certainly not the only Bible character who fell prey to covetousness. Achan coveted the wedge of gold and the Babylonian garment, then paid the price for his sin. Judas coveted thirty pieces of silver and valued it more than his relationship with Jesus.

Along with people and possessions, we also covet *position*. Cain coveted his brother's position of acceptance in the Lord but was unwilling to do what it took to find that acceptance himself.

A friend of mine, a successful writer, told me that she

once hosted a Christmas open house for the women of her church. As the women walked through her spacious, book-lined office, one woman said, "If only I had surroundings like this, I could write a masterpiece too!"

Let me tell you, friend: Most people who are good at their work make the work look easy. But every star athlete has invested hours of practice and pain. Every best-selling author has spent endless hours in solitary research and work. Every singer who fills a concert hall has sung to small crowds and smiled through the pain of a sore throat. Most people who find success *earn* it.

Stop coveting other people's success. God wants you to get excited about the work He's called *you* to do. When John the Baptist was in prison, his worried disciples came to him. What had them upset? Not the fact that their leader was in mortal danger of losing his head, but the fact that Jesus' preaching was eclipsing John's ministry. "Rabbi," they told John, "He who was with you beyond the Jordan, to whom you have testified—behold, He is baptizing, and all are coming to Him!" (John 3:26 NKJV).

Even workers in Christian ministry are not immune to the sin of covetousness. When Paul was in prison, his colleagues engaged in sinful competition for his place in ministry (Phil. 1:15). It's a sad fact, but true—many churches in America pray for revival, but they certainly don't want it coming to the church down the street.

What would happen to churches in America if *believers* had zeal enough to live by the Ten Commandments? We'd see a revival of personal holiness and traditional values. We'd also see a resurgence of purity, power, and purpose!

COVETOUSNESS IS THE FIRST STEP

The tenth commandment is of prime significance because covetousness causes us to break the other nine commandments. The first commandment forbids us to place any other gods before God, but a covetous man will put the god of gold before the Almighty.

The second commandment says we shall make no graven images, but the covetous man bows before his material possessions. If you were to put records of his house payment, his car payment, and his vacation expense statement next to his tithing record, you'd see that greed is his idol.

The third commandment forbids taking the name of the Lord in vain, but Ananias and Sapphira, who coveted glory and praise as well as money, walked into church and lied in the name of God.

The fourth commandment reminds us to keep the Sabbath holy, but have you noticed that most malls and amusement parks do more business on Sunday than any other day? Mankind's love of money and pleasure is far greater than its love for the Master of the universe.

The fifth commandment requires us to honor our parents, but recently I read a newspaper story about a teenage girl who stole twenty-eight thousand dollars from her grandmother, who had worked all her life to save that amount. The girl and her friend spent most of the money in one wild shopping spree and a week at Disneyland.

The sixth commandment forbids murder, but Judas loved money enough to sell the Son of God for thirty pieces of silver. Some of you are killing yourselves and your families for the love of money.

The seventh commandment forbids adultery, but prostitution, the world's oldest profession, is driven by the lust for money and the lust of the flesh. Our modern age mistakes lust for love. Due to the drive of lust and pleasure, we have debased love to the level of a glandular function.

The eighth commandment forbids stealing, but all theft is driven by the love of material things. Wrote the prophet Zechariah, "This is the curse that goes out over the face of the whole earth: 'Every thief shall be expelled'" (Zech. 5:3 NKJV). If you are covetous, you will break all ten commandments in your lust for things!

THOU *SHALT* COVET?

Is it ever *right* to covet? Yes!

In his letter to the Corinthian church, Paul wrote: "Covet earnestly the best gifts: and yet shew I unto you a more excellent way" (1 Cor. 12:31 KJV). His command to covet may seem a little strange until you realize that an emotional fire drives covetousness.

When misused, *any* drive can destroy a man . . . but when used wisely, it can build him up.

I must not fear fire . . . I must know how to use it.

I must not fear sex . . . I must know its proper place.

I must not fear anger, but I must know when it is appropriate.

I must not fear covetousness, but I must know which things I should earnestly desire.

In the battle of life, when victory hangs in the balance,

you must call upon an inner power if you are going to win. You must be motivated by something that drives you to give more than you've ever given. What should be your driving force? Passionate desire, which is the same thing as "coveting earnestly"!

Turn your desire for inappropriate things toward God-ordained targets. Go after your godly goals with an intensity that will terrify your opposition, the devil.

Remember this, my friend: Good is the enemy of better, and better is the enemy of best. Paul said, "Covet earnestly the best gifts," and second best is never good enough for a child of God!

Until the church of Jesus Christ covets holiness and earnestly desires to see the lost brought to Christ, America will continue to swim in a moral sewer. Until God's people earnestly covet righteous men in government, godless, immoral neopagans and sexual predators will rule Washington, D.C.

Until we earnestly covet the right to life, abortion will be the law of the land.

Until we earnestly covet economic sanity, Congress will continue to spend this nation into bankruptcy!

Until we earnestly covet a public school system where the Ten Commandments are allowed *in* and condoms, crack, and Colt .45s are *out*, our school grounds will continue to host terroristic students who were never taught "Thou shalt not kill."

In a letter to the Philippian church, Paul confessed the overriding goal of his life: "I press toward the goal for the prize of the upward call of God in Christ Jesus" (Phil. 3:14 NKJV). Spiritual victory demands that we *press*!

In the game of basketball, a *full-court press* requires the team to play with maximum effort. As soon as the opponent brings the ball in bounds, each team member tries his best to eat his opponent's lunch. Everyone presses his assigned man, allowing no rest or sanctuary on the court.

In the New Testament, Scripture tells us of four men who literally ripped the roof off a house in order to lower a sick friend to Jesus, who was teaching inside. That's pressing!

Press! Do the impossible! Reach out in faith! If you want what you've never had, you must do what you've never done! You must press toward the prize with a passion.

The best will not yield to mediocre effort. Diamonds have to be dug out. Education has to be sought out. The devil has to be run out! In James 4:7 (NKJV), the disciple wrote, "Resist the devil and he will flee from you." *Resist* is an active verb. You must resist the evil one in Jesus' name!

Right now, God is looking down at you from heaven. Will you allow covetousness to destroy you . . . or press you to the next level of divine excellence? The choice is yours.

Journal, Page Seven

Summoned by a mighty blast from the golden trumpet, I joined the others of the angelic host in the throne room of heaven. The Father turned to the Son, and His voice rumbled like thunder as He whispered: "It is time."

I don't know if any human heart can comprehend what we all felt in that moment. We had known this moment would come; it had been part of the Father's plan from the beginning, even before the dawn of time. But somewhere in my deepest heart, as I observed the men created in God's image, I had hoped they would understand the concepts they had been given. They had ignored the strong voice of conscience, they had neglected the set of seven complete laws, they had been blind to the deeper meaning of the sacrificial systems, and the chosen people had neglected their responsibility as examples.

Did they really believe that an all-powerful God delighted in their slaughter of helpless, dumb beasts? 'Twas not the animals or the incense or the blood that pleased him, but their obedience.

I remember one day when I walked among men in a little village in Mesopotamia. A young mother sat beneath a tree with her child, a boy not more than two years old. "Bow like this," she said, bending from the waist with her hands clasped before her. "And keep your eyes down."

The little boy laughed and imitated his mother, and for a while the two of them made a game out of their lesson.

Within the hour, the reason for the mother's behavior became clear. A caravan approached from the desert, and a prince of the region passed by with his retinue.

Acting out of respect and honor, the mother and her young son bowed as the mighty man passed by. The boy, not understanding which rider was the prince, happily bowed to several men in the entourage.

And I realized something profound. The little boy had no idea what the bow meant or why it was important for him to learn this act of respect, but the mother had known that the great man would soon pass by. It did not matter that the boy was young and naive; he would grow into understanding. Within a few years he would realize that the prince held the power of life and death and deserved respect.

In the same way, the Father's Law was a teacher for His children. Some of them learned and understood that the Prince would soon pass by; others continued to bow without understanding.

In time, however, surely they will come to recognize the Prince of Peace . . .

CHAPTER

THE AGE
OF GRACE

The other day I heard a story of a minor league baseball player who was playing his first game in center field. He made two errors. The overbearing manager leaped out of the dugout and shouted, "Sit down; I'll show you how to play center field!"

As the manager took the player's glove, a hitter stepped up to the plate. The first ball was a high fly and got lost in the sun. A runner scored.

The second pitch resulted in a grounder between first and second base. The manager ran after it and collided with the right fielder, who just happened to be the team's star hitter. The man was injured and had to be taken out of the game.

The third pitch resulted in a line drive that hit the manager between the eyes and knocked him out. As they carried him off the field on a stretcher, he looked into the dugout and spied the rookie. "Boy," he said, trying to focus his vision, "you've got things so messed up in center field nobody can play that position!"

Ah, my friend, is that how you feel? Have you been made to feel guilty for your own and other people's mistakes? Then you need to bathe in God's cleansing ocean of grace!

THE AMAZING POWER OF GRACE

The cord of redemption continued to wind through time, unbroken by man's faithlessness or God's judgment. While the children of Israel offered sacrifices of animals as a picture of the Sacrifice to come, God prepared to send His Son to take the place of all men in death, so they might be fully reconciled, redeemed, and restored to the place where God intended man to live at creation—in fellowship with Himself.

This next age is called the Age of Grace because Jesus Christ brought the fullness of grace to mankind. John 1:16–17 (NKJV) tells us, "And of His fullness we have all received, and grace for grace. For the law was given through Moses, but grace and truth came through Jesus Christ."

What is grace? You've probably heard the acronym: God's Riches At Christ's Expense. Grace is God's freely bestowed love and protection for undeserving sinners. Grace is something you and I don't deserve, but through God's matchless love, He grants grace to us.

The Age of Grace began with the preaching of John the Baptist and will continue until the second coming of Jesus Christ. We are living in the Age of Grace as I write this book. We do not know how long this age will last, but we know it will not end until: the church has been taken away from the earth at the Rapture; the revealed Antichrist has established his earthly kingdom; and the prophesied events of the Tribulation and Great Tribulation have come to pass.

Like each preceding age, the Age of Grace began favorably. John the Baptist preached of the coming kingdom of God, and Christ preached the gospel throughout Jerusalem and Judea. At Calvary, Jesus defeated Satan on the cross. His death opened the gates of salvation to anyone who would walk through, Jew or Gentile, man or woman, slave or free man. Fifty days after Jesus ascended to heaven, the Holy Spirit descended at Pentecost and empowered believers to spread the gospel throughout the world.

The test of this age? To see if man will be obedient to the faith of the gospel. Romans 1:5 (NKJV) tells us, "Through Him we have received grace and apostleship for obedience to the faith among all nations for His name." Hebrews 11:6 (NKJV) adds, "Without faith it is impossible to please Him, for he who comes to God must believe that He is, and that He is a rewarder of those who diligently seek Him."

In the Age of Grace, God has a threefold purpose: to save all who will believe, to call out a people for His name, and to build the church.[1]

Listen to how James explained the purpose for this age in Acts 15:13–17 (NKJV):

And after they had become silent, James answered, saying, "Men and brethren, listen to me: Simon has declared how God at the first visited the Gentiles to take out of them a people for His name. And with this the words of the prophets agree, just as it is written:

'After this I will return
And will rebuild the tabernacle of David, which has fallen down;
I will rebuild its ruins,
And I will set it up;
So that the rest of mankind may seek the LORD,
Even all the Gentiles who are called by My name,
Says the LORD who does all these things.'"

To accomplish His purpose in this era, God intends for His people to preach the gospel. For this work He has called and equipped men and women. The apostle Paul explained in Ephesians 4:7–8, 11 (NKJV):

But to each one of us grace was given according to the measure of Christ's gift. Therefore He says:

"When He ascended on high,
He led captivity captive,
and gave gifts to men."

. . . And He Himself gave some to be apostles, some prophets, some evangelists, and some pastors and teachers.

God uses ordinary people, endowed with His supernatural gifts, to reach the lost for Christ. He also uses angels to work in people's lives. Hebrews 1:14 (NKJV) says, "Are they not all ministering spirits sent forth to minister for those who will inherit salvation?"

AN INCREDIBLE PICTURE MARKS THE BEGINNING OF THE AGE

Let's look back to Genesis, to an event that transpired in the Garden of Eden. Speaking to the serpent, Satan, after the Fall, God said:

> And I will put enmity
> Between you and the woman,
> And between your seed and her Seed;
> He shall bruise your head,
> And you shall bruise His heel. (Gen. 3:15 NKJV)

God was foretelling that Christ, the Messiah, would be born supernaturally. The One who would crush the serpent's head would be a child, or the "Seed" of the woman. The seventeenth revelation of truth is this: *God would be incarnated in human flesh!*

Think about it! When Eve ate the forbidden fruit, sin entered the world by woman. But by woman would also come the Savior of the world. A woman would be the mother of God!

By woman came the curse, but by woman also came the Christ, who would forever break the bondage of sin. "Therefore if the Son makes you free, you shall be free indeed" (John 8:36 NKJV).

By woman Paradise was lost, but by woman also came the One who would restore us to Paradise! On the cross,

Jesus told the repentant thief hanging by His side, "Assuredly, I say to you, today you will be with Me in Paradise" (Luke 23:43 NKJV).

My heart fills with holy awe when I consider the implications of these words: "But when the fullness of the time had come, God sent forth His Son, born of a woman, born under the law" (Gal. 4:4 NKJV). The advent of the Age of Grace is marked by one of the most astounding and incredible pictures the world has ever seen. God sent the chief angelic messenger to visit a young girl in a town called Nazareth:

> Now in the sixth month the angel Gabriel was sent by God to a city of Galilee named Nazareth, to a virgin betrothed to a man whose name was Joseph, of the house of David. The virgin's name was Mary. And having come in, the angel said to her, "Rejoice, highly favored one, the Lord is with you; blessed are you among women!"

> But when she saw him, she was troubled at his saying, and considered what manner of greeting this was.

> Then the angel said to her, "Do not be afraid, Mary, for you have found favor with God. And behold, you will conceive in your womb and bring forth a Son, and shall call His name JESUS. He will be great, and will be called the Son of the Highest; and the Lord God will give Him the throne of His father David. And He will reign over the house of Jacob forever, and of His kingdom there will be no end." (Luke 1:26–33 NKJV)

Mary, the young woman who received this astonishing news, was Jewish and obeyed God as she followed the Law. She was not perfect or sinless, for she herself spoke of the need for a Savior (Luke 1:47), but surely she knew that a Messiah had been promised. The prophets had even predicted that He would be born of a virgin: "Therefore the Lord Himself will give you a sign: Behold, the virgin shall conceive and bear a Son, and shall call His name Immanuel" (Isa. 7:14 NKJV).

I believe that at some point Mary knew that her beloved Son would give His life for mankind. She had seen the program of sacrifices; she had heard the words of the prophets. The Bible tells us that she "pondered in her heart" all the miracles surrounding her Son's birth, and she stood by her Son throughout His ministry . . . and His death.

The eighteenth revelation of truth is contained in the images of two trees—one found in the Garden of Eden, the other atop a rocky hill known as Golgotha.

The first tree brought sickness and corruption. The second tree brought eternal healing.

The first tree brought poverty. The second tree brought the blessings of Abraham.

The first tree brought rejection and expulsion from Paradise. The second tree brought acceptance by God the Father and entrance into eternal heaven.

The first tree brought death to mankind. The second tree brought us life.

The first tree was pleasant to the eyes. The second tree was harsh, a symbol of judgment and death. The bloodied man hanging upon it was the spotless Lamb of God, slaughtered for the sins of man. The sight was horrific enough to make a man turn his eyes away. Scripture tells us:

> He has no form or comeliness;
> And when we see Him,
> There is no beauty that we should desire Him.
>   (Isa. 53:2 NKJV)

God forbade man to eat of the first tree. Of the second tree, God says, "Whosoever will may come." In Psalm 34:8 (NKJV), the psalmist extended the invitation:

> Oh, taste and see that the LORD is good;
> Blessed is the man who trusts in Him!

God's provision of redemption for the Age of Grace and all ages to come is Christ's death at Calvary. Men of previous ages have by faith looked forward to the sacrifice of the Lamb; today we look back to that sacrifice with eyes of faith and gratitude. Through the cross of Christ, we have been brought back to God, released from the curse that ended the Age of Innocence, freed from our inability to keep the laws of God and human government. Paul wrote, "Christ has redeemed us from the curse of the law, having become a curse for us . . . that the blessing of Abraham might come upon the Gentiles in Christ Jesus, that we might receive the promise of the Spirit through faith" (Gal. 3:13–14 NKJV).

All who believe on Jesus Christ will be fully redeemed, reconciled, and restored to fellowship with God. The cross atop Calvary's mountain is the hub of history, the apogee of eternity, the point and purpose of creation. The cross fulfilled all the requirements of the Mosaic Law. Christ's blood paid for Adam and Eve's sin in the Garden; his death atoned for every broken human law.

> And you, being dead in your trespasses and the uncircumcision of your flesh, He has made alive together with Him, having forgiven you all trespasses, having wiped out the handwriting of requirements that was against us, which was contrary to us. And He has taken it out of the way, having nailed it to the cross. (Col. 2:13–14 NKJV)

Hallelujah for the cross!

THE SOURCE OF GRACE

My friend, apart from the act of turning to Christ in surrender, your salvation doesn't depend on anything you do or don't do. Grace is a gift, and it springs from the blood of Jesus Christ alone.

You are not saved because you crawled down the aisle of a church and kissed the big toe of St. Peter's statue. You're not saved because you joined the church or went under the baptismal waters or were sprinkled as a baby. Getting wet in a church no more makes you a child of God than a bar of soap and some water transforms a pig into a poodle.

The old hymn tells the truth:

> There is a fountain filled with blood;
> Drawn from Immanuel's veins.
> And sinners, plunged beneath that flood,
> Lose all their guilty stains.[2]

You Have to Think to Believe

One day the head of a university astronomy department was conversing with the dean of the divinity school. In a rather patronizing way, the astronomy professor concluded, "Now, let's face it. Boil away the chicken fat, and what is the basis of Christianity? Love your neighbor as you love yourself. It's just the Golden Rule, right?"

"Yes, I suppose that's true," the dean answered. "Just as in astronomy it all boils down to 'Twinkle, Twinkle, Little Star.'"

Why do we tend to oversimplify the most important issues in life? Someone once observed that 5 percent of people think, 15 percent *think* they think, and the remaining 80 percent would rather die than think. Many people are of the opinion that Christians are people who check their brains at the church door in order to believe in Christ, but nothing could be further from the truth.

Christianity is neither a faith of oversimplification or uncritical thinking. When the Bible challenges men and women to believe in Jesus Christ as their personal Savior, it appeals for faith that satisfies the *intellect*, the *emotions*, and the *will*. An unreasonable faith, a heartless faith, or an inactive faith is not a biblical faith. It's easy for most people to dismiss the rational component of faith because they harbor a suspicion that faith and reason are almost opposites.

Biblical faith certainly goes beyond reason, but it does not *contradict* reason. It starts from a rational foundation. An object of faith must be worthy of trust. An ice-skater who puts his faith in thin ice gets a frigid dunking because he didn't examine the evidence well enough. An investor who puts her faith in the advice of a swindler takes an equally chilling bath for her unreasonable trust.

Is Christian faith reasonable? Can we verify its tenets in any meaningful way? Christianity springs from the Bible, which is rooted in historical events rather than myths or legends. Scholars and skeptics have subjected the Bible to intensive archaeological and literary investigation. The factual details and the cultural milieu the Bible presents are true.

Secular sources as well as the New Testament reported that Jesus was a historical figure. The claim that He rose from the dead as evidence that God accepted His sacrifice for sins is the best—though obviously supernatural—explanation of the empty tomb. A claim made at the time said the body disappeared from a scaled, guarded tomb, and no credible evidence to the contrary ever appeared, although powerful political and religious establishments had vested interests in disproving the resurrection.

Through the intervening centuries, the teachings of Jesus and His disciples have formed the foundation of countless individual lies and of classical western civilization. Based upon the biblical evidence, it is reasonable to believe in Jesus as Savior.

YOU HAVE TO LOVE TO BELIEVE

A college man took a portrait of his new girlfriend to a photography studio. He wanted more than one copy of her picture so he could post them at strategic places at home and at school. When the studio owner removed the photograph from its frame, he noticed an inscription on the back: "My dearest John, I love you with all my heart. I love you more and more each day. I will love you forever and ever. I am yours for all eternity." It was signed "Marsha." Beneath the signature was a P.S.: "If we ever break up, I want this picture back."

Obviously, Marsha's emotional commitment to John wasn't what it needed to be. At first glance it looked okay, but her whole heart wasn't in it.

In Matthew 22:37 (NKJV) Jesus said that the greatest command of the Old Testament was Deuteronomy 6:5: "You shall love the LORD your God with all your heart, with all your soul, and with all your mind." Jesus identified an emotional commitment—love—as the primary response we need to make to God. The Old Testament law understood love to be first a function of the heart, then a function of the entire personality, and finally a function of the mind.

The English word *wholehearted* may capture the idea that Jesus wanted to express about the kind of love we need to have for God. Wholehearted love is a loyal love. Ultimately, loyalty is what was missing from Marsha's love for John. When our faith in Jesus as our Savior is wholehearted in its extent and loyal in its intensity, it has touched our emotions as it should.

Faith that has a proper emotional dimension also satisfies certain primary emotional needs. Faith in Jesus as Savior produces a deep sense of peace with God. Jesus told His disciples, "Let not your heart be troubled; you believe in God, believe also in Me . . . Peace I leave with you, My peace I give to you" (John 14:1, 27 NKJV). The *shalom* kind of peace Jesus referred to is personal wholeness with perfect harmony among all the parts of our lives. Wholehearted faith leads to this kind of peace.

Wholehearted faith also leads to joy. Jesus encouraged His disciples to pray in faith by saying, "Until now you have asked nothing in My name. Ask, and you will receive, that your joy may be full" (John 16:24 NKJV). Joy is more than a fleeting feeling of happiness. The Greek term translated "joy" is related to the word for "grace." The ideas are inseparable when applied to faith. Joy is an abiding sense of well-being and satisfaction based on God's grace rather than current circumstances.

YOU HAVE TO CHOOSE TO BELIEVE

In a bygone time, a young lady was enjoying her first transatlantic cruise. She always dined at a table from which she could watch an attractive young man she had noticed on the first evening out. He was flattered by her obvious attention and summoned the courage to approach her. "Pardon me," he said, "it may be my imagination, but I have the impression you keep looking in my direction. Is there something wrong?"

Blushing demurely, she answered, "Oh, no. It's just that I can't help but notice how much you resemble my first husband."

Startled, the young man blurted out, "How many times have you been married?"

She gave him an innocent smile and answered, "Oh, I haven't been—yet."

I have to admire that young woman's willingness to boldly act upon faith. For faith to be complete it must choose and act on its choice. Consider our shipboard romantic—she observed and learned about the young man, and when the opportunity presented itself, she chose to act.

If I am to exercise faith in Jesus as my Savior from sin, my intellect must believe the facts of the gospel, my emotions must respond with love and gratitude, and my will must choose to receive the gift of eternal life offered me by God the Father. The activities of our will can be looked at as deciding, receiving, and responding.

Decision is the activity of the will in response to the information gathered and evaluated by the mind. When Elijah was frustrated because the Israelites vacillated between worshiping the Lord and Baal, he asked them, "How long will you falter between two opinions? If the LORD is God, follow Him; but if Baal, then follow him" (1 Kings 18:21 NKJV). Then the prophet gave the people a demonstration of God's power and Baal's impotence. They decided in favor of the Lord.

Reception and response are the passive and active sides of the decision to trust Jesus as Savior. God has been offering the gift of forgiveness of sins and eternal life throughout all the dispensational ages. When any person decides that the Word of God is true and that he wants to receive God's grace, he must remove the barriers and allow God to give the gift of eternal life. He receives it and responds to the gift of grace with gratitude and good works.

WE ARE FREE, BUT NOT FREE TO SIN

Grace drove John Newton, a slave trader, to write one of the most beloved songs in history:

> Amazing grace! how sweet the sound,
> That saved a wretch like me!
> I once was lost, but now am found,
> Was blind, but now I see.[3]

Grace is greater than all your sin. Paul wrote, "Where sin abounded, grace abounded much more" (Rom. 5:20 NKJV). If God's grace can forgive Moses, David, and Paul—each of whom was a murderer—then God's grace can forgive you. If you've had an abortion, delved into the occult, or fallen into sexual sin, you can rest in the certainty that God's grace is sufficient.

Please understand this—we are forgiven for all our sin, no matter how terrible, but God's forgiveness is not blanket permission to sin. If we look back to Genesis, we will see another picture that contains the nineteenth revelation of truth: *God will discipline erring believers.*

You may be familiar with the story told in Genesis 27. Isaac's twin sons, Jacob and Esau, were rivals from the moment of their birth. Isaac favored Esau, but Rebekah favored Jacob. Through a conspiracy of trickery, Rebekah and Jacob managed to steal the blessing of the firstborn, which was Esau's by right. As you might expect, when Esau learned of their deception, he was angry enough to kill his brother. Jacob had to flee from his family's camp.

When Jacob stole his brother's birthright, he got everything he wanted but lost everything he had. He never saw his parents again. He spent every day glancing back over his shoulder, wondering if Esau would arrive to kill him. Finally, God crippled him by touching his thigh (Gen. 32:24–32).

Your choices do have consequences!

But, Pastor, you may be thinking, *I'm under grace. I'm saved. I'm washed in the blood of the Lamb, and all my sins are forgiven!*

All true, but still your choices have consequences. The writer of Hebrews assured us that a loving Father will discipline the children of God:

> If you endure chastening, God deals with you as with sons; for what son is there whom a father does not chasten? . . . Now no chastening seems to be joyful for the present, but painful; nevertheless, afterward it yields the peaceable fruit of righteousness to those who have been trained by it (Heb. 12:7, 11 NKJV).

When Samson chose Delilah over obedience to God's command, he paid the price.

When David took another man's wife, he paid the price.

When Adam and Eve chose to eat the forbidden fruit, they paid the price.

You can't plant wild oats and pray for crop failure! You can't escape the consequences of your choices. Even if you're the president of the United States, know this: God will demand an accounting! "Take note," says the Scripture, "you have sinned against the LORD; and be sure your sin will find you out" (Num. 32:23 NKJV).

WHY DON'T WE ENJOY THE BENEFITS OF GRACE MORE OFTEN?

If grace is so powerful to equip the saints for service, why aren't more churches overflowing with grace-filled

Christians? I'll tell you why—because the enemy of grace is rebellion. Most denominations have an element of rebellion amongst their people. The New Testament church at Galatia was no exception. Let's look at part of the letter Paul wrote to them:

> O foolish Galatians! Who has bewitched you that you should not obey the truth, before whose eyes Jesus Christ was clearly portrayed among you as crucified? This only I want to learn from you: Did you receive the Spirit by the works of the law, or by the hearing of faith? Are you so foolish? Having begun in the Spirit, are you now being made perfect by the flesh? Have you suffered so many things in vain—if indeed it was in vain? Therefore He who supplies the Spirit to you and works miracles among you, does He do it by the works of the law, or by the hearing of faith? (Gal. 3:1–5 NKJV)

The people in the church at Galatia were saved and Spirit-filled, but they had set aside the grace of God in order to try and *work* toward their salvation. They set aside the truth that salvation does not come from human deeds, but through faith in Christ. Neglecting the grace of God, they were rebelling against the things they had been taught. How did Paul know they were bewitched and rebellious? Because they had fallen into legalism.

Legalism can be defined as following man-made rules in an attempt to obtain righteousness with God. Legalism is Satan's theology at work in the church of Jesus Christ.

God hates legalism! If man-made rules could save mankind, why would Jesus have to die? Legalism takes

our eyes off the cross and focuses our attention upon ourselves. Legalism makes us think we're not such bad
people; in fact, it makes us think we're pretty holy. Just
look at all the good things we're doing! And look at all the
bad things we're *not* doing! Legalists have a mile-long
Don't list. They don't dance, they don't chew, and they
don't run with folks who do . . .

Legalism divides churches and separates parents and
children. Why? Because if my righteousness is based on my
set of rules, if *your* set doesn't conform to *my* set, I will
judge you as unrighteous.

Legalism destroys love. Legalistic churches aren't soul-
winning churches because they don't have time to love the
lost—they're too busy judging them! They get upset when
lost people behave like lost people—as if they could behave
like anything else! Legalists are sour, self-righteous, arro-
gant, loveless Pharisees who control each other with religious rules.

Every church has its own tendencies toward legalism.
You couldn't catch some Christians tapping both feet at the
same time lest they be accused of dancing, but they won't
hesitate to make the telephone lines hum with gossip.
Trouble is, they call this malicious slander "sharing prayer
requests" or even "telephone ministry."

I know what I'm talking about because I was raised in
a legalistic Pentecostal church. We had a list of rules, and at
the top of our list we added an Eleventh Commandment:
Thou shalt not have fun. If something was fun, we thought
it had to be sinful!

I grew up with a colossal catalog of forbidden activities.
No movies. No ball games. No board games, not even

Monopoly (and to this day I haven't figured out why that was on the *verboten* list).

After school, we used to play a game with marbles called "Keeps." We'd draw a circle in the sand, and if you flicked your marble so that it knocked someone else's marble out of the circle, you got to keep that player's marble. Well, one day after school my mother told me I couldn't play Keeps any more. It was gambling, and it was forbidden.

I couldn't believe it. "Mom," I said, "can you show me in the Bible where it says I can't play marbles?"

My mother didn't miss a beat. "Yes," she said, a mischievous twinkle in her eye. "John 3:7 and John 5:28. Both those verses begin 'Marble not'!"

This Age Will End in Failure

Despite the encroachment of legalism and rebellion in the body of believers, the Age of Grace is a marvelous miracle, and millions have come to the Savior in this era. Despite these many victories, this age will end in twofold failure.

First, the nation of Israel has rejected the Messiah and the gospel. God offered the gospel first to the children of Israel, but they rejected the message:

> These twelve Jesus sent out and commanded them, saying: "Do not go into the way of the Gentiles, and do not enter a city of the Samaritans. But go rather to the lost sheep of the house of Israel." (Matt. 10:5–6 NKJV)

But the Jews weren't alone in their failure to follow God's plan. The early church began to fail God almost immediately after its foundation. From a study of Paul's epistles, we see that division, strife, immorality, greed, and apostasy crept swiftly into the early church, and the situation didn't improve much in later years.

History reveals that the church continued to fail by not preaching the truth and not being an example of godliness. Who can explain the organized church's disgraceful actions during the Crusades and the Inquisition? The blood of innocent people stained the hands and robes of clerics, while thousands of true Christians and Jews were massacred for not parroting the man-made creeds of the day.

Greed moved into the church, from the highest offices down to the lowest, and pardon for sin was bought and paid for with everything from gold to chickens. A reformation did sweep through the church, but the reformers were forced to pay for their courageous stands with their lives. Bible-believing ministers like Jan Hus were burned at the stake for daring to proclaim that the Bible, not man, was the ultimate religious authority. William Tyndale was strangled and burned for daring to print an English Bible the common man could read. And John Wycliffe, another reformer, was so hated that after his death ecclesiastical leaders had his body exhumed so they could burn his bones and drown his ashes. But they could not stop the truth that Wycliffe preached. The author of *Fox's Book of Martyrs* sums up the strength of Wycliffe's testimony in the following passage:

> But these and all others must know that, as there is no
> counsel against the Lord, so there is no keeping down

of verity [truth], but it will spring up and come out of dust and ashes, as appeared right well in this man; for though they dug up his body, burned his bones, and drowned his ashes, yet the Word of God and the truth of his doctrine, with the fruit and success thereof, they could not burn.[4]

Even in our day we have seen Christian leaders confess to everything from greed to sexual immorality. The church is made up of imperfect people, and Scripture warns us that in the last days many false teachers will come (2 Peter 2). We should not be surprised when we find sin in the camp.

Don't misunderstand—God has always had righteous servants who were faithful unto death. Men and women throughout the ages have sacrificed their time, their riches, and even their lives to reach a fallen world with the gospel. But the church, the bride of Christ, has never been all God intended her to be.

DON'T EXCUSE SIN

Just because others are falling into sin does not mean we can afford to lower our standards. We are still called to be holy examples to the fallen world around us.

At the beginning of his ministry, Jesus told His disciples, "As long as I am in the world, I am the light of the world" (John 9:5 NKJV). At the end of His ministry, however, He told them, "You are the light of the world" (Matt. 5:14 NKJV).

As Christians, we are required to be light. Light exposes and reveals. It cannot coexist with darkness.

Paul asked, "What communion has light with darkness?" (2 Cor. 6:14 NKJV). None! But the church of Jesus Christ in America, in an effort to please the world, has hidden its light under a bushel basket. We have become carnal, compromising, and cowardly in the day of battle. We have offended God with our casual Christianity.

Scripture reveals that this age will end with great apostasy. Writing to his student, Timothy, Paul warned:

> I charge you therefore before God and the Lord Jesus Christ, who will judge the living and the dead at His appearing and His kingdom: Preach the word! Be ready in season and out of season. Convince, rebuke, exhort, with all longsuffering and teaching. For the time will come when they will not endure sound doctrine, but according to their own desires, because they have itching ears, they will heap up for themselves teachers; and they will turn their ears away from the truth, and be turned aside to fables. (2 Tim. 4:1–4 NKJV)

JUST AS IN THE DAYS OF NOAH, WARNING, RESCUE, AND JUDGMENT BEGIN

In the latter days, as God's prophetic stopwatch ticks away the remaining moments of the Age of Grace, the Father will nod to the Son, who will rise from His throne. He will not return to earth at this point, but He will appear in the clouds for an instant while the trumpet of God rings throughout heaven. And at that moment, all believers in Christ, dead and living, will rise through the clouds to be with Him.

Genesis depicts this wonderful event, known as the

Rapture, not once, but twice! Let's look first at how Noah and the ark reveal the truth of God's judgment and His escape for the righteous.

God sent the Flood to destroy all flesh because mankind had thoroughly rejected Him, but He does not judge the righteous along with the wicked. If you study the actual ark, Noah's means of deliverance, you'll see several significant facts:

1. *The ark was a manifestation of God's grace.* The boat was a God-ordained means of escape from the coming judgment upon mankind.

2. *The ark had only one door.* In the Age of Grace, there is only one means by which we can claim God's favor. Jesus said, "I am the door. If anyone enters by Me, he will be saved" (John 10:9 NKJV).

3. *All men were invited into the ark.* God issued Noah an invitation, not a command: "Then the LORD said to Noah, 'Come into the ark, you and all your household, because I have seen that you are righteous before Me in this generation'" (Gen. 7:1 NKJV). Jesus is a gentleman. He does not bully His way into people's lives. You must accept His invitation for salvation.

4. *The ark had only one window, located within eighteen inches of the roof of the ark.* "You shall make a window for the ark, and you shall finish it to a cubit from above; and set the door of the ark in its side. You shall make it with lower, second, and third decks" (Gen. 6:16 NKJV). The people on the ark could not look out at the frightening storm; they could look only up toward their Savior! When the Tribulation and judgment begin upon earth, the believers in heaven will not see the anguish of

those left behind. We will be with the Savior, preparing for the marriage supper of the Lamb.

ENOCH: A MAN FOR ALL SEASONS

Look closely for the twentieth revelation of truth: *The life of Enoch vividly portrays the Rapture!*

Let's look at Genesis 5:24 (NKJV): "And Enoch walked with God; and he was not, for God took him." Enoch did not die—God suddenly snatched him off the earth and took him to heaven! This miraculous event is going to happen again, and very soon. The trumpet of God shall sound, the dead in Christ shall rise, and we're going to the city where roses never fade.

In Hebrews 11:5 (NKJV), Paul wrote:

> By faith Enoch was taken away so that he did not see death, "and was not found, because God had taken him"; for before he was taken he had this testimony, that he pleased God.

Notice this—after God took him, Enoch was missed! His family and neighbors looked for him, but they couldn't find him anywhere.

On the first Sunday after the Rapture, churches all across America will be packed to the walls with people who were left behind. They'll be looking for us, but they won't find us anywhere . . . on earth. We, the bride of Christ, will be standing before the heavenly Groom, opening our hope chests to display the treasures we have laid up in heaven.

Let's look a little deeper into the story of Enoch. In Genesis 5:21–22 (NKJV) we read: "Enoch lived sixty-five years, and begot Methuselah. After he begot Methuselah, Enoch walked with God three hundred years, and had sons and daughters."

Did Enoch not walk with God *before* he fathered Methuselah? We can't be sure, but apparently Enoch received a revelation from God at the time of his baby's birth. When they brought the infant to him, he named the baby *Methuselah*, which literally means "When he is dead it shall come."

It was the Flood, and Enoch's prophecy proved true. Noah's flood commenced in the year Methuselah died.

Think of it—a child brought his father to God! A baby is a mighty force, my friend. An infant's tiny fingers, unable to hold the lightest article, can grasp the hearts of all who visit. A baby's small feet, unable to take a single step, can march into your affection. A baby's eyes, which cannot differentiate between one person and another, can instantly captivate your own.

Once an infant enters a home, he will become the center of attention and affection. Enoch's tiny son must have turned the heart of the father toward God. From what Scripture tells us, we can surmise that Enoch did more than accept congratulations upon the birth of his son—he determined to make his life as pure as the baby in his arms. After begetting Methuselah, Enoch began to walk with God.

Are you a father? If so, do your children see you walking toward the house of God or on the highway to hell? Never forget, Dad, that your children are watching and listening. If you use profanity, your children will curse. If you speak untruths, they will lie. If you commit adultery, they will grow up to cheat on their spouses. If you neglect your financial responsibilities, your children will grow up to be deadbeats.

Enoch walked with God, and we know that two people cannot walk together unless they are agreed (Amos 3:3). Enoch walked in harmony with God, and his is one of the most outstanding biographies recorded in Scripture. Of his 365 years on earth, Enoch walked with God for three hundred of those years, then he was translated without dying, just as Elijah was (2 Kings 2).

Notice this—God did not walk with Enoch, but Enoch walked with God. He went where God went, not vice versa. He surrendered his will, for God does not force His company upon us. God will never force you to obey Him, for He respects man's free will. But He will place you in a position where you will have to make a choice.

Jonah had a choice when he knelt in the belly of the great fish: He could either preach in Nineveh as God had commanded, or prepare to be digested. As desperate as he was, Jonah had a choice.

When Paul walked over that dusty Damascus road and covered his eyes before the blinding glory of God, he had a choice. He could either follow God's command and go to Straight Street and prepare to preach the gospel, or go to Main Street and prepare to sit as a blind man with a beggar's cup in his hand.

The psalmist wrote, "I delight to do Your will, O my God, and Your law is within my heart" (Ps. 40:8 NKJV). Are you pounding your head against a wall as you resist God's call? Stop fighting God's will; instead, learn to delight in it.

Enoch walked with God, so he made steady progress.

Enoch was a man of faith, for without faith it is impossible to please God. His was a happy life, for when you walk with God, nothing can cause you to be afraid. David wrote:

> Yea, though I walk through the valley of the shadow of
>   death,
> I will fear no evil;
> For You are with me. (Ps. 23:4 NKJV)

In the presence of God is fullness of joy. Weeping may endure for a night, "but joy comes in the morning" (Ps. 30:5 NKJV). If your face looks like a reprint of the book of Lamentations, you need joy! You need to begin walking with God!

Enoch's little baby bore a message from God to everyone who ventured into Enoch's house. What do you suppose the neighbors thought when they realized Enoch had named his son, "When he dies it shall come"? I'm sure they mocked Enoch when he spoke of God's coming judgment, just as they mocked him when he prophesied of the second coming of Christ. Jude 14 (NKJV) tells us, "Now Enoch, the seventh from Adam, prophesied about these men also, saying, 'Behold, the Lord comes with ten thousands of His saints.'"

Enoch is the longest-living human on record. Besides living 365 years on earth, he has now lived more than five thousand years in heaven! Many Bible scholars believe he and Elijah, the only other human translated to heaven without tasting death, will return to earth as the two witnesses portrayed in Revelation 11. In the latter part of the Great Tribulation, they will preach about God's coming judgment and be killed for their faithfulness to God's truth.

Other men have visited heaven and then returned to earth. Paul and John went to heaven and returned (2 Cor. 12:1–7; Rev. 4:1). At the Rapture, all believers will go to heaven and live there until they return to earth with Christ at His second coming.

Enoch's message when he comes to the earth during the Tribulation will be the same message he preached to his contemporaries before the Flood: God has a set time for judgment! God's mercy has limits! Payday is coming!

Jesus Paid It All

Immediately after the Rapture of all believers, every Christian will stand before the judgment seat of Christ, also called the *bema* seat. We will be judged there, not for our sins, but for the works we accomplished in Christ's name.

In ancient Greece, the *bema* seat was never used as a judicial bench where criminals were pardoned or punished. The word refers instead to a raised platform in the sports arena on which the umpire sat. From this platform he rewarded all contestants and winners. As Christians, we run the race set before us. Eventually, we will be ushered to the *bema* seat to stand, not before heads of state, but before the Son of God.

At this judgment seat, Jesus will not judge whether or not we are saved, for everyone before the *bema* seat is a believer. Paul says the believer's *works* will be brought into judgment to see whether they are good or bad. Bible scholar Dwight Pentecost observed that Paul did not use the usual word for *bad* (*kakos* or *poneras*), either of which would signify that which is ethically or morally evil, but rather a word which means "good for nothing," or "worthless."[5] The Lord does not intend to punish us for sins, but to reward deeds done in His name.

This is why Paul wrote, "But I discipline my body and bring it into subjection, lest, when I have preached to others, I myself should become disqualified" (1 Cor. 9:27 NKJV). Paul wasn't worried about losing his salvation, but that his deeds might be found to be worthless.[6]

John the Revelator wrote:

> Let us be glad and rejoice and give Him glory, for the marriage of the Lamb has come, and His wife has made herself ready. And to her it was granted to be arrayed in fine linen, clean and bright, for the fine linen is the righteous acts of the saints. (Rev. 19:7–8 NKJV)

The marriage supper of the Lamb will take place right after our appearance before the Lord's judgment seat, and we will wear the wedding garments we have prepared while on earth. You are constructing your wedding garment right now, piecing it together with your righteous acts! You may stand before the Lord at the *bema* seat in a beautiful wedding gown . . . or you may be wearing just enough for a bikini! Your service to God here will determine the quality of your reward there.

Some people teach that at the judgment seat of Christ, God will punish believers for all the sins they commit after they accept Jesus Christ as Savior. This concept implies that when an individual accepts Christ, the blood of Jesus washes away all sin from the time of birth until that moment. However, from that moment on, he must answer to God for every sin.

We must cast off this teaching because Scripture plainly teaches that God does not blot out some of our sins and leave others for us to face on Judgment Day. In Isaiah 44:22 (NKJV) we read:

I have blotted out, like a thick cloud, your transgressions,
And like a cloud, your sins.

The psalmist said:

As far as the east is from the west,
So far has He removed our transgressions from us. (Ps.
    103:12 NKJV)

My favorites are found in both the Old and New Testaments:

For I will forgive their iniquity, and their sin I will
    remember no more. (Jer. 31:34 NKJV)
For I will be merciful to their unrighteousness, and their
    sins and their lawless deeds I will remember no more.
    (Heb. 8:12 NKJV)

Another false teaching about the Lord's judgment seat is that if a believer confesses his sins, he's forgiven the sin he confesses, but if he refuses or forgets a sin, God will punish him for it at the judgment seat. We must reject this concept as well, for the reasons mentioned above. If Christ is going to present me with a list of sins at His judgment seat, His death on the cross was meaningless.

Elvina M. Hall wrote:

> For nothing good have I
> Whereby Thy grace to claim—
> I'll wash my garments white
> In the blood of Calvary's Lamb.
> Jesus paid it all,
> All to Him I owe,
> Sin had left a crimson stain,
> He washed it white as snow.[7]

Paul wrote, "There is therefore now no condemnation to those who are in Christ Jesus" (Rom. 8:1 NKJV). Christ took *all* my judgment at Calvary. If He took all my judgment, there is no sin judgment to face at the judgment seat of Christ. That's the power of God's grace!

Anyone can accept or reject grace. John the Revelator looked into heaven and recorded the invitation offered to every living man, woman, and child:

> And the Spirit and the bride say, "Come!" And let him who hears say, "Come!" And let him who thirsts come. Whoever desires, let him take the water of life freely. (Rev. 22:17 NKJV)

AFTER THE RAPTURE, THE ANTICHRIST WILL APPEAR

Scripture tells us that the Rapture will be preceded by apostasy and a great falling away from the faith. Paul wrote:

Let no one deceive you by any means; for that Day will not come unless the falling away comes first, and the man of sin is revealed, the son of perdition. (2 Thess. 2:3 NKJV)

After the rise of apostasy, after the Rapture, the "son of perdition," or the Antichrist, will be revealed. The third chapter of Genesis foretold and pictured his arrival on the world stage. Look at the twenty-first revelation of truth:

> And I will put enmity
> Between you and the woman,
> And between your seed and her Seed;
> He shall bruise your head,
> And you shall bruise His heel. (Gen. 3:15 NKJV)

God was speaking to Satan, and He said He would put enmity, or hatred, "between your seed and her Seed." We have already seen that Jesus Christ was the Seed of the woman—so who was the seed of Satan?

He is the Antichrist, the son of Satan.

What is his name? No one knows . . . yet. But we do know many things about him.

- We know he will come from a revived Roman Empire, probably the European Union.

- We know he will use military force to gain and maintain world supremacy (Dan. 11:38). I found it interesting that the European Union, which until the summer of 1999 had not maintained or established a military force, has decided to do so. According to a plan announced at the European Union summit meeting in June 1999, by late 2000, a sixty-thousand-strong, five-nation Eurocorps based in Strasbourg, France, will have a "soft-spoken foreign and security policy czar."[8]

- We know his agenda will include a one-world religion, one-world currency, and one-world government.

- We know he will make a treaty with Israel and break it after three and one-half years (Dan. 9:27).

- We know he will require every living human to take his mark in the right hand or on the forehead (Rev. 13:16–17).

- We know he will set up an image of himself in the Temple in Jerusalem (Matt. 24:15–16).

- We know he will be the object of an assassination attempt and will suffer a mortal wound (Rev. 13:3).

- We know he will try to destroy the Jewish people.

- We know he will be defeated at Armageddon (Dan. 11:40–41, 44–45).

- We know he will be bound forever in the lake of fire (Rev. 19:20).

- We know he is already defeated! He and his father, Satan, are defeated forever!

Pictures of the Antichrist appear throughout the Bible. Revelation 13:6 (NKJV) tells us that the Antichrist will open his mouth "in blasphemy against God, to blaspheme His name, His tabernacle, and those who dwell in heaven."

The account of the Antichrist's final days is as vivid as any revelation in Scripture. As the Antichrist, indwelled by Satan, marshals his massive army for the battle of Armageddon, he will look into heaven at the angels who had the opportunity to follow him in his first rebellion against God. He will look at Christ, to whom Satan once offered the kingdoms of the world. He will look up at the believers who stand with their Lord, and he will say, "Look, all of you! Look where you would be if you had followed me! You would be rulers of the earth! I *forbid* God to send his Son to earth to reign. I am God here! I rule and reign in this city! Jerusalem is *mine!*"

Why does the Antichrist covet Jerusalem? What inspires his hatred for the Jews? The answer is simple: God chose the nation of Israel so He would have a repository of divine truth for generations to come. Through Israel God has given the world the Word of God, the patriarchs, the prophets, Jesus Christ, and the apostles. There would be no Christianity without Jewish contribution.

Satan's purpose in this battle is to exterminate every Jew on the face of the earth. The Lord Jesus Christ is returning to earth to rule over the seed of Abraham, Isaac, and Jacob. If Satan, through the Antichrist, can destroy the Jews, there is no reason for Jesus to return, and Satan could continue as the world ruler. But the Antichrist cannot stop what God has already decreed.

BATTLE SCENE:
GOD DRAWS THE NATIONS TO MEGIDDO

In Joel, God said, "I will also gather all nations, and bring them down to the Valley of Jehoshaphat" (Joel 3:2 NKJV).

Speaking through Zechariah, God said:

> Behold, I will make Jerusalem a cup of drunkenness to all the surrounding peoples, when they lay siege against Judah and Jerusalem . . . I will gather all the nations to battle. (Zech. 12:2, 14:2 NKJV)

The battle of Armageddon will begin on the plains of Megiddo to the north, continue down through the Valley of Jehoshaphat on the east, cover the land of Edom to the south and east, and revolve around Jerusalem. Fighting will begin almost immediately. The Antichrist's enemies will lay siege to Jerusalem, then overrun her defenses and city and wreak the havoc Zechariah so vividly described. They will take captives, murder, rape, and pillage until the streets run red with blood.

The Antichrist, who will be chasing the Jews who are fleeing Jerusalem for Petra, will hear of the trouble and direct his military juggernaut toward Armageddon to face the army of 200 million advancing from China to capture the oil-rich Persian Gulf.

But news from the east and the north shall trouble him; therefore he shall go out with great fury to destroy and annihilate many. And he shall plant the tents of his palace between the seas and the glorious holy mountain [Jerusalem]. (Dan. 11:44–45 NKJV)

After hearing about the advancing eastern army and the attack on Jerusalem, the Antichrist will advance from the territory of the defeated king of the South to Armageddon, a natural battlefield, to face the armies from the north and east.

LIVE-ACTION FOOTAGE: GOD DISPATCHES THE CAVALRY

Then God, who has patiently borne the blasphemies of the Antichrist, will say, "Son, take the armies of heaven—the angels and the church—and return to earth as the King of kings and Lord of lords. Go and make Your enemies your footstool. Go and rule the earth with a rod of iron. Go and sit upon the throne of Your father, King David."

Then will come the final invasion, not from the north, south, east, or west, but from heaven. It is the invasion described in Revelation 19, the attack led by Jesus Christ, the Lamb of God, the Lion of Judah, and the Lord of Glory!

Then the Lion of Judah shall mount His milk-white stallion, followed by His army wearing crowns and dazzling robes of white. I will be in that army, for it is composed of the loyal angels of God and those who were raptured with the church! This is the day Enoch foretold:

"Behold, the Lord comes with ten thousands of His saints" (Jude 14 NKJV).

John the Revelator told us that Jesus "had in His right hand seven stars, out of His mouth went a sharp two-edged sword, and His countenance was like the sun shining in its strength" (Rev. 1:16 NKJV). Mounted upon a white horse, the King of kings will descend onto the battlefield at Armageddon. As He comes, His eyes will be like blazing fire, and the armies of heaven will follow Him. Out of the Messiah's mouth will come a sharp two-edged sword, the Word of God with which He created the world out of chaos, raised Lazarus from the dead, and rebuked the unruly wind and waves on the Sea of Galilee. Just as God defeated Nimrod with the tongue, He will conquer the Antichrist with the tongue. His spoken word will crush His enemies in milliseconds.

He is the mighty conqueror, and of His kingdom there shall be no end!

When Jesus begins His descent, two opposing forces will be drawn up in battle array on the mountains of Israel—the armies of the Antichrist and the army of the kings of the east.

At that point, the two armies will turn from each other and direct their weapons toward Christ himself. John the Revelator said: "And I saw the beast, the kings of the earth, and their armies, gathered together to make war against Him who sat on the horse and against His army" (Rev. 19:19 NKJV).

Jesus Christ, leading the armies of heaven, will dismount from His white horse and step out onto the Mount of Olives, cleaving the mountain in two. The terrified inhabitants of Jerusalem, who have been brutalized by the invading armies, will flee the city through the gap in the ancient mountain.

John the Revelator told us that the mire of mingled blood and mud will form a lake that reaches to the bridle of a horse: "And the grapes were trodden in the winepress outside the city," John wrote, "and blood flowed from the winepress in a stream about 180 miles long and as high as a horse's bridle" (Rev. 14:20, NLT). This blood will flow from the veins of men who came to destroy Israel but were themselves destroyed by God.

Daniel foretold the outcome of the Antichrist's encounter with Jesus: "He [the Antichrist] shall even rise against the Prince of princes; but he shall be broken without human means" (Dan. 8:25 NKJV).

Paul also gave us a word of prophecy:

And then the lawless one [the Antichrist] will be revealed, whom the Lord will consume with the breath of His mouth and destroy with the brightness of His coming. (2 Thess. 2:8 NKJV).

John the Revelator wrote:

Then the beast [Antichrist] was captured, and with him the false prophet who worked signs in his presence . . . These two were cast alive into the lake of fire burning with brimstone. And the rest were killed with the sword which proceeded from the mouth of Him who sat on the horse. And all the birds were filled with their flesh. (Rev. 19:20–21 NKJV)

The Antichrist won't stand a chance! He who invaded Jerusalem, who murdered and killed those who would not worship him, who conquered the world, will be cast alive and forever into the lake of fire with the false prophet! And "that serpent of old, who is the Devil and Satan" will be bound by an angel and cast "into the bottomless pit, and shut . . . up . . . so that he should deceive the nations no more till the thousand years were finished" (Rev. 20:2–3 NKJV).

Returning to the earth with the church, Jesus will clean house. Not only will the Antichrist and the false prophet be thrown into hell, but Satan himself will be put away for a thousand years. Every hostile force that would challenge Christ's right to rule the earth will be eradicated.

THE FAMILY REUNION

There is one more beautiful revelation of truth in Genesis that pertains to the Age of Grace: *The story of Joseph is a picture of the second coming of Jesus Christ.*

Consider the names of Joseph and Jesus—both come from the same Hebrew root meaning "salvation."

God sent Joseph from his father's house to a strange land so that his family might be fed in a time of drought and famine. God dispatched Jesus from the right hand of the Father to the earth as "living water" and the "bread of life" (John 4:10, 6:48 NKJV).

Joseph's brothers rejected and betrayed him. His siblings sold him into the hands of his enemies, and Jacob's favorite son became a slave. Judas betrayed Jesus, Peter denied Him, and Thomas doubted Him. The Bible tells us,

"He came to His own, and His own did not receive Him" (John 1:11 NKJV).

Joseph's brothers sold him for twenty shekels of silver, the price of a slave (Gen. 37:28). Judas "sold" Jesus for thirty pieces of silver (Matt. 26:15), the usual price of a slave.

Joseph was falsely accused of attempted rape and sent to prison (Gen. 39:19–20). Jesus was falsely accused of treason and sent to prison and death.

After leaving prison, Joseph was exalted to the right hand of Pharaoh. After leaving the tomb, Jesus was exalted to the right hand of God.

At every point, Joseph walked the exact path Jesus trod generations later. Read the Genesis story carefully, and you'll discover that Joseph's brothers traveled to Egypt three times before the man who had worn the coat of many colors dropped his disguise. When Pharaoh's vizier abandoned his masquerade and revealed himself, he said, "I am Joseph, your brother." His brothers then wept openly and bitterly.

The Jewish people, the chosen family of God, have now entered Israel for the third time. The first time, they came with Joshua. After the exile, the Hebrews entered the land a second time with Nehemiah in order to rebuild the walls of Jerusalem and reestablish the nation. In 1948, the Jews entered Israel for the third time when the United Nations recognized their statehood. As foreseen by the prophet Isaiah, a nation was born in a day (Isa. 66:8).

Just as Joseph revealed his identity to his brothers on their third visit, the 1948 return of Israel has prepared the way for the revelation of the Messiah. As we study the pictures God has placed in the book of Genesis, we know that the moment when the people of Israel will discover the identity of Messiah lies before us. On His third visit to His brothers, He will reveal Himself.

And, like Joseph's brothers, the children of Israel will weep openly with bitter tears. Zechariah said, "Yes, they will mourn for Him as one mourns for his only son, and grieve for Him as one grieves for a firstborn" (12:10 NKJV).

AMAZING GRACE IS AVAILABLE IN EVERY AGE

There is no message in the Word of God that can heal, inspire, encourage, and bring joy unspeakable like the message of grace, the unmerited favor of God. Grace has been available in every dispensational age.

The next revelation of truth is this: *Grace is freely available to you; it has always been available to anyone who desired it.*

Grace was available in the Age of Innocence, even in the Garden of Eden. It revealed itself when God promised that the Seed of the woman would crush the serpent's head. God gave hope before He dispensed judgment—that's grace!

Grace was available in the Age of Conscience. Before God sent the Flood to destroy all flesh, He told Noah to build an ark, a way of escape before judgment. That's grace!

Grace was available in the Age of Human Government. Even before Nimrod and his cronies began to build the Tower of Babel, God instituted the plan of redemption, revealing it through a system of sacrifices.

Grace was available in the Age of Promise. In the midst of a kingdom of idolaters, God called Abram and instituted an unconditional covenant to form a nation of kings and priests unto God. That's grace.

Grace was available in the Age of the Law. Through the sacrifices of atonement, the people were forgiven of sin, and through those same sacrifices God painted a portrait of the Lamb who would come to remove the curse of sin once and for all. The Age of Law ended with the Lamb of God, Jesus Christ, at Calvary. He paid a debt He did not owe because you and I owed a debt we could not pay. That's grace!

Grace is available in this age that bears its name. Any man or woman or child who will may come to the Savior and accept His free gift of forgiveness and mercy.

Grace will be available even during the Tribulation. Millions who have never heard the gospel will hear it from angels. In Revelation 14:6 (NKJV), John wrote: "Then I saw another angel flying in the midst of heaven, having the everlasting gospel to preach to those who dwell on the earth— to every nation, tribe, tongue, and people."

God will give everyone who has not heard the gospel an opportunity to be saved. That's grace!

Journal, Page Eight

I have never, not once in the span of eternity, picked up a sword. I'm more of a recording angel—I suppose the English word would be scribe. But when I heard the sound of trumpets and saw the vision of the Son mounted upon His white horse, surrounded by the armies of saints and countless angelic warriors—well, it was enough to make me want to toss aside my pen and enlist in the advancing army! I might have done so, if not for a stern glance from Michael, who reminded me that someone would have to record the vision so all will know that the things that came to pass were the things that were foretold from the time before time.

And yet human words fail me now. How can I describe the fierce majesty of the Lord, the exuberant victory of the saints, the astounding gratitude of those who resisted the evil one, and his false Christ? I would write with the tongues of angels, but then this page would be worthless to you.

Until I can sit with you and speak of the terrible beauty of that day of war and victory, content yourselves with the words John the Revelator wrote after he visited us in the heavenly realm:

"Now I saw heaven opened, and behold, a white horse. And He who sat on him was called Faithful and True, and in righteousness He judges and makes war. His eyes were like a flame of fire, and on His head were many crowns. He had a name written that no one knew except Himself. He was clothed with a robe dipped in blood, and His name is called The Word of God. And the armies in heaven, clothed in fine linen, white and clean, followed Him on white horses" (Rev. 19:11–14 NKJV).

CHAPTER

THE AGE
OF THE KINGDOM

The advent of the Age of the Kingdom will be a time of
great rejoicing for God's people. Jesus Christ, the Lord of
Glory, will come again and defeat the son of Satan, the
Antichrist. Jesus will regather, regenerate, and restore faithful Israel. He will call the Jewish remnant hiding from the
Antichrist's persecution in Petra and welcome them back
into Jerusalem, His Holy City. Isaiah prophesied:

> For the LORD will comfort Zion,
> He will comfort all her waste places;
> He will make her wilderness like Eden,
> And her desert like the Garden of the LORD;
> Joy and gladness will be found in it,
> Thanksgiving and the voice of melody . . .
> For you shall go out with joy,
> And be led out with peace;
> The mountains and the hills
> Shall break forth into singing before you,
> And all the trees of the field shall clap their hands.
> (Isa. 51:3, 55:12 NKJV)

We who have returned in the armies of heaven will follow our King as He revisits His promised land. The barren, devastated earth around Jerusalem will miraculously burst forth with new life as the Messiah passes by. We will breathe in the scents of sweet jasmine, the Rose of Sharon, and the Lily of the Valley. The faithful Jews who have anticipated His coming will follow us, rejoicing in the arrival of their long-awaited Messiah. What a victory parade that will be!

The dispensational Age of the Kingdom, commonly known as the Millennium, will be a time of heaven on earth. For the first time since man walked in the Garden of Eden, men will know what it is like to enjoy the direct rule of God.

Like the previous ages, this era will have a favorable beginning. For the first time since the creation of Eden, man will be free from Satan, his fallen angels, and demons. God's angel will have bound the devil and cast him into the bottomless pit, there to remain for one thousand years (Rev. 20:2–3). Men and women born during this time will still possess a sinful nature, but the ability to overcome sin will be greater because there will be no satanic power or influence, no sickness, disease, or pain. The saints who return with Christ in the army of God will rule and reign over cities and provinces, and Christ Himself will reign from Jerusalem, the Holy City.

As wonderful as conditions on earth will be, this age will still have a test: Will the children born into this age obey Christ and conform to the will of God, or will they go their own way?

The Purpose of the Millennium

God has several reasons for instituting an earthly kingdom over which His Son will reign. First, He has promised to reward His children. Jesus said:

> His lord said to him, 'Well done, good and faithful servant; you have been faithful over a few things, I will make you ruler over many things. Enter into the joy of your lord. (Matt. 25:23 NKJV)

Second, God promised Abraham that Israel would become a mighty nation and that his seed would someday own the Promised Land forever (Gen. 13:14–15). Israel rightfully owns all the land God gave to Abraham by blood covenant: "from the river of Egypt to the great river, the River Euphrates," and "from the wilderness and Lebanon . . . even to the Western Sea" (Gen. 15:18; Deut. 11:24 NKJV). Ezekiel 48:1 established the northern boundary of Israel as the city of Hamath; verse 28 established the southern boundary as the city of Kadesh. In modern terms, Israel rightfully owns all of present-day Israel, all of Lebanon, half of Syria, two-thirds of Jordan, all of Iraq, and the northern portion of Saudi Arabia. When Messiah comes, the seed of Abraham will receive every square inch of that land.

Third, God will establish the millennial kingdom to answer millions of believers' prayers. Jesus taught His disciples to pray, "Thy kingdom come" (Luke 11:2 KJV). This is a plea that God would soon establish His earthly kingdom!

Finally, God will establish a millennial kingdom to

prove a point. In the Millennium God will redeem creation, resulting in an earth filled with docile wild animals, plentiful crops, and pure water. The world will know one thousand years of peace, joy, holiness, glory, comfort, justice, health, protection, freedom, and prosperity. Satan will not be able to work havoc on earth. King Jesus Himself will rule from Jerusalem, and immortal Christians with godly wisdom will rule other cities.

Despite all these things, man's fallen nature will *still* pull him into sin and disobedience.

The Millennium will be a one-thousand-year lesson in man's ultimate depravity. The humanistic idea that man can improve himself to the point of perfection will be proven false once and for all; the concept of utopia will disappear like the blues on a warm spring day. Although Christians will live in their resurrected bodies, the Tribulation believers who go into the Millennium in mortal bodies will bear children throughout the thousand years. The children, grandchildren, and great-grandchildren of the Millennium will possess a sinful nature, and they will have to choose whether or not to accept Christ as authority and Savior.

All seven dispensational ages reinforce one indisputable fact: Without God, man has no hope.

1. The Age of Innocence ended with willful disobedience (Gen. 3).

2. The Age of Conscience ended with universal corruption (Gen. 6).

3. The Age of Human Government ended with occultism at the Tower of Babel (Gen. 11).

4. The Age of Promise ended with God's people enslaved in Egypt (Ex. 1).

5. The Age of Law ended with the creatures killing their Creator upon a rugged tree (Matt. 27).

6. The Age of Grace will end with worldwide apostasy (1 Tim. 4:1–3).

7. The Age of the Kingdom will end with an attempt to destroy God Himself (Rev. 20).[1]

How the Millennium Begins

Daniel 12:11–12 indicates there will be a period of seventy-five days between Christ's second coming and the institution of His millennial reign. Dr. S. Franklin Logsdon explains it this way:

> We in the United States have a national analogy. The President is elected in the early part of November, but he is not inaugurated until January 20th. There is an interim of 70-plus days. During this time, he concerns himself with the appointment of Cabinet members, foreign envoys and others who will comprise his government. In the period of 75 days between the termination of the Great Tribulation and the Coronation, the King of glory likewise will attend to certain matters.[2]

The Judgment of the Nations

Before Christ establishes His millennial kingdom, several events must occur, among them a judgment. At this point, the twenty-fourth revelation of truth found in Genesis will come to vivid, colorful life: *God will keep his promise to Abraham, blessing those who blessed the Jews, and cursing those who cursed the children of Abraham.* This will occur at an event known as the Judgment of the Nations.

After the defeat of the Antichrist, Jesus will sit on His throne, then every mortal individual living on earth at that time will pass before Him. This is not the Great White Throne Judgment, at which every unbeliever will be judged for his deeds, but a judgment of the Gentile nations of earth for the manner in which they treated the Jewish people and Israel (Gen. 12:1–3). Let's see how Jesus described it:

> When the Son of Man comes in His glory, and all the holy angels with Him, then He will sit on the throne of His glory. All the nations will be gathered before Him, and He will separate them one from another, as a shepherd divides his sheep from the goats. And He will set the sheep on His right hand, but the goats on the left.
>
> Then the King will say to those on His right hand, "Come, you blessed of My Father, inherit the kingdom prepared for you from the foundation of the world: for I was hungry and you gave Me food; I was thirsty and you gave Me drink; I was a stranger and you took Me in; I was naked and you clothed Me; I was sick and you visited Me; I was in prison and you came to Me."
>
> Then the righteous will answer Him, saying, "Lord, when did we see You hungry and feed You, or thirsty and give You drink?" . . .

And the King will answer and say to them, "Assuredly, I say to you, inasmuch as you did it to one of the least of these My brethren, you did it to Me."

Then He will also say to those on the left hand, "Depart from Me, you cursed, into the everlasting fire prepared for the devil and his angels: for I was hungry and you gave Me no food; I was thirsty and you gave Me no drink". . .

Then they also will answer Him, saying, "Lord, when did we see You hungry or thirsty or a stranger or naked or sick or in prison, and did not minister to You?"

Then He will answer them, saying, "Assuredly, I say to you, inasmuch as you did not do it to one of the least of these, you did not do it to Me."

And these will go away into everlasting punishment, but the righteous into eternal life. (Matt. 25:31–37, 40–42, 44–46 NKJV)

Here the Lord will judge the Gentiles according to how they treated Jesus' "brethren," or the Jews, from the time of Genesis 12 to the Judgment of the Nations. The Gentiles who live during the Tribulation will answer for their treatment of the Jewish people and Israel. You will recall that during the Tribulation, God sealed a believing remnant of Israel, 144,000 strong, to witness during the entire seven-year period (Rev. 7:1–8). In Matthew 24:14 (NKJV), Jesus told us that this remnant will preach "the gospel of the kingdom . . . in all the world as a witness to all the nations, and then the end will come." These believing Jews are successful in their endeavors, for in Revelation 7:9–17, we see that a great multitude has been redeemed during the dark Tribulation period.

Upon a casual reading of Matthew's passage, you might think these Gentiles are being judged by their works—if they gave food and water to the ministering Jews, they would be allowed to obtain eternal life. This idea, however, contradicts the entire body of Scripture, for nowhere does God allow man to be saved through his own efforts. We are saved through faith in Jesus Christ, and our salvation *results* in good works. The works of kindness and compassion detailed in Jesus' words are not the criteria upon which these people are judged, but evidence of the transformation of their hearts.

God will look at each individual who has come out of Tribulation terror and ask, "How did you treat the witness who came to visit you? Did you give him food and water and listen to his message? Or did you call the authorities and attempt to have him cast into prison?" I believe that society will be so dark and dismal and paranoid that kindness and compassion will be found only in those whose hearts the Spirit of God has regenerated.

After this judgment, the "goats" will follow the Antichrist and the False Prophet into the lake of fire and brimstone. As they followed him in life, they will follow him in eternity. The "sheep" who know the Good Shepherd, Jesus, will follow Him to a glorious marriage feast.

Does God Really Bless Those Who Bless Israel?

Here's the twenty-fifth revelation of truth, pictured for us in the story of Jacob and Laban as recorded in Genesis 29–31: *God blesses Gentiles through the Jewish people.*

In the Genesis story, Jacob agreed to work seven years for Laban in order to earn the right to marry Laban's daughter Rachel. Aided by darkness and a heavy wedding veil, Laban deceived Jacob and gave his daughter Leah in marriage instead. Jacob was forced to work another seven years for Rachel's hand.

Over the years, Laban changed Jacob's wages ten times and began to look with disfavor on him. Fearful of his future prospects, Jacob fled with Leah and Rachel, their children, and all their possessions. When Laban heard that Jacob had fled, he followed. When he finally caught up with his son-in-law, he asked why Jacob had left his camp. Jacob answered, "You have changed my wages ten times, each time to my hurt, and you deceived me into marrying your homely daughter."

Laban, Jacob's Gentile employer, answered: "Please stay, if I have found favor in your eyes, for I have learned by experience that *the LORD has blessed me for your sake*" (Gen. 30:27 NKJV, italics added). Laban knew from first-hand experience that God blessed Gentiles through the Jewish people.

In Acts 10 the Bible declares that Cornelius, a Roman centurion who lived in Caesarea and gave alms to the Jewish people, was a man of "good reputation among all the nation of the Jews" (10:22 NKJV). Cornelius was a righteous man who benefitted from the principle of "I will bless those that bless you." How did God bless him?

Soon after Christ's ascension back into heaven, God gave the apostle Peter a vision of a prayer shawl descending from heaven held by the four corners. All manner of four-footed and wild beasts and creeping things and fowls of the air crawled inside the prayer shawl. This vision broke down the religious barrier forbidding Jews from associating with Gentiles in spiritual matters.

Understanding the message of the vision, Peter went to the house of Gentile Cornelius, preached the gospel, and rejoiced when those in Cornelius's household were saved. "While Peter was still speaking these words, the Holy Spirit fell upon all those who heard the word. And those of the circumcision [the Jews] who believed were astonished, as many as came with Peter, because the gift of the Holy Spirit had been poured out on the Gentiles also" (Acts 10:44–45 NKJV).

What made this possible? A Roman Centurion—a Gentile—blessed the Jewish people, and God opened the windows of heaven and poured upon him and his house blessing he could not contain.

WHY DON'T I HEAR MUCH ABOUT THE MILLENNIUM?

Though it is not often preached from Sunday pulpits, the Bible has much to say about the Millennium. It is known in Scripture as "the world to come" (Heb. 2:5 NKJV), "the kingdom of heaven" (Matt. 5:10 NKJV), "the kingdom of God" (Mark 1:14 NKJV), "the last day" (John 6:40 NKJV), and "the regeneration" (Matt. 19:28 NKJV). Jesus told His disciples, "Assuredly I say to you, that in the regeneration, when the Son of Man sits on the throne of His glory, you who have followed Me will also sit on twelve thrones, judging the twelve tribes of Israel" (Matt. 19:28 NKJV).

The twenty-sixth revelation of truth contains a beautiful picture of this regeneration: *In the book of Genesis, the Sabbath, a time of rest, foreshadows the Millennium.* God commanded His people to observe a rest after six work days, six work weeks, six work months, and six work years. In God's eternal plan, the earth will rest after six thousand years as He ushers in the millennial kingdom of the Messiah.

The Millennium will be a time of rest for the people of God. Hebrews 4:8–9 (NKJV) tells us: "For if [Jesus] had given them rest, then He would not afterward have spoken of another day. There remains therefore a rest for the people of God."

The prophet Isaiah echoed the thought:

And in that day there shall be a Root of Jesse,
Who shall stand as a banner to the people;
For the Gentiles shall seek Him,
And His resting place shall be glorious. (Isa. 11:10 NKJV)

ISRAEL IS NOT FORGOTTEN

We would be remiss, my friend, if we thought the Millennium was nothing but a time of celebration and rest for Christians. The twenty-seventh revelation of truth in Genesis will come to pass in the Age of the Kingdom: *Israel will enjoy a glorious, triumphant future.*

Blessing I will bless you, and multiplying I will multiply your descendants as the stars of the heaven and as the sand which is on the seashore; and your descendants shall possess the gate of their enemies. In your seed all the nations of the earth shall be blessed, because you have obeyed My voice. (Gen. 22:17–18 NKJV)

God's revelation to Abraham concerning his seed validates the biblical concept of two Israels, one physical and the other spiritual. God mentions two separate and distinct elements: the stars of the heavens and sand of the sea.

The "stars of the heaven" represent the church, or *spiritual* Israel. As light, stars rule the darkness, which is the commission of the church. Jesus said, "You are the light of the world" (Matt. 5:14 NKJV). Jesus is called "the Bright and Morning Star" (Rev. 22:16 NKJV). Daniel 12:3 (NKJV) tells us:

Those who are wise shall shine
Like the brightness of the firmament,
And those who turn many to righteousness
Like the stars forever and ever.

Stars are heavenly, not earthly. They represent the church, the spiritual descendants of Abraham.

The "sand of the sea," on the other hand, represents an earthly kingdom.

Both stars and sand coexist at the same time, and neither ever replaces the other. Just so, the nation of Israel and spiritual Israel, the church, coexist at the same time and do not replace each other. In Revelation 7:4–8, physical Israel is represented by twelve tribes and 144,000 people whom

God sealed to preach the gospel during the Great Tribulation.

Isaiah 40:1 (NKJV) clearly states this distinction: " 'Comfort, yes, comfort My people!' says your God." Take a close look at the formal English. Whom is God addressing? It is obvious that one group is being comforted and another is offering comfort.

Logic tells us we cannot be comforting and comforted at the same time. The people being comforted in this verse are "My people," or the Jewish people. The next verse makes this plain:

> Speak comfort to Jerusalem, and cry out to her,
> That her warfare is ended,
> That her iniquity is pardoned. (Isa. 40:2 NKJV)

The group comforting Israel is *spiritual* Israel, the church. The two Israels will merge on the day when the Messiah literally enters the physical city of Jerusalem.

When will Israel welcome its Messiah? Look at Romans 11:25 (NKJV): "For I do not desire, brethren," Paul wrote, "that you should be ignorant of this mystery, lest you should be wise in your own opinion, that blindness in part has happened to Israel until the fullness of the Gentiles has come in."

The word translated "fullness" is the Greek word *pleroma.* The word refers not to a numerical capacity, but to a sense of *completeness.*

"The completion of the mission to the Gentiles will result in, or lead to, Israel's 'fullness' or 'completion' (Rom. 11:12), her 'acceptance' (Rom. 11:15)," write the authors of *Hard Sayings of the Bible.*

Paul proclaims this future realization of God's intention as "a mystery" (Rom. 11:25) . . . The most
instructive parallel to this text—which envisions the
grafting of both Gentile and Jew into the same olive
tree—is Ephesians 3:3–6, where Paul says that the
content of the "mystery of Christ" is the inclusion of
the Gentiles as fellow heirs of the promise with Jews in
the new community of Christ's body.[3]

Bible scholars agree that Paul's statement that "all Israel
will be saved" means Israel "as a whole," not every single
individual. Just as "the fullness of the Gentiles" (Rom. 11:25)
does not mean that every single Gentile will accept Jesus as
Messiah, even so not every single child of Israel will place his
or her faith in Christ. But when the "fullness of the Gentiles"
has come, that is, when the Age of Grace is complete, then
God will remove the Jews' blindness (Rom. 11:10) to the
identity of Messiah and "all Israel will be saved" (Rom.
11:26 NKJV).

"What is also clear from the whole thrust of the discus-
sion in Romans 9–11," write the authors of *Hard Sayings of
the Bible*, "is that God's purposes for the salvation of Israel
will be realized in no other way and by no other means than
through the preaching of the gospel and the response of
faith."[4]

THE NEW MILLENNIUM MAP

The children of Abraham will come home to a country
whose geography has drastically changed. The nation will
be greatly enlarged, and the desert will become a fertile

plain. A miraculous river will flow east to west from the Mount of Olives into both the Mediterranean and the Dead Sea, but that sea will be dead no longer!

Hear how Ezekiel described it:

> When I returned, there, along the bank of the river, were very many trees on one side and the other. Then he said to me: "This water flows toward the eastern region, goes down into the valley, and enters the [Dead] sea. When it reaches the sea, its waters are healed. And it shall be that every living thing that moves, wherever the rivers go, will live. There will be a very great multitude of fish, because these waters go there; for they will be healed, and everything will live wherever the river goes. It shall be that fishermen will stand by it from En Gedi to En Eglaim; they will be places for spreading their nets. Their fish will be of the same kinds as the fish of the Great Sea, exceedingly many. (Ezek. 47:7–10 NKJV)

Ezekiel described fishermen catching all the species of fish at En Gedi (a city on the Dead Sea) that can be caught in the Mediterranean Sea. Indeed, the Dead Sea shall live, as will everything during the millennial kingdom when the Giver of Life sits upon the throne of His Father, King David.

Trees will grow on each side of this river flowing out of the Temple Mount, and John the Revelator tells us that these trees will bear twelve kinds of fruit, one for each month of the year. The leaves of these trees will be used for the healing of the nations (Rev. 22:2). Isaiah said that we will enjoy unparalleled health:

In that day the deaf shall hear the words of the book,
And the eyes of the blind shall see out of obscurity and
out of darkness. (Isa. 29:18 NKJV)

Listen to the beautiful picture Zechariah painted of the
regenerated land:

And in that day it shall be
That living waters shall flow from Jerusalem,
Half of them toward the eastern sea
And half of them toward the western sea;
In both summer and winter it shall occur . . .

All the land shall be turned into a plain from Geba to
Rimmon south of Jerusalem. Jerusalem shall be raised up
and inhabited in her place from Benjamin's Gate to the
place of the First Gate and the Corner Gate, and from the
Tower of Hannanel to the king's winepresses.

The people shall dwell in it;
And no longer shall there be utter destruction,
But Jerusalem shall be safely inhabited . . .

And it shall come to pass that everyone who is left of all
the nations which came against Jerusalem shall go up
from year to year to worship the King, the LORD of hosts,
and to keep the Feast of Tabernacles. (Zech. 14:8, 10–11,
16 NKJV)

Jerusalem, the apple of God's eye, will become the joy of
the world, for Jesus will reign there. The city will become the

international worship center, and people from all over the world will make pilgrimages to worship in the holy temple. Kings, queens, princes, and presidents shall come to the Holy City so "that at the name of Jesus every knee should bow, of those in heaven, and of those on earth, and of those under the earth, and that every tongue should confess that Jesus Christ is Lord, to the glory of God the Father" (Phil. 2:10–11 NKJV).

The prophet Micah sketched a wonderful picture of the millennial kingdom, and the poetry of his verse has inspired the inscription of his words on many a public building. But Micah wasn't describing the United Nations, London, or New York; the prophet was writing about God's millennial capital, Jerusalem:

> Now it shall come to pass in the latter days
> That the mountain of the LORD's house
> Shall be established on the top of the mountains,
> And shall be exalted above the hills;
> And peoples shall flow to it.
> Many nations shall come and say,
> "Come, and let us go up to the mountain of the LORD,
> To the house of the God of Jacob;
> He will teach us His ways,
> And we shall walk in His paths."
>
> For out of Zion the law shall go forth,
> And the word of the LORD from Jerusalem.
> He shall judge between many peoples,
> And rebuke strong nations afar off;
> They shall beat their swords into plowshares,
> And their spears into pruning hooks;

Nation shall not lift up sword against nation,
Neither shall they learn war anymore. (Mic. 4:1–3 NKJV)

The Holy City, now six miles in circumference, will occupy an elevated site and will be named *Jehovah-Shammah*, meaning "THE LORD IS THERE" (Ezek. 48:35 NKJV) and *Jehovah Tsidkenu*, meaning "THE LORD OUR RIGHTEOUSNESS" (Jer. 33:16 NKJV).

Can you imagine one thousand years of perfect peace? Mankind will cease from strife, and the lion shall lie down by the lamb without even showing his claws! Satan will be bound in the bottomless pit, and earthly problems will fade away.

BY WHAT RIGHT DOES JESUS CHRIST RULE THE EARTH?

Two particular portions of Genesis foreshadow Jesus' right to rule the earth. Both are beautiful scenes in the lives of two Jewish patriarchs, and both contain the twenty-eighth revelation of truth: *Jesus Christ rules the earth by royal right of inheritance.*

God promised Abraham, "I will make you exceedingly fruitful; and I will make nations of you, and kings shall come from you" (Gen. 17:6 NKJV). God was revealing how He planned to eventually rule over all the earth—through a king of His appointment.

In Genesis 49 Jacob the patriarch called his twelve sons around his bed to give them a final blessing and to speak a prophetic word over each of them. His word over Judah is especially provocative:

Judah, you are he whom your brothers shall praise;
Your hand shall be on the neck of your enemies;
Your father's children shall bow down before you . . .

The scepter shall not depart from Judah,
Nor a lawgiver from between his feet,
Until Shiloh comes. (Gen. 49:8, 10 NKJV)

The word *Shiloh* may be rendered "he whose right it is to rule." Jacob thus prophesied that a man who had the right to be king would come out of Judah's lineage.

In 2 Samuel 7:16 (NKJV), God made this promise to King David: "And your house and your kingdom shall be established forever before you. Your throne shall be established forever." There are three important words in this verse: *house, kingdom,* and *throne.* "Your house" designates the descendants of David who would sit on his throne. "Your kingdom" represents the kingdom of Israel. "Your throne" is David's royal authority, the right to rule as God's representative. Twice in this one verse God assured David that his dynasty, kingdom, and throne would last *forever.*

The gospel of Matthew opens with God breaking a silence of more than four hundred years. God proclaimed Jesus' royal lineage to Israel by saying, "The book of the genealogy of Jesus Christ, the Son of David, the Son of Abraham" (Matt. 1:1 NKJV).

If Jesus Christ is the Son of Abraham, He is the Blessor promised to Abraham through whom all the families of the earth should be blessed (Gen. 12:3). If Jesus Christ is the Son of David, He is the one who has the right to rule. He is Shiloh!

The angel of the Lord told the Virgin Mary:

Do not be afraid, Mary, for you have found favor with God. And behold, you will conceive in your womb and bring forth a Son, and shall call His name JESUS. He will be great, and will be called the Son of the Highest; and the Lord God will give Him the throne of His father David. And He will reign over the house of Jacob forever, and of His kingdom there will be no end. (Luke 1:30–33 NKJV)

Jesus Christ was born, lived as a Jewish rabbi, and was crucified by the Roman government on a Roman cross. When He ascended into heaven, God the Father said to Him, "Sit at My right hand, till I make Your enemies Your footstool" (Matt. 22:44 NKJV).

Jesus Christ rules the Millennium because He alone is worthy. He rules by heritage, by holy decree, and by divine appointment. Blessing and honor and glory and power be to Him who will sit on the throne of His father, David!

THE KING AND HIS VICE-REGENT

Though Jesus Christ will be supreme ruler during the Millennium, some prophetic passages strongly suggest He will be aided by a second in command: David, the man after God's own heart![5]

Let's look at the Scripture:

But they shall serve the LORD their God,
And David their king,
Whom I will raise up for them. (Jer. 30:9 NKJV)

Jeremiah wrote four hundred years after David's death, so he could not have been referring to David's earthly reign. Let's look at what else Scripture says:

> I will establish one shepherd over them, and he shall feed them—My servant David. He shall feed them and be their shepherd. And I, the LORD, will be their God, and My servant David a prince among them . . .

> David My servant shall be king over them, and they shall all have one shepherd; they shall also walk in My judgments and observe My statutes, and do them. (Ezek. 34:23–24, 37:24–25 NKJV)

> Afterward the children of Israel shall return and seek the LORD their God and David their king. They shall fear the LORD and His goodness in the latter days. (Hos. 3:5 NKJV)

But King David won't be the only ruler. Aiding him will be:

- The church (1 Cor. 6:3).
- The apostles (Matt. 19:28).
- Nobles (Jer. 30:21).
- Princes (Isa. 32:1; Ezek. 45:8–9).
- Judges (Zech. 3:7; Isa. 1:26).
- Lesser authorities (Zech. 3:7).[6]

If there is a lesson here for us, the waiting church, it is that those who are faithful now will be given greater responsibility in heaven. "Well done, good and faithful servant," the master told the servant who multiplied the talents he had been given. "You have been faithful over a few things, I will make you ruler over many things. Enter into the joy of your lord" (Matt. 25:23 NKJV).

THE MILLENNIUM IS WONDERFUL, BUT IT ISN'T HEAVEN

Does the Millennium sound like heaven on earth? Think again. Millions of babies will be born during this thousand years, and they will be babies just like you and I once were, prone to sin and bent toward trouble. Though the Christian parents who live during the Millennium will teach their children right from wrong, some of these children will exercise their free will to choose wrong. Though Satan will be bound, mankind will still have a fleshly tendency to resist the law of authority.

Some citizens of the Millennium, Zechariah reported, will "not come up to Jerusalem to worship the King, the LORD of hosts," so "on them there will be no rain" (14:17 NKJV). Christ will have to rule with "a rod of iron" (Rev. 19:15 NKJV).

Dr. Rene Pache explains the situation:

> As beautiful as the Millennium is, it will not be heaven . . . Sin will still be possible during the thousand years. Certain families and nations will refuse to go up to Jerusalem to worship the Lord. Such deeds will be all the more inexcusable because the tempter will be absent and because the revelations of the Lord will be greater.[7]

Unfortunately, just as men failed in previous ages, mankind will fail during this period too. Though many will obey Christ, others will rebel against God and His righteousness. At the end of the Millennium, Satan will be released from the bottomless pit in order to give mankind a final opportunity to follow someone other than God. Free will, remember? Mankind always has a choice.

At the end of the Millennium, Satan will be free from his prison, and thousands of people from all the nations of the earth will believe his lies and follow him. They will gather around Jerusalem, Christ's capital city, and wage a great war:

> Now when the thousand years have expired, Satan will be released from his prison and will go out to deceive the nations which are in the four corners of the earth, Gog and Magog, to gather them together to battle, whose number is as the sand of the sea. They went up on the breadth of the earth and surrounded the camp of the saints and the beloved city. (Rev. 20:7–9 NKJV)

What will make these people follow Satan? Who can understand what drives men to sin? For those who are living in earthly bodies, even as we are now, the law of sin is like the law of gravity. No matter how much we want to rise above it, it draws us down. It is only through the power of Christ that we can rise above sin at all.

The Age of the Kingdom will be a time similar to the Age of Innocence. In a perfect environment that God created, Adam and Eve chose to sin. Under ideal circumstances—an abundant earth, no sickness, and no war—the human heart will prove that it remains unchanged unless regenerated by the power of Christ. When Satan is loose on the earth, many will turn their backs on the God who has sustained them and follow the evil one.

Notice that Revelation mentions Gog and Magog in this verse describing the final conflict, but this is not the same Gog-Magog war described in Ezekiel 38–39. J. Vernon McGee believed that "the rebellion of the godless forces from the north will have made such an impression on mankind that after one thousand years, the last rebellion of man bears the same label—Gog and Magog."[8] Just as we have called two conflicts "World War I" and "World War II," the people may call this last battle "Gog-Magog II."

These people will mount an army and advance against Jerusalem, where Jesus rules and reigns. There they will learn that rebellion always ends in destruction. To purge creation of the evil effects of sin finally and forever, God will destroy the earth with great heat and fire. Peter wrote:

> The heavens will pass away with a great noise, and the elements will melt with fervent heat; both the earth and the works that are in it will be burned up . . . Nevertheless we, according to His promise, look for new heavens and a new earth in which righteousness dwells. (2 Peter 3:10, 13 NKJV)

John the Revelator saw that "fire came down from God out of heaven and devoured them. And the devil, who deceived them, was cast into the lake of fire and brimstone where the beast and the false prophet are. And they will be tormented day and night forever and ever" (Rev. 20:9–10 NKJV).

Our enemy—the one who has tormented, tempted, and tested Christians for generations—will be put away permanently. He will enter hell for the first time—during the Millennium he was chained in the bottomless pit, and today he roams the earth, seeking those he may lead into deception. But at the end of the Age of the Kingdom, praise God, Satan the Destroyer will receive God's permanent justice.

As judgment for sin, fire will come down from out of heaven and devour the millennial earth. The rebels who chose to side with Satan will be destroyed. God will bring an end to rebellion as all rebels, human and immortal, face judgment and are confined to eternal hell and torment. And then God will create a new heaven and a new earth.

> "For as the new heavens and the new earth
> Which I will make shall remain before Me," says the
>   LORD,
> "So shall your descendants and your name remain.
> And it shall come to pass
> That from one New Moon to another,
> And from one Sabbath to another,
> All flesh shall come to worship before Me," says the
>   LORD.
> "And they shall go forth and look
> Upon the corpses of the men
> Who have transgressed against Me.
> For their worm does not die,
> And their fire is not quenched.

They shall be an abhorrence to all flesh." (Isa. 66:22–24
NKJV)

Notice what happened when Satan rebelled against God
in eternity past. He courted allies among the angelic host,
he led a revolt against the armies of heaven, and he lost!
God defeated Satan prior to the creation. Satan could not
force God from His throne.

In the Age of Innocence, God defeated Satan in the
Garden of Eden. Though Satan persuaded Eve and Adam to
eat the forbidden fruit, God's promise quelled him: "The
Seed of the woman shall crush your head."

In the Age of Conscience, God defeated Satan when Satan
controlled the thoughts and impulses of all men except Noah
and his family. Noah found grace in the eyes of the Lord.

In the Age of Human Government, God defeated Satan
when He confused the language of men at Babel. The city
and tower purposely designed to supplant the worship of
the one true God had to be abandoned.

In the Age of Promise, God defeated Satan when He
struck the Egyptians with plagues and mocked their heathen gods. Satan was powerless to prevent the Israelites'
liberation!

In the Age of the Law, God defeated Satan in the wilderness. When Satan tempted Jesus with the kingdoms of this
world, Jesus responded, "It is written . . ." Jesus used the
Word of God to defeat Satan three times!

At the dawn of the Age of Grace, God defeated Satan at
Calvary. Because of Calvary, demons tremble at the mention
of Jesus' name. When He arose victorious over death and
corruption, death, hell, and the grave were finished.

In the Age of the Kingdom, God will defeat Satan when Christ returns to rule and reign during the Millennium. An angel will bind Satan for a thousand years and seal him in the bottomless pit.

When the Age of the Kingdom concludes, God will finally, permanently defeat Satan. The Bible tells us:

> The devil, who deceived them, was cast into the lake of fire and brimstone where the beast and the false prophet are. And they will be tormented day and night forever and ever. (Rev. 20:10 NKJV)

The Prince of Darkness is defeated!

The powers and principalities of Satan's dominion are defeated!

The demons of hell are defeated!

God kicked Satan out of heaven, and you have the authority to kick him out of your life. Do it! Remember this—Satan is a loser!

If Satan has the gall to remind you of your past failures, remind him of his future. He is a defeated foe!

Journal, Page Nine

There are times, I must confess, that I feel a strange stirring in my heart when I think of you humans. Were I not sinless in action and thought, I might call this stirring jealousy, but I cannot be jealous of those I love. And I do love you, for I love all that the Father loves, and the Father loves you.

Yet still I am wistful as I consider the future to come. I cannot see it, for only God is omniscient and all-seeing. He has seen the future, and He has described it in some detail, but you have as much access to that information as I. It is all contained in the Scripture, scattered in luminous word pictures and sound sonnets throughout the writings of the prophets.

I know that after the Age of the Kingdom, when God exiles the evil one and his minions to the lake of fire and settles the question of sin eternally, you humans will be like us of the heavenly host. You will not be angels, but you will have bodies like Christ's when He appeared to the disciples after His resurrection. He ate, He drank, and He was recognized by His friends and loved ones. But the heavenly body is incorruptible. It will never wear out or weaken, and it can travel through space and solid material at the speed of thought.

Like us, you will know contentment and joy at being in the presence and service of God, the Three-in-One. Your minds will be quick and able to fathom the mysteries of the universe, your hearts will brim with feelings and desires— albeit godly desires. The sin nature and the weakness that tempted you in ages past will be gone, wiped away forever by the transforming power of God.

Perhaps one day you and I will join hands and travel to the edges of the new cosmos. God has promised a new heaven and a new earth to explore, and . . . well, as long as I'm confessing, I may as well lay bare my heart.

I'm curious about you. How does it feel to be redeemed? How can your fragile human heart contain the joy of gratitude? The gulf between depravity and redemption is so great, I can't imagine traversing it upon the wings of love.

Someday, you and I must talk.

THE WORLD
THAT WILL BE

God has saved the best for last. After the dispensational eras are finished, eternity will be a time of endless perfection and eternal life. It will not only have a favorable beginning, but a glorious continuation and no end. There will be no further need for testing or trials.

Two events, however, bridge the Age of the Kingdom and Eternity. These are the Last Resurrection and the Great White Throne Judgment.

THE LAST RESURRECTION

The *first* resurrection includes three waves of ingathering. The first wave to be resurrected were those who came out of their graves at the Crucifixion. The second wave will be the Rapture of the church, and the third wave will be those who are converted in the Tribulation. They will be taken into heaven in the middle of that seven-year period. Jesus Himself explained it to us:

> Do not marvel at this; for the hour is coming in which all
> who are in the graves will hear His [the Son of God's]

voice and come forth—those who have done good, to the resurrection of life, and those who have done evil, to the resurrection of condemnation. (John 5:28–29 NKJV)

Daniel wrote:

And many of those who sleep in the dust of the earth
    shall awake,
Some to everlasting life,
Some to shame and everlasting contempt. (Dan. 12:2
    NKJV)

Those who would wake to "contempt," however, will rise at the end of the millennial kingdom: the Last Resurrection.

In Revelation 20:5–6 (NKJV) we learn that the Millennium will separate these two resurrections:

But the rest of the dead did not live again until the thousand years were finished. This is the first resurrection. Blessed and holy is he who has part in the first resurrection. Over such the second death has no power, but they shall be priests of God and of Christ, and shall reign with Him a thousand years.

The second resurrection is the resurrection of the unjust, when every remaining soul is called to stand before the awe-inspiring throne of God. There are no future judgments for believers. Christians were rewarded or reproved at the *bema* seat of Christ. The Great White Throne Judgment is for those who have rejected the Savior.

THE GREAT WHITE THRONE JUDGMENT

The prophet Daniel peered through the periscope of prophecy and saw this terrible, final accounting. Daniel 7:9–10 (NKJV) records his vision:

> I watched till thrones were put in place,
> And the Ancient of Days was seated;
> His garment was white as snow,
> And the hair of His head was like pure wool.
> His throne was a fiery flame,
> Its wheels a burning fire;
> A fiery stream issued
> And came forth from before Him.
> A thousand thousands ministered to Him;
> Ten thousand times ten thousand stood before Him.
> The court was seated,
> And the books were opened.

The Great White Throne Judgment will be held in an intermediate place, somewhere between heaven and earth. It cannot occur on the earth because the earth will be gone (2 Peter 3:10). It will not occur in heaven because sinners would never be permitted in the throne room of a holy God.

Christ Himself is the One sitting on the throne. In John 5:27–29 (NKJV), Jesus said:

> [The Father] has given [the Son] authority to execute judgment also, because He is the Son of Man. Do not marvel at this; for the hour is coming in which all who

are in the graves will hear His voice and come forth—
those who have done good, to the resurrection of life,
and those who have done evil, to the resurrection of
condemnation.

In Revelation 20:12–13 (NKJV) John continued to describe
the Great White Throne Judgment, saying:

And I saw the dead, small and great, standing before
God, and books were opened. And another book was
opened, which is the Book of Life. And the dead were
judged according to their works, by the things which
were written in the books. The sea gave up the dead who
were in it, and Death and Hades delivered up the dead
who were in them. And they were judged, each one
according to his works.

Notice that God has two sets of books. The Book of
Life contains the name of every person who accepted Jesus
Christ while he or she was on the earth. When the wicked
dead approach the Great White Throne, Jesus will first look
for their names in the Book of Life. Obviously, they will not
be recorded there. Then He will open the "books" that contain written records of the wicked's every word, thought,
and deed.

BUT I DON'T BELIEVE IN HELL

Are you one of those folks who doubts the existence of hell?
Well, my friend, what you believe has no bearing on reality.

Poison kills whether you believe in it or not. Frost freezes whether you believe in it or not. The world is round, whether you believe it or not. And hell is a reality.

Fact: Jesus talked about hell twice as often as He talked about heaven. Paul believed in hell, and wrote:

> The Lord Jesus is revealed from heaven with His mighty angels, in flaming fire taking vengeance on those who do not know God, and on those who do not obey the gospel of our Lord Jesus Christ. These shall be punished with everlasting destruction from the presence of the Lord and from the glory of His power. (2 Thess. 1:7–9 NKJV)

Hell, sometimes known as *Sheol* or *Hades*, is not to be confused with the lake of fire. In this life, the ungodly die and go to hell, where they wait until they are brought to the Great White Throne for final judgment (Rev. 19:20, 20:10, 14, 15). After judgment, the hand of God will place Satan, fallen angels, demons, and all ungodly persons into the eternal lake of fire for rejecting Jesus Christ as the Son of God (Rev. 20:15; Jude 6–7).

In a secular society where there is no absolute right or wrong, many people scoff at the concept of a literal hell designed for those who violate the law of God. But Jesus believed in hell, and so did the prophets. Let's examine the Scriptures about hell, the abiding place of the lost before they face judgment before the Great White Throne. We can learn nine truths about hell from studying the parable Jesus told in Luke 16:19–31.

1. *Hell is a literal place.* Notice that Jesus begins this

story by saying, "There was . . ." The story is a literal tale of two beggars—Lazarus, who begged in this life, and the rich man, who begged throughout eternity.

2. *Christ's parable verifies the extreme difference in eternity for the righteous and the ungodly.* This teaching is not a condemnation of wealth; it is a condemnation of any person who rejects Jesus Christ.

3. *This parable confirms that the saved before Calvary were carried by angels into Paradise* (Luke 16:22; 23:43). After Calvary the righteous go to heaven (2 Cor. 5:8; Phil. 1:21–23; Rev. 6:9–11).

4. *Hell is a place of eternal agony.* The unsaved go to hell when they die and are in a conscious state of eternal torment (Luke 16:23–28; Deut. 32:22; 2 Sam. 22:6; Isa. 14:9–11). Hell is a place of weeping and wailing and gnashing of teeth.

5. *Hell is a place without mercy.* The rich man in hell cried out, "Have mercy on me, and send Lazarus that he may dip the tip of his finger in water and cool my tongue; for I am tormented in this flame" (Luke 16:24 NKJV). In hell, you will hear the bloodcurdling screams of millions hour after hour, day after day, week after week, year after year . . . for all eternity.

6. *Hell is a place without escape.* Jesus said, "Between us and you there is a great gulf fixed, so that those who want to pass from here to you cannot, nor can those from there pass to us" (Luke 16:26 NKJV). After you arrive in hell, the prayers of ten thousand saints cannot lift you out.

7. *People in hell are aware of people on earth.* The rich man begged for someone to warn his family, "for I have five brothers, that he [Lazarus] may testify to them, lest they also

come to this place of torment" (Luke 16:28 NKJV). People in hell are conscious. They know who they are, and where they are. They remember the terrible things they did on earth.

8. *Souls are immortal in hell and heaven* (Luke 16:22–23, 20:38; 2 Cor. 5:8).

9. *Hell is located in "the lower parts of the earth"* (Ps. 63:9; Eph. 4:8–10 NKJV), also called "the heart of the earth" (Matt. 12:40 NKJV). It is a bottomless pit of eternal darkness. It is a city whose inhabitants are murderers, rapists, child molesters. The tortured citizens of hell are depraved.

John the Revelator concluded his description of the Great White Throne Judgment by saying, "Then Death and Hades were cast into the lake of fire . . . And anyone not found written in the Book of Life was cast into the lake of fire" (Rev. 20:14–15 NKJV).

Paul wrote:

> For as in Adam all die, even so in Christ all shall be made alive . . . Then comes the end, when He delivers the kingdom to God the Father, when He puts an end to all rule and all authority and power. For He must reign till He has put all enemies under His feet. The last enemy that will be destroyed is death . . .
>
> "O Death, where is your sting?
> O Hades, where is your victory?" (1 Cor. 15:22, 24–26, 55 NKJV)

After the Great White Throne Judgment, death and hell are finished, and eternity looms. The best is yet to come. Glory!

ETERNITY DAWNS FRESH AND NEW

What is God's purpose in establishing eternity? Finis Dake wrote:

> To be all in all again, as before rebellion began with Lucifer and Adam, and to carry out His eternal plan of having creations and kingdoms which are willingly subject to Him and consecrated to the same end that He, Himself is consecrated to, which is the highest good of being for all in all the universes—that is the purpose of God in the future eternal dispensation.[1]

In this age without end there will be no failure, no judgment for sin, and no further need of redemption. Christ's redemption will have sufficed for all mankind, through all eternity.

Look at the next revelation of truth in Genesis: *The perfect creation and fellowship Adam enjoyed in Eden is a living portrait of heaven!* The Creator will have come full circle and restored His creation so that it reflects His original intention. The beings who live with Him—angels and humans—have been tested. Though the humans could not merit perfection on their own, they have chosen surrender to Christ instead of rebelling against God.

The Old Testament prophet Isaiah caught a glimpse of this restored creation, and recorded God's thoughts about what He would bring to pass:

> For behold, I create new heavens and a new earth;
> And the former shall not be remembered or come to mind.

> But be glad and rejoice forever in what I create;
> For behold, I create Jerusalem as a rejoicing,
> And her people a joy.
> I will rejoice in Jerusalem,
> And joy in My people;
> The voice of weeping shall no longer be heard in her,
> Nor the voice of crying. (Isa. 65:17–19 NKJV)

God will present us with a new heaven and a new earth, to which a New Jerusalem will descend from heaven. John the Revelator wrote:

> Now I saw a new heaven and a new earth, for the first heaven and the first earth had passed away. Also there was no more sea. Then I, John, saw the holy city, New Jerusalem, coming down out of heaven, prepared as a bride adorned for her husband. And I heard a loud voice from heaven saying, "Behold, the tabernacle of God is with men, and He will dwell with them, and they shall be His people, and God Himself will be with them and be their God."(Rev. 21:1–3 NKJV)

Speaking of Jesus Christ, the apostle John said: "And the Word became flesh and dwelt [tabernacled] among us, and we beheld His glory, the glory as of the only begotten of the Father, full of grace and truth" (John 1:14 NKJV).

Writing to a primarily Jewish audience, John used the Greek word *sk'enos* (meaning "shelter" or "covering") and the metaphor of a tabernacle to describe Christ's incarnation. The same word appears in Revelation 21:3, when the New Jerusalem comes down from heaven. John said,

"Behold, the tabernacle of God is with men." We will be able to talk with God in the cool of the day as Adam did in the Age of Innocence. The sinlessness of Eden will be recreated on earth, and in immortal resurrection bodies we will fellowship with God forever.

Not only will we commune with God, but we will enjoy fellowship with other believers. Jesus said we would sit down with the patriarchs of Genesis: "And I say to you that many will come from east and west, and sit down with Abraham, Isaac, and Jacob in the kingdom of heaven" (Matt. 8:11 NKJV).

In the rest of this chapter, I want to give you a guided tour of the place God is preparing for the righteous. I want to whet your appetite to go there—because you may not be ready to meet God.

I once heard about a little boy who was born blind. Through his eight years on earth, he never saw his mother's face, the blinding glory of a winter snow, or the soft colors of a summer sunset. His mother tried her best to describe these things for him, but though he seemed to understand, she wondered if her words were really adequate.

Then the boy's mother heard about a fabulous doctor who had made great strides in optical operations. She took her son to see him, and within a few weeks the boy was scheduled for surgery. He went into the operating room, underwent the deep sleep of anesthesia, and then lay in his hospital room for a few days with bandages covering his eyes.

Finally the doctor came to his room and began to unwrap the bandages. After the last one was lifted away, the doctor moved to the shuttered windows and gradually adjusted the light. Once the child's eyes had focused, he climbed out of bed and ran to the window, then leaned over the sill, breathing in the scents and sights he had only imagined. "Oh, Mother," he said, staring at the park below where a fountain splashed and children played in the bright sunlight. "Why didn't you tell me I was living in such a beautiful world?"

With tears in her eyes, his mother said, "Sweetheart, I tried. But words weren't enough to paint the picture."

If there is any message of this chapter, of this entire book, it is this: Words aren't enough to paint the picture of what God has planned for His children. The word pictures in the Bible are but shadows of what is to come; and the words on this page are but symbols to describe the reality of heaven. I apologize to God for the pathetic job of description I am about to undertake, but at least I can identify with Paul, who enjoyed a guided tour of heaven. That brilliant writer tried to describe heaven, and finally resorted to saying:

> Eye has not seen, nor ear heard,
> Nor have entered into the heart of man
> The things which God has prepared for those who love
> Him. (1 Cor. 2:9 NKJV)

Dream what you will, my friend, and make those dreams as big as you can. Then know that you haven't even begun to dream of the richness and depth and breadth of heaven and eternity.

WHAT WON'T BE IN HEAVEN

Heaven will be a wonder because of the things we'll miss. First, there will be no sorrow or sickness there. Just as there was no sorrow or sickness in Eden before the Fall, in heaven we will live without physical weakness and corruption. John the Revelator wrote: "And God will wipe away every tear from their eyes; there shall be no more death, nor sorrow, nor crying. There shall be no more pain, for the former things have passed away" (Rev. 21:4 NKJV).

Heaven is a place without cancer wards, cardiac units, and emergency rooms. You won't find any twisted, arthritic limbs in heaven . . . and no asthma patients wheezing for breath. There are no blind eyes in heaven, and no deaf ears. There are no wheelchairs, no crutches, and no drugstores. Heaven is a society of absolute physical perfection.

Jesus said, "Behold, I make all things new" (Rev. 21:5 NKJV). In heaven, I'll have a new body, a new name, a new mansion in New Jerusalem, and a new nature. I'll drink new wine at the marriage supper of the Lamb, and I'll sing a new song to the King of kings and Lord of lords.

Notice what else is missing in heaven—John wrote, "Also there was no more sea" (Rev. 21:1 NKJV). Why wouldn't heaven have a sea? You'll have to remember that John was in exile on the Isle of Patmos at the time he wrote the Revelation. The sea separated him from the church, his family, his friends, all he loved. He was lonely, forsaken, and homesick. But in heaven there is nothing to separate us from the people we hold dear!

Incidentally, we can have victory over separation even now. Though sometimes we are separated from loved ones, we are never separated from our loving Savior. Paul wrote:

> For I am persuaded that neither death nor life, nor angels
> nor principalities nor powers, nor things present nor

things to come, nor height nor depth, nor any other created thing, shall be able to separate us from the love of God which is in Christ Jesus our Lord. (Rom. 8:38–39 NKJV)

There is no sin in heaven! We in America have taken to calling sin a "mistake," but sin is a cancer of the soul. You must either eradicate the cancer, or the cancer will eradicate you! Today we laugh at the power of sin to destroy while we swim in a moral sewer of divorce, rape, murder, drug addiction, gangs, pornography, abortion, suicide, and welfare deadbeats. Thank God, there will be none of those social diseases in heaven. Sin will be forever gone!

Another wonder of heaven is our means of arriving there—death. Everyone wants to go to heaven, but no one wants to die to get there! Know this—death is certain. The writer of Hebrews assured us, "It is appointed for men to die once, but after this the judgment" (Heb. 9:27 NKJV).

Friend, *if you're not ready to die, you're not ready to live.*

Years ago, while I was in seminary, I was running around the track of the high school where I had graduated in Houston, Texas. I met a friend, a fellow with whom I had played high school football. After we talked a while, I asked him what he was going to do with his life.

"First I'm going to college," he said.

"Okay. What then?"

"Then I'm going to law school."

"What then?"

"Then I'm going to make a lot of money."

I laughed. "What then?"

"Then I'll get married, and then I'll have kids."

"What then?"

"Well, I suppose my children will get married and leave home."

"What then?"

He scratched his head. "Then I'll retire and travel a while. I'll be ready to have some fun."

"What then?"

His smile faded as he looked at me. "I suppose someday I'll get around to dying."

"What then?"

For that question he had no answer.

If you were to walk through the door of death tonight, where would you be? There's no great mystery about what happens after death. If you're a believer, the first thing you will see as you approach death is the dazzling lights of squadrons of angels who have come to escort you home. Luke 16:22 tells us that the angels carried the beggar directly into Abraham's bosom.

In spirit form, you will get up from your deathbed and look back at the empty shell of your lifeless body. An angel will say, "The Father is waiting for you." Holding the angel's hand, you will pass through the walls of whatever room you are in. As you ascend upward, the earth will fade into the distance as you rise into space.

As you approach the second heaven, Satan's throne, the powers and principalities in high places will scatter in terror, saying, "Here comes a child of God covered with the blood of Jesus Christ! Don't touch!" The angels of God will remain before and behind you, safely escorting you to the throne of God.

The next thing you will feel as you reach heaven's gate is the hand of God the Father wiping every tear from your eye. Earth is a place of trials, tension, turmoil, and terror, but you will leave all of that behind as you enter heaven. And as God escorts you into the throne room, you will hear the voice of a great multitude, the saints who have gone before you, saying, "Hallelujah, for the Lord God omnipotent reigns!"

To the repentant thief who hung by His side on the cross, Jesus said, "Today you will be with Me in Paradise" (Luke 23:43 NKJV). Paul said that "to be absent from this body [is] to be present with the Lord" (2 Cor. 5:8 NKJV). There's no soul sleep, no purgatory, no interim place. Our spirits will be with the Lord in heaven, and our bodies will be reunited with our spirits at the Rapture, when the saints of God will resurrect with new, incorruptible bodies.

If, however, you die without confessing Jesus Christ as Savior, no amount of prayers or candles will get you out of hell and into Paradise. The souls of the lost go to hell, there to remain until the last resurrection, when the wicked will resurrect to face the White Throne Judgment. Payday is coming! The lost who mock God now will give an account.

When you confess Christ, you become part of God's royal family. You receive the gift of eternal life, with a heavenly mansion in New Jerusalem.

Just think of it! If a man on earth had a heavenly mansion, he would build a twelve-foot fence around it and keep attack dogs in the yard just to keep people out. But the King of Glory has built mansions of splendor and said to the people of earth, "Whosoever will, let him come!"

THE NEW JERUSALEM:
GOD'S GOLDEN, GLORIOUS CITY

In Revelation chapters 21 and 22, John offered a panoramic view of the new Jerusalem:

> Then one of the seven angels who had the seven bowls filled with the seven last plagues came to me and talked with me, saying, "Come, I will show you the bride, the Lamb's wife." And he carried me away in the Spirit to a great and high mountain, and showed me the great city, the holy Jerusalem, descending out of heaven from God, having the glory of God.

> Her light was like a most precious stone, like a jasper stone, clear as crystal. Also she had a great and high wall with twelve gates, and twelve angels at the gates, and names written on them, which are the names of the twelve tribes of the children of Israel: three gates on the east, three gates on the north, three gates on the south, and three gates on the west.

> Now the wall of the city had twelve foundations, and on them were the names of the twelve apostles of the Lamb. And he who talked with me had a gold reed to measure the city, its gates, and its wall. And the city is laid out as a square; its length is as great as its breadth. And he

measured the city with the reed: twelve thousand fur-
longs [about fourteen hundred miles]. Its length, breadth,
and height are equal.

Then he measured its wall: one hundred and forty-four
cubits [about two hundred feet], according to the measure of a man, that is, of an angel.

And the construction of its wall was of jasper; and the
city was pure gold, like clear glass. The foundations of
the wall of the city were adorned with all kinds of precious stones: the first foundation was jasper, the second
sapphire, the third chalcedony, the fourth emerald, the
fifth sardonyx, the sixth sardius, the seventh chrysolite,
the eighth beryl, the ninth topaz, the tenth chrysoprase,
the eleventh jacinth, and the twelfth amethyst. The
twelve gates were twelve pearls: each individual gate was
one pearl. And the street of the city was pure gold, like
transparent glass.

But I saw no temple in it, for the Lord God Almighty and
the Lamb are its temple. The city had no need of the sun
or of the moon to shine in it, for the glory of God illu-
minated it. The Lamb is its light.

And the nations of those who are saved shall walk in its
light, and the kings of the earth bring their glory and
honor into it. Its gates shall not be shut at all by day
(there shall be no night there). And they shall bring the
glory and the honor of the nations into it. But there shall
by no means enter it anything that defiles, or causes an

abomination or a lie, but only those who are written in the Lamb's Book of Life.

And he showed me a pure river of water of life, clear as crystal, proceeding from the throne of God and of the Lamb. In the middle of its street, and on either side of the river, was the tree of life, which bore twelve fruits, each tree yielding its fruit every month. The leaves of the tree were for the healing of the nations.

And there shall be no more curse, but the throne of God and of the Lamb shall be in it, and His servants shall serve Him. They shall see His face, and His name shall be on their foreheads. There shall be no night there: They need no lamp nor light of the sun, for the Lord God gives them light. And they shall reign forever and ever. (Rev. 21:9–27; 22:1–5 NKJV)

John described the New Jerusalem as a city that is foursquare and fourteen hundred miles up, down, and across (Rev. 21:15–18). It would extend from the northernmost point of Maine to the southern tip of Florida, and from the Atlantic Ocean on the east to the western Rocky Mountains. It is as large as all of Western Europe and half of Russia. Each street is one-half the length of the diameter of the earth. The levels rise one mile above the others, equaling eight million miles of beautiful golden avenues. The twelve gates of pearl are built upon twelve jeweled foundations (Rev. 21:14), and they will open to believers from every kindred, tribe, and nation.

The citizens of Jerusalem, that ancient city which has

seen so much suffering, will exchange streets that have flowed with blood for streets of pure gold! The desert sun will yield to the light of the Lamb, and the hatred of warring nations to the peace of God! The protective walls of Jerusalem, which were built and rebuilt with much toil and struggle, will be replaced by walls designed solely for beauty and glory. The tree of life, not seen or enjoyed since Eden, will grow in the center of the city. Nations will no longer look upon Jerusalem with jealousy or resentment, but will look to it for the light of God's glory.

A CENSUS OF THE NEW JERUSALEM

Who will live in this holy city? The angels, Gentiles who have placed their faith and trust in Christ, and redeemed Israel. Although the New Jerusalem is a wedding present from the Bridegroom to His bride, Israel is invited to dwell within these beautiful walls.[2]

In Hebrews 11, the "roll call of faith," the author testified of Jewish saints who placed their faith in God and obeyed His commands. They are invited to dwell in His heavenly city: "But now they desire a better, that is, a heavenly country. Therefore God is not ashamed to be called their God, for He has prepared a city for them" (Heb. 11:16 NKJV).

Most people want to go to heaven for the same reason they want to go to Florida—the weather is good, and most of their relatives are there! But consider this amazing fact—though polls tell us that 92 percent of Americans believe in heaven, few are making preparations to go there. In churches across America we sing "When We All

Get to Heaven," but that only proves you can sing a lie as well as tell one.

Jesus said that many would stand before Him at the judgment seat and protest the fact that they aren't going to heaven: "Many will say to Me in that day, 'Lord, Lord, have we not prophesied in Your name, cast out demons in Your name, and done many wonders in Your name?'" (Matt. 7:22 NKJV)

Jesus' response? "And then I will declare to them, 'I never knew you; depart from Me, you who practice lawlessness!'" (Matt. 7:23 NKJV)

Just as the ark was the only way to be saved from the judgment of the Flood, Jesus Christ is the only way to enter heaven. Jesus Himself said, "I am the way, the truth, and the life. No one comes to the Father except through Me" (John 14:6 NKJV).

How many people will be dwelling on the new earth, in the new heaven, and in the heavenly city? Bible scholar Harold Willmington has devised a formula by which we can take an informal "census" of heaven's future residents. He estimates that approximately forty billion people have lived on our planet since Adam's creation. With that figure, we can extrapolate a rough formula:

Several anthropologists and sociologists have calculated that as many as 70 percent of all humans born never live to celebrate their eighth birthday; they are killed by disease, war, starvation, etc. What happens to the souls of all these little ones? Various verses make it clear that they go to be with Jesus. (See 2 Sam. 12:23, Matt. 18:1–6, 10; 19:14; Luke 18:15–17.) Now, add to this figure the millions of babies murdered by abortion each year, 40 million worldwide[3] . . . Abortion is now the number one cause of death in the U.S. These victims of abortion, like those children dying outside the womb, also go to be with Christ. Finally, let us suggest that 10 percent of those 40 billion human beings born on the earth accept Christ as Savior sometime after reaching the age of accountability. Put this figure with the rest and total it up.[4]

As of 1988, the column would read:

28,000,000,000 (those who died before age eight) +
600,000,000 (aborted babies from 1973–1988) +
1,200,000,000 (10 percent of survivors who
accept Christ as Savior) =

29,800,000,000

If you were disenchanted by the low figure of only 10 percent who accept Christ, notice that the total figure indicates that nearly three-fourths of all human beings will enjoy heaven and the new earth!

HEAVEN IS A REAL PLACE

There are some who say heaven is a state of mind, a dream, or an abstraction, but Jesus Himself called heaven a real place. He came from heaven to earth and then returned to heaven, where He awaits the day when His church shall join Him in the mansions He has prepared for His own.

Jesus calls heaven "a house, a dwelling place." It is not an illusion. It's just as real as the home in which you live right now.

In Acts 1:11 (NKJV), the angel told the disciples, "Men of Galilee, why do you stand gazing up into heaven? This same Jesus, who was taken up from you into heaven, will so come in like manner as you saw Him go into heaven."

Did Jesus go up into a state of mind? Did He enter an abstraction? No! Jesus went to a real place, an eternal home, a place of perfection God has prepared as a reward for those who love Him.

Jesus prayed, "Our Father in heaven . . ." (Luke 11:2 NKJV). He did not say, "Our Father in a state of mind" or "an eternal illusion." His Father and ours was and is in heaven, a real place.

Stephen saw heaven as he was being stoned to death. The Bible tells us, "But he, being full of the Holy Spirit, gazed into heaven and saw the glory of God, and Jesus standing at the right hand of God" (Acts 7:55 NKJV). Stephen closed his eyes, died, and went to be with Jesus.

Believers can claim heaven as home. Paul writes, "For our citizenship is in heaven, from which we also eagerly wait for the Savior, the Lord Jesus Christ" (Phil. 3:20 NKJV).

Our names are written in heaven. Jesus said, "Nevertheless do not rejoice in this, that the spirits are subject to you, but rather rejoice because your names are written in heaven" (Luke 10:20 NKJV).

Our treasures are stored in heaven. "Do not lay up for yourselves treasure on earth . . . but lay up for yourselves treasures in heaven, where neither moth nor rust destroys and where thieves do not break in and steal" (Matt. 6:19–20 NKJV).

Consider this final revelation of truth: *Abraham yearned for the New Jerusalem!*

> By faith Abraham obeyed when he was called to go out to the place which he would receive as an inheritance. And he went out, not knowing where he was going. By faith he dwelt in the land of promise as in a foreign country, dwelling in tents with Isaac and Jacob, the heirs with him of the same promise; for he waited for the city which has foundations, whose builder and maker is God. (Heb. 11:8–10 NKJV)

Abraham obeyed God and went looking for his Promised Land, but he was also looking for heaven! The Israelites did not possess the land of Canaan in his lifetime, so he looked forward to the New Jerusalem in faith! He looked forward to the place of rest, the time when we would spend an eternity praising the God who called him out of idolatry and the land of Ur.

WHAT WILL WE DO IN ETERNITY?

We're not going to sit around heaven and pluck harps all day. No indeed! Scripture tells us that heaven will be a very busy place for active people.

Heaven will be a place of rejoicing. We will sing praise to God for all he has done (Isa. 44:23; Rev. 14:3, 15:3).

Heaven will be a place of reunion. We will not only know each other, but we will also be able to talk to the Old

Testament prophets, Adam and Eve, the apostles, and the Lord Jesus Himself! Christian families that have been separated by death will be reunited!

Heaven will be a place of serving (Rev. 22:3, 7:15).

Heaven will be a place of learning (1 Cor. 13:9–10). If you enjoy learning new things, exploring new worlds, or visiting new places, heaven will be the perfect place for you. Imagine being able to fly to new planets where no man has gone before . . . or exploring a continent on the new earth. Best of all, we will learn about God, about our Savior, and His plan for us. The holy Scriptures will come together in our minds, and all mysteries will be revealed.

Heaven will be a place of joy and perfection. "But when that which is perfect has come," Paul wrote, "then that which is in part will be done away" (1 Cor. 13:10 NKJV).

Heaven will be a place of unbelievable real estate. Jesus taught, "In My Father's house are many mansions; if it were not so, I would have told you" (John 14:2 NKJV). My heavenly mansion will make the Taj Mahal look like a mud hut!

Heaven is the place where Jesus is. "Beloved, now we are children of God; and it has not yet been revealed what we shall be, but we know that when He is revealed, we shall be like Him, for we shall see Him as He is" (1 John 3:2 NKJV). Consider this:

- Mary saw Jesus as a baby in Bethlehem's manger.

- John the Baptist saw Him as a candidate for baptism.

- The disciples saw Him as *Rabbi*—their master and teacher.

- Rome saw Him as an insurrectionist.

- At Calvary, the citizens of Jerusalem saw Him as a common criminal.

- The Pharisees saw Him as a drunkard, a liar, and a heretic.

- Contemporary society sees Him as an ordinary man.

But when we get to heaven, we shall see Him as He is! We will see Jesus as:

- The Lord of Glory, high and lifted up, full of grace and truth!

- The Alpha and Omega, the First and the Last.

- The Lamb of God, the Light of the World, and the Lion of Judah.

- The Fairest of Ten Thousand . . . the Bright and Morning Star.

- The Great I AM, the Great Physician, and the Great Shepherd.

- The King of kings and the Lord of Lords.

BETTER THAN A CINDERELLA STORY

There once was a prince who disguised himself as a poor man and went out into the world to find a bride who would love him for himself alone, not for his power and wealth.

He found a job as a common laborer and fell deeply in love with a farmer's daughter. He asked the farmer for permission to marry his daughter, and felt his heart break when the farmer said, "No, you can't marry my girl. You are only a common laborer."

The daughter, however, saw her suitor with the eyes of love. She agreed to run away with the disguised prince, and they were married in a village not far away from her home. Unbeknownst to the bride, the prince sent a message to his father the king and informed him of his marriage. Thrilled beyond words, the king prepared a wedding reception for his son and new daughter-in-law.

The morning after their honeymoon, the groom turned to his bride and suggested a trip to the royal city. The bride agreed but was flabbergasted when the king's royal carriage met them at the city gates. Royal guards surrounded them as the carriage made its way through streets lined with jubilant citizens, and the king's musicians played wedding songs when she alighted from the carriage.

"What does this mean?" she asked her groom.

The prince gently took her hand and answered, "I am the king's son. You married me in obscurity and loved me as a common man. Now all the wealth, honors, and power of the kingdom are yours. You are royalty!"

Jesus Christ came to earth in obscurity as deep as that fictional prince's. He lived as a common man, a carpenter's son. He came to earth to win a bride, the church.

When you confess Christ, you become a part of God's family. By right of marriage, you are granted a mansion and a royal position. You are granted a home in heaven that will satisfy your soul for eternity.

ONLY JESUS CAN SATISFY YOUR SOUL

Satisfaction is yet another wonder of heaven. Nothing in this world satisfies absolutely, but heaven will still the yearning in your soul.

America is a hedonistic society, and pleasure is her god. Our slogan? *If it feels good, do it . . . or buy it.*

But life on earth teaches us that pleasure doesn't satisfy. Lord Byron lived for enjoyment and delighted in every sensual pleasure known to man. Three months before dying he wrote: "My days are in the yellow leaf; the flowers and fruits of Love are gone; the worm—the canker, and the grief are mine alone!"[5] He died miserable.

Unbelief and intellectualism do not satisfy. At the end of his life, Voltaire, a godless French philosopher, cried out that he was "abandoned by God and man." On his deathbed, he wept in despair: "Oh Christ! Oh, Jesus Christ!" The woman who was hired to nurse him refused to ever again care for the dying because she feared "witnessing another such scene as the death of Voltaire."[6]

Money doesn't satisfy. Jay Gould, one of the richest men in America, said on his deathbed, "I suppose I am the most miserable man on earth."

Fame doesn't satisfy. Clarence Darrow, probably the greatest criminal lawyer America has ever known, told a graduating class: "If I were a young man, I would chuck it all. I would commit suicide. I would get out of this wretched life . . . It isn't worth what it cost."

As a marked contrast, through thousands of years Christian saints have expressed statements of joy and confidence on their deathbeds. Ludwig van Beethoven, the brilliant deaf composer, was a fervent Christian. As he lay dying, Beethoven confidently said, "I shall hear in heaven."[7]

Jan Hus, the great Bohemian reformer, stood in the midst of the howling flames where church leaders had condemned him to die. "I call God to witness that I have neither taught nor preached what has falsely been laid to my charge," he told the crowd gathered to observe his execution. "The end of all my preaching and writings was to induce my fellow men to forsake sin. In the truth which I have proclaimed, according to the Gospel of Jesus Christ, . . . I will, this day, joyfully die."[8]

Hundreds of devout Christians have faced death confidently because they had steadfast faith in heaven . . . and in the One who has prepared it for us. Only Jesus can satisfy your soul! Satisfaction doesn't come from power, possessions, or profits. Only Jesus can satisfy us, and He will be in heaven. I don't even need my heavenly mansion and God's other benefits—as long as Jesus is there, I'll be satisfied eternally.

THE WONDER OF ETERNITY

There was a time when you did not exist . . . but now there will never be a time when you do not. When the Caesars ruled Rome, you were not. When Columbus sailed to the New World, you were not. When the Founding Fathers established America, you were not. But from the day of your conception, there will never come a day when you will not *be* somewhere.

You will either be in Paradise or in hell—in heaven or

in the bottomless pit. And wherever you make your final home, you will exist there for eternity.

Our minds cannot grasp the concept of a million years—or ten million. In eternity, time will cease to exist, and we will no longer speak of hours and days and weeks and years. I find it hard to conceive of a language without past and present tense, but all will change in eternity.

A few years ago I stood in a Dallas hospital beside the bed of a little girl who was dying. Her father stood by my side, and in the last moments of that little girl's life, she lifted up her hand and said, "Daddy, I see a beautiful house out there. I see pretty flowers, and people dressed in white. They look so happy, Daddy. Take me there."

Her father clutched her little hand. With tears in his eyes, he said, "Sweetheart, you're looking into heaven. You are seeing the mansion Jesus has prepared for you."

She tightened her hand around her father's. "Daddy, there's Jesus. He is holding His arms out to me. Daddy—Jesus is here."

And then, as I watched, that little girl exhaled her last breath. One moment she was with us, and in the next she had gone . . . and walked into the arms of Jesus.

Heaven is wonderful, my friend. I hope you're ready to go there.

NOTES

INTRODUCTION

1. Andy Warhol (1928–87), U.S. pop artist. Quoted from *The Columbia Dictionary of Quotations*. Copyright © 1993, 1995, 1997, 1998 by Columbia University Press. All rights reserved.

CHAPTER 1

1. George Will, "The Gospel from Science," *Newsweek*, 9 November 1998, 88.
2. Ibid.
3. Frances Welch, "'To Deny Religion Would Be Unscientific': Me and My God: Kitty Ferguson talks to Frances Welch," *Sunday Telegraph*, 11 April 1999.
4. Ibid.
5. Richard N. Ostling, "Galileo and Other Faithful Scientists," *Time*, 28 December 1992, 42.
6. Ibid.
7. Gregg Easterbrook, "What Came Before Creation?" *U.S. News & World Report*, 20 July 1998, 44.
8. John Haught, "Religion and Physics Are No Longer Mutually Exclusive," *Washington Times*, 4 March 1996, 24.
9. Harold Willmington, *Basic Stages in the Book of Ages* (Lynchburg, VA: Thomas Road Bible Institute, 1975), 20.

10. Ibid.
11. Finis Jennings Dake, *Dake's Annotated Reference Bible* (Lawrenceville, GA: Dake Bible Sales, Inc., 1963), 58.
12. Ibid., 52.
13. Grant Jeffrey, ed., *Prophecy Marked Reference Study Bible* (Grand Rapids, MI: Zondervan Publishing House, 1999), 4.

CHAPTER 2

1. Mike Mason, *The Mystery of Marriage* (Portland, OR: Multnomah Press, 1985), 47.
2. Walter C. Kaiser Jr. et al., *Hard Sayings of the Bible* (Downers Grove, IL: InterVarsity Press, 1996), 93-94.
3. Ibid., 98.
4. Ibid., 98.
5. Ibid., 91–92.
6. Eddie Chumney, *The Seven Festivals of the Messiah*, <http://www.geocities.com/Heartland/2175/chap8.html>.

CHAPTER 3

1. John Bartlett, ed. *Familiar Quotations* (Boston: Little, Brown and Co., 1980), 856.
2. Excerpted from *The American Heritage Dictionary of the English Language, Third Edition*, electronic edition. Copyright © 1992 by Houghton Mifflin Company.
3. List adapted from Willmington, *Basic Stages in the Book of Ages*, 46.
4. Will St. John, "A Theory for Noah, the Flood, and Eden," *London Free Press*, 4 April 1999, C5.
5. Richard Ostling, "Analysis: In Search of Noah's Flood," <http://www.nandotimes.com/noframes/story/0,2107,10011-17209-116857-0,00.html>, Copyright © 1999 Associated Press.
6. Harold Willmington, *Willmington's Bible Handbook* (Wheaton, IL: Tyndale House Publishers, 1997), 11.

7. Ibid., 12.
8. Ibid.
9. Walter C. Kaiser Jr. et al., *Hard Sayings of the Bible,* 110–111.
10. Filby quoted in Willmington, *Basic Stages in the Book of Ages,* 46–47.
11. [Author not available], "Noah's Story Still Holds Water," *Dallas Morning News,* 28 February 1998, 3G.
12. Ibid.
13. "Special Report from Chuck Colson on the InnerChange Freedom Initiative," <http://www. prisonfellowship.org/prison.html>.
14. Source: <http://www.abortionfacts.com>. In 1998 there were 1,210,883 recorded abortions.
15. [Author not available], "Conscience," *Business Daily* (Philippines) 27 May 1998.

CHAPTER 4

1. Walter C. Kaiser Jr. et al., *Hard Sayings of the Bible,* 116.
2. Charles Colson, "Battle in Kosovo Fails 'Just' Warfare Principles," *USA Today,* Prison Fellowship Online, <http://www.prisonfellowship.org/prison.html>.
3. Anne Rochell Konigsmark, "'Ma'am,' 'Sir' Forced by Law, If You Please," *Atlanta Journal-Constitution,* 16 June 1999, A1.
4. Associated Press, "LA to Legislate Respect in School," *Newsday,* 16 June 1999, A52.
5. Alan Unterman, *Dictionary of Jewish Lore and Legend* (London: Thames and Hudson, 1991), 32.
6. Willmington, *Willmington's Bible Handbook,* 13.
7. Dake, *Dake's Annotated Reference Bible,* 9.
8. Harold Willmington, *Survey of the Old Testament* (Wheaton, IL: Victor Books, 1987), 53.
9. Charles Dyer and Angela Elwell Hunt, *The Rise of Babylon* (Wheaton, IL: Tyndale House, 1991), 50.

10. [Author not available], "Senator Bennett Invokes Tower of Babel Imagery," *Salt Lake City Tribune*, 4 May 1999.
11. Dake, *Dake's Annotated Reference Bible*, 309.

CHAPTER 5

1. Willmington, *Willmington's Bible Handbook*, 14.
2. Willmington, *Basic Stages in the Book of Ages*, 75.
3. Ibid.
4. "The Mayflower Compact," *The Encarta® 99 New World Almanac* © Copyright 1998, Helicon Publishing Ltd. All rights reserved.
5. Walter C. Kaiser Jr. et al., *Hard Sayings of the Bible*, 126.
6. Willmington, *Willmington's Bible Handbook*, 19, 21.
7. Margaret Murray, *The Splendour That Was Egypt* (London: Sidgwick & Jackson, 1963), 105–108.
8. Margaret Bunson, *The Encyclopedia of Ancient Egypt* (New York: Facts on File, 1991), 99.
9. Murray, *The Splendour That Was Egypt*, 108.
10. Bunson, *The Encyclopedia of Ancient Egypt*, 197.

CHAPTER 6

1. Willmington, *Willmington's Bible Handbook*, 54.
2. Gary L. Bauer, Edwin Meese III, "The Commandments and the Constitution," *Washington Times*, 11 October 1998, B4.
3. Tessie Borden, "Candidates Express Mixed Views on Commandments, Gun Controls," *Tampa Tribune Online*, 18 June 1999.
4. Associated Press, "Colorado Can Keep Ten Commandments Monument," *USA Today*, 28 May 1996, online version.
5. Dan Luzadder, "Modest Monument Proposal Raising Heck in Statehouse," *Denver Rocky Mountain News*, 1 March 1997, 5A.
6. Anne Belli Gesalman, "Off the Wall? Judges Defend Displays, but Critics Reply: Thou Shalt Not," *Dallas Morning News*, 5 July 1997, 1G.

7. Ibid.
8. Ibid.
9. Tom Jarriel, Hugh Downs, Barbara Walters, "God's Laws, America's Laws," *20/20* transcript, 16 October 1997.
10. Ibid.
11. Ibid.
12. Dr. Laura Schlessinger and Rabbi Stewart Vogel, *The Ten Commandments: The Significance of God's Laws in Everyday Life* (New York: Cliff Street Books, 1998), xxv–xxvi.
13. Ibid., 92–93.
14. Michelle Green, "On the Cover: Fate's Captive," *People,* 5 December 1988, 56.

CHAPTER 7

1. Dake, *Dake's Annotated Reference Bible,* 61.
2. "There Is a Fountain," words by William Cowper (1731–1800). Public Domain.
3. "Amazing Grace," words by John Newton (1725– 1807). Public Domain.
4. *Fox's Book of Martyrs,* Database © 1996, NavPress software.
5. J. Dwight Pentecost, *Things to Come* (Grand Rapids, MI: Zondervan Publishing House, 1964), 223.
6. Ibid., 224.
7. "Jesus Paid It All," words by Elvina M. Hall (1820–1889). Public Domain.
8. *New York Times* report, "European Union Plans to Create Military Power for Peace Missions," *Tampa Tribune,* 4 June 1999.

CHAPTER 8

1. Harold Willmington, *The King Is Coming* (Wheaton, IL: Tyndale House Publishing, 1988), 241–242.
2. S. Franklin Logsdon, *Profiles of Prophecy* (Grand Rapids, MI: Zondervan Publishing House, 1964), 81.

Notes

3. Walter C. Kaiser Jr. et al., *Hard Sayings of the Bible,* 569–570.
4. Ibid.
5. Willmington, *The King Is Coming,* 250.
6. (Adapted) Ibid.
7. Rene Pache, *The Return of Jesus Christ* (Chicago: Moody Press, 1955), 428.
8. J. Vernon McGee, *Revelation, Chapters 14–22* (Nashville: Thomas Nelson Publishers, 1991), 152.

CHAPTER 9

1. Dake, *Dake's Annotated Reference Bible,* 62.
2. Willmington, *The King Is Coming,* 300.
3. The Web site <www.abortionfacts.com> estimates the total of abortions worldwide numbers between 36 and 53 million.
4. Ibid., 304.
5. "Lord Byron," *The Columbia Dictionary of Quotations* is licensed from Columbia University Press. Copyright © 1993, 1995, 1997, 1998 by Columbia University Press. All rights reserved.
6. Grant R. Jeffrey, *Heaven: The Mystery of Angels* (Toronto: Frontier Research Publications, Inc., 1996), 216.
7. Ibid., 221.
8. W. N. Schwarze, *John Hus: The Martyr of Bohemia* (New York: Fleming H. Revell, 1915), 134–135.

From Daniel to Doomsday

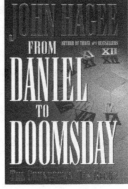

In his most provocative and comprehensive book about end times, Dr. John Hagee counts down the prophetic minutes from the time of Daniel through the twentieth century. While Wall Street revels in economic euphoria and proclaims that all is well, *From Daniel to Doomsday* reports on the rumblings of the coming Rapture in such current world events as:

- The collapse of the Asian and Pacific Rim economies
- The expanding threat of cyber terrorism and germ warfare
- The continuing moral decay among national leaders
- The devaluing of human life through the practice of abortion

The Day of Apocalypse. The End of the World. Call it what you will, but with the new millennium, people's thoughts have turned toward Christ's final reckoning. *From Daniel to Doomsday* not only interprets the times but also unveils what has yet to occur before that fateful moment when every unredeemed individual must face God on Judgment Day.

ISBN 0-7852-6966-5 • Hardcover • 320 pages
ISBN 0-7852-6818-9 • Paperback • 320 pages

His Glory Revealed

This seven-week devotional explores the feasts of Israel: The Feast of the Passover, The Feast of Unleavened Bread, The Feast of Firstfruits, The Feast of Pentecost, The Feast of Trumpets (Rosh Hashanah), The Feast of Atonement (Yom Kippur), and The Feast of Tabernacles. *His Glory Revealed* helps readers understand not only the meaning of each of these feasts but also the prophetic significance of each festival.

ISBN 0-7852-6965-7 • Hardcover • 192 pages

Three Books in One Volume

This collection combines three of Dr. Hagee's books: *Beginning of the End, Final Dawn Over Jerusalem,* and *Day of Deception.*

In *Beginning of the End,* Dr. Hagee takes a close look at the 1995 assassination of Israeli prime minister Yitzhak Rabin and explains how it fits into events prophesied centuries ago in the Bible.

In *Final Dawn Over Jerusalem,* Dr. Hagee tells how his life changed the night he took a bold stand against terrorism and anti-Semitism in his hometown. Though his life was threatened, his property destroyed, and his peace of mind rocked, Dr. Hagee was able to uncover spiritual insights for all believers, as well as a blueprint for the rapidly approaching end times.

In *Day of Deception,* Dr. Hagee reveals deception at work in America's government, schools, media, culture, and even our religious institutions. This book shows readers how to discern truth from falsehood and how to appropriate the power of God to emerge victorious over deceptions.

ISBN 0-7852-6761-1 • Hardcover • 688 pages

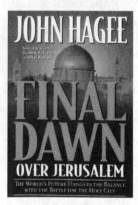